Software Engineering
and CASE

Other McGraw-Hill Books of Interest

Software Engineering and CASE

Bridging the Culture Gap

Tom Flecher

Jim Hunt

McGraw-Hill, Inc.

New York San Francisco Washington, D.C. Auckland Bogotá
Caracas Lisbon London Madrid Mexico City Milan
Montreal New Delhi San Juan Singapore
Sydney Tokyo Toronto

Library of Congress Cataloging-in-Publication Data

Flecher, Tom.
    Software engineering and CASE : bridging the culture gap / by Tom
Flecher and Jim Hunt.
        p. cm.
    Includes index.
    ISBN 0-07-021219-8 (h)
        1. Computer-aided software engineering.   2. Management information
systems. I. Hunt, Jim.   II. Title.
    QA76.758.F55   1993
    005.1'068'4—dc20   93-16410
                                                                                               CIP

1 2 3 4 5 6 7 8 9 0   DOC/DOC   9 9 8 7 6 5 4 3

ISBN 0-07-021219-8

*The editors for this book were Jeanne Glasser and Sally Anne Glover.
The production supervisor was Katherine G. Brown. This book was set
in Century Schoolbook. It was composed by TAB Books.*

Printed and bound by R.R. Donnelley amd Sons Company.

To my parents, William and Dorothy Flecher.

Tom Flecher

To Marilyn, Susan, Scott, and my mother, Juanita Hunt, for all their support over the years, which made this book possible.

Jim Hunt

Contents

Preface

Are you trying to make a difference within your organization but don't know where to start? Are you having trouble implementing the new technologies of software engineering (SE) and computer aided software engineering (CASE)? Do you ever worry about the strength of the information systems (IS) profession? All of these questions are addressed in this book, and in an integrated manner.

Many of today's IS departments are at a crucial crossroad. We're faced with the dilemma of continuing to stay the course with existing tools, techniques, and associated cultural norms or striking out into new horizons.

If we "stay the course," our IS department will continue to satisfy (or perhaps pacify) management by addressing the majority of fires and hot needs. As they say, "If it ain't broke, don't fix it." Somehow, most IS organizations are able to get by year after year with a high maintenance burden, high error rates, and many confrontations with the user community. Why upset the apple cart in these turbulent times?

If you do "strike out" into new tools and techniques, what risks do you face? Software engineering and CASE have gotten a lot of press over the past few years, and not all of it has been positive. Could your organization be the next disappointment? Is it truly worth the risk? Why not wait until next year when this new stuff is truly tested out?

A "stay-the-course" policy is very similar to the federal government's action towards our national debt. The government likes to talk a lot about reducing the debt, but no one actually seems to be doing anything about it. We all know that a huge debt is unhealthy for our nation, but there never seems to be a good time to attack the debt. First there's a war in the Middle East, then a recession, then an election. There's never a perfect time to get started. As time goes on, the situation simply gets worse. The solution is simple—reduce spending and/or raise taxes. However, this strategy takes a cultural change of major proportions.

The IS department's view of software engineering is very similar. We all know about our universally poor productivity and performance records. We all know they won't get better by leaving them alone. Most of us never seem to have the time or the opportunity to start making them better. Yet, surprisingly, most of us know how to solve the problem.

Many IS organizations have shown that software engineering techniques and CASE tools can dramatically help in this area. However, like the national debt, this is not a quick fix. The solution is not just to install the tools, but also to provide significant training and to modify the IS culture to properly support the new approaches.

The techniques, tools, and training aspects of SE/CASE are thoroughly addressed in this book. It provides a background to those who have not had the opportunity or desire to keep up with advances, but the primary focus of the book is squarely on the cultural aspects of IS. We first define the ideal IS culture, then provide guidance on how to install this ideal culture.

However, please don't follow this advice verbatim. The definition and implementation of culture cannot be standardized. It's not like installing a software program on a PC, where you can simply follow the installation steps and expect to be successful. Every organization is different, and each will provide a different set of opportunities and challenges. To change your culture, use this book as a starting place for your own strategy and work plan. Don't use this book as a cookbook. It's not a substitute for thinking. Think of the book as a guide.

This book provides many checklists and work plans, but you'll need to customize these instruments for your own organization. The process involves a high degree of commitment and lots of hard work, but the results will be fruitful. Remember, SE/CASE implementation is a major undertaking; there's a lot at risk—perhaps even your long-term career within the IS profession!

Acknowledgments

It's almost impossible to author a book about Information Services (IS) culture without obtaining a lot of ideas, insight, and concepts from other people. After all, culture is about how people feel, interact, and behave. You can't theorize this topic; you need to experience it. So, for those who were directly and indirectly involved, thank you all for your contributions. Special thanks also goes to Jim Dudziak, Jim Wicker, Marty Springer, John Berendt, and Lori Meola for listening to, building on, and supporting the evolutionary development of many of my ideas.

The seeds of this book were sown some eight years ago by Clint Alston. Mr. Alston is a true visionary whose conceptual ideas and words of support inspired me to take up the challenge of putting my ideas to paper. Thank you, Clint. This book is a fruit of your mentoring.

Finally, no book can be written without the support and understanding of a loving wife and family. During the writing of this book, there were countless weekend mornings when my wife Patricia had to deal with the combination of Melissa, Michael, Sara, and Jill without my help. Thank you, Pat, for your support. Also, thank you, kids, for staying out of my study!

Tom Flecher

Acknowledgments

It would be impossible to thank all of those who have contributed to the contents of this book. However, I'm especially grateful to those courageous people who are out there every day making CASE and other technology-useful tools improve how we do our business.

I'm also grateful to the companies where I've had the opportunity to work on CASE projects; those businesses have been my learning ground for what I've attempted to pass on in these pages.

I'm especially grateful for the sacrifices of my wife, who put up with all the long hours I had to dedicate to this book's completion.

Finally, I'm grateful to you, the reader, for your willingness to push open the envelope of your thinking and always be looking for a better way, for it's only through an attitude of continuous improvement that we can grow.

Jim Hunt

Introduction

Focus of the Book

Software engineering (SE), in the form of structured analysis and design (SA&D), has been with us now for more than 20 years. More advanced variations of SA&D (e.g., information engineering, rapid application development) have been around for the past five to eight years. Software engineering's computerized counterpart, computer aided software engineering (CASE) technology, has been around for almost 10 years. The integration of these technologies has now matured to the point where a few corporations are finding tangible value and benefit from implementing the technologies.

However, a significant portion of recent SE/CASE implementation attempts have been less than successful. The typical response towards implementation failure has been to blame the problems on the shortcomings of the technology. This was an acceptable excuse a few years ago, but it's no longer valid. The technology has matured far beyond this point. Although not perfect, the technology does, in fact, work.

Based on our combined consulting experiences assisting MIS clients with the implementation of SE/CASE, implementation failures can be traced to one, if not to both, of the following scenarios:

1. The effect that SE/CASE technology has on the MIS culture is overlooked or disregarded.

2. The glitzy part of software engineering, the CASE tool, is overemphasized, thereby downplaying SE methods, techniques, and approaches.

Implementation of software engineering and CASE will change the ideological foundation of an MIS organization. It will challenge an MIS organization's fundamental beliefs, assumptions, and behaviors concerning the development and maintenance of systems. Understanding and proactively dealing with a change in the MIS culture is paramount for success. Experience has proven that, in this area, it's "Pay me now (through planning, presentations, counseling) or pay me later (through loss of productivity, turnover, loss of a job)."

From a technical perspective, a typical, and most likely unsuccessful, SE/CASE implementation plan goes something like this:

1. Form a CASE committee.

2. Bring in CASE vendors for demonstrations.

3. Select/purchase a tool.

4. Receive training on the tool/techniques.

5. Pilot test the tool.

6. Declare department-wide adoption.

This approach is quick, straightforward, and simple, even though on occasion it has taken many months or several years to actually select the tool. This approach, however, implies doing the same thing to ourselves that we've done to our users for years—getting to the "code" as quickly as possible.

Within MIS culture, there's a constant temptation to select, build, or buy solutions before applying the appropriate analysis. Remember, this is the primary reason to implement software engineering and CASE in the first place! Organizations want to structure the development and maintenance process, but they're not structuring the process of selecting and implementing technology for the MIS function.

Selecting and implementing CASE technology is not much different from selecting and implementing user software packages. Would you quickly select a few software vendors and then "pilot test" their payroll packages for your Human Resources department? We hope not! You'd be surprised at the number of requests we get to coordinate such a process! This "CASE-off mentality" has to change.

Software engineering and CASE represents a system for creating and maintaining systems—a meta-system from those so inclined to think in "meta-terms." During this process, you need to identify your system's objective (e.g., improve your ability to use MIS for competitive advantage), define requirements, design a solution, and plan for the implementation. You can be truly successful only with a top-down assessment of where you are today, a vision of where you want to be in the next five years, and a plan to get you there.

Unfortunately, this book doesn't present a quick fix to the selection and implementation of SE/CASE. We wish it could. However, the intent is to present the most expedient, best approach based on solid organizational change-management principles and varied experiences implementing SE/CASE.

This book presents an approach that you'll be able to fine-tune and use. The end result of this approach will be an implemented software engineering infrastructure—complete with methods, procedures, tools, and a supportive culture. Please note: We do not discuss the relative merits of specific SE/CASE technologies (e.g., IEW/ADW versus IEF) within this book. There are a variety of books and articles that address this area.

This book is a blend of practical experience and theoretical concepts concerning the technical and cultural transition to software engineering and CASE. The backbone of the approach described in this book is based on CGA's previously proprietary SYS*CASE approach. The publication of this book removes the proprietary nature of the approach; however, the new name, IC/VISION, will be trademarked and the details copyrighted.

The focus of this book is on providing a firm theoretical basis for developing a strategy and a plan for action. The book is truly a blend of conceptual behavioral models and practical guides for action. As with any approach of this nature, this is not a substitute for thinking. We provide a work plan complete with checklists, questionnaires, and sample deliverables, but you'll need to customize them to your unique organization. The process involves a high degree of commitment and lots of hard work, but the results will be fruitful. Remember, SE/CASE implementation is a major undertaking; there's a lot at risk—perhaps even your job!

Who Should Use This Book?

This book is aimed at two primary audiences:

1. MIS management interested in implementing SE/CASE.
2. Those responsible for SE/CASE's selection and implementation (i.e., what we later refer to as the transition team).

This book is not geared to the project manager looking for a few tools to help augment an upcoming project. That need represents a tactical look at SE/CASE. This book takes a strategic look at the technology from the departmental level.

In addition, some chapters of this book would be appropriate for non-MIS types to get a better grasp of the new technology—especially those who are responsible for and/or affected by a SE/CASE implementation and corresponding cultural shift. These chapters include:

- Chapter 5.
- Chapter 6.
- Chapter 7.

A critical success factor in the implementation of SE/CASE is that MIS management understands what's going on—not from a detailed perspective, but from a global perspective. For success, MIS management needs:

- An understanding of the software engineering components.
- An overview of the implementation and selection process.
- An appreciation for dealing with the cultural aspects.

Without this knowledge, the initiative will most likely result in CASE shelfware and departmental disarray. By reading chapters 4, 5, 6, and 7, MIS management will be able to quickly obtain this valuable insight, which provides the thrust behind the transition team's activities.

MIS management's responsibility, as outlined in this book, is to sponsor the selection and implementation process, not the tool selected. All too often, management buys into a name, a product, or a vendor without knowing how or why the selection was made. In the final analysis, it should make no difference to management which tool is selected, just that the selection process produced the appropriate result.

If you're the person responsible for selecting and implementing the technology, consider yourself a change agent. This is a very exciting and demanding role. Be prepared to learn a lot about technology, politics, and human interactions. Be prepared to keep a proper perspective on all three. The biggest sin of a change agent is getting overly enamored with the technology. Sure, its fun, new, and exciting. However, remember that the technology doesn't get the work done—people do. It's these people who will resist and manipulate the agent of change. It's your job to see that they don't.

The change agent needs to share with MIS management the same understanding of software engineering components, an overview of the selection and implementation process, and an appreciation for dealing with the cultural aspects. The primary difference is that the change agent also needs to be able to implement the initiative. He or she needs a course of action to follow. This book provides guidance and it outlines an approach to making SE/CASE happen. This path is found in chapter 8.

Like any approach, however, this book is no substitute for thinking. A change agent still needs to understand the concepts and plans presented here and customize them for the specific organization.

1

The "Typical" CASE Selection/Implementation Initiative

Stages of a "Typical" CASE Implementation

From the beginning of our profession, there has been a tendency for MIS professionals to jump right to the physical aspect of a particular problem or situation. "Why aren't Suzy and John coding yet" is a universally accepted axiom around MIS organizations and, not so surprisingly, for more than just the code! A corollary is the "analysis-by-paralysis" axiom that's used to make people feel guilty about not jumping right into physical aspects of a problem.

Both of these axioms help to establish a mind-set for action. We like to think we're active, results-oriented people. This is a noble quest, but not well founded. The fruits of our actions are generally short-sighted, sometimes successful, always popular, very American, but never quite visionary. As stated succinctly in the Fram oil filter commercials of late, "Pay me now or pay me later." We continue to pay with high maintenance, disgruntled users, and missed opportunities.

The "jump-to-the-code" philosophy can be seen in many different aspects of MIS beyond the coding activity. Many organizations fill their training curriculums with "how-to" training classes, completely ignoring the associated educational classes needed to build a firm foundation of the "why." Organizations also implement quality assurance programs that focus on policing the end deliverable and ignoring the process.

"Jumping to the code" is exactly what many organizations are doing when implementing SE/CASE. There's this mysterious force that impels organizations to quickly purchase a CASE product, receive "how-to" training, run a pilot, and implement the product. There are a few lucky organizations that are successful with this approach, but for many, "shelfware" is the ultimate result.

In our experiences, we've seen this cycle all too often. It's driven by the earlier-mentioned axioms and supported by aggressive CASE vendors. As a "typical" CASE selection/implementation process unfolds, it goes through a series of steps designed to get a tool quickly selected and implemented. These steps directly affect management's perception of the new technology along the way. Figure 1.1 breaks this process into four distinct phases: hype, realization, tuning, and reevaluation.

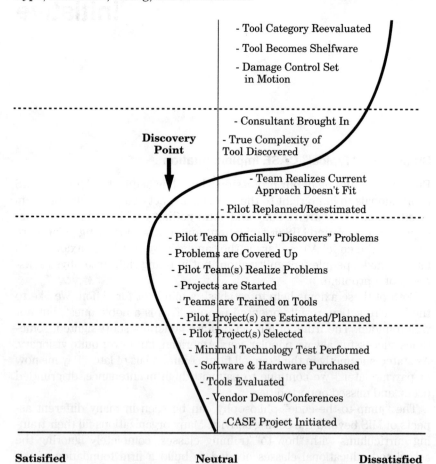

- Tool Category Reevaluated

- Tool Becomes Shelfware

- Damage Control Set
  in Motion

**Discovery
Point**

- Consultant Brought In

- True Complexity of
  Tool Discovered

- Team Realizes Current
  Approach Doesn't Fit

- Pilot Replanned/Reestimated

- Pilot Team Officially "Discovers" Problems

- Problems are Covered Up

- Pilot Team(s) Realize Problems

- Projects are Started

- Teams are Trained on Tools

- Pilot Project(s) are Estimated/Planned

- Pilot Project(s) Selected

- Minimal Technology Test Performed

- Software & Hardware Purchased

- Tools Evaluated

- Vendor Demos/Conferences

-CASE Project Initiated

Satisified   **Neutral**   **Dissatisfied**

Figure 1.1 Typical CASE implementation cycle.

Hype phase

During the early days of the CASE selection/implementation initiative, vendors are typically brought in to show off their wares. During this process, the MIS organization is educated in a few software engineering principles (at least those helpful to the vendor's cause), and tool demonstrations are held. These demonstrations spur the evaluation process; a very fun process for those so inclined to attend CASE conferences in warm, sunny spots. A tool is eventually selected and a pilot project designated. On occasion, a very small project is run through the tool to validate the concepts.

All of these activities build a positive and quickly moving momentum for the initiative. Management is very satisfied with progress and has confidence in the team/committee who selected the tool, even though management really doesn't understand the concepts and principles behind the technology. There's a feeling that something good is starting to happen and that if you don't move fast enough to capitalize on this good feeling, then nothing will ever happen. Momentum is very important to maintain.

Realization phase

Next, the organization enters a phase where they begin to realize what they did to themselves. The tool is solid, but the pilot project team realizes that the organization really doesn't understand the basics behind the tool—software engineering. Concepts like decomposition, normalization, encyclopedia integration, and transform analysis appear to impede progress.

In an effort to "prop up the tool decision," these issues are largely ignored or covered up. Management is given only superficial information about the potential problems, in effect isolating them from the situation. After all, the tool does provide some intangible value and there's no reason to alarm management. After all, the pilot team usually consists of many of the organization's brightest and best. They should be able to figure it all out. This situation continues, building up pressure. The project team does a good job of hiding the problems until they reach what we facetiously refer to as the "discovery point."

The discovery point is where political protocol says that it's time to admit to the problems. The team knew about them all along, but now its time to be surprised. Up until this point, satisfaction was steadily climbing, or at least holding steady. Once the discovery point is hit, there's a huge drop in confidence. This phenomenon is very similar to the financial markets of old (or even of present). Right before the crash of 1929, there was very strong confidence in the market. However, once the market started to slide and people realized the problems, confidence fell far below what was appropriate for the financial situation. This same effect happens within an MIS organization implementing CASE. Paradoxically, the better the pilot team is in hiding the problems, the deeper the surge in confidence will be.

Usually, the problems are blamed on physical aspects of the CASE tool—something tangible and easy to explain. Examples include lack of LAN support, inability to model a specific object, and processing speed. Make no mistake; these are all real issues with the CASE tools of today, and will be at least for the next few years. However, these problems alone should not kill the energy and momentum of a pilot project team.

Tuning phase

In an effort to save the pilot project and the CASE initiative, the pilot project is reestimated and replanned. During this process, the organization begins to understand that their current approach (referred to as a methodology or ideology) and skills for development don't fit the new paradigm of SE/CASE. In addition, other problems are uncovered concerning the encyclopedia integration and user involvement.

It's at this point that a consultant is brought in to save the project, and along with it the CASE initiative. Many times the project is saved, but the doubts cast over the CASE technology linger long after the project. Even though the project team might eventually feel that the technology was valuable, the political stigma attached to it drains any momentum. The organization is dissatisfied with the technology.

Reevaluation phase

The reevaluation phase starts with damage control. In an attempt to save careers, the specific tool is savaged, further disintegrating confidence in the technology. For it's far nicer to blame a technology than to blame people or the process that got you there. This is just human nature. After all, no technology is perfect, and CASE is relatively immature. If it were perfect, there would be no need for human intervention (i.e., MIS professionals). The users could simply interact with the tool and out would come the code.

This is the potential point of no return for the specific CASE technology. In essence, it becomes "shelfware." Depending on the champions and sponsors within the organization, either the CASE initiative is dropped or redirected towards some other tool. Witness the number of organizations switching from ADW to IEF and vice-versa. The champions saw the benefits, but knew that the name had to change in order to build back confidence in the technology. The process is then restarted with another tool selection and pilot test. Most organizations are much more successful on the second attempt due to lessons learned on the first. We have found that many of these lessons are culture based. These lessons will be further developed in chapter 5.

Of course, not every organization that follows this path meets with the same demise. As we mentioned earlier, some organizations who follow this path are successful. Perhaps they're skillful, perhaps lucky. In either event, the percentage of success is low compared to what it should be. Considering the cost, both financially and politically, a different approach is probably called for.

Common Pitfalls

There are two fundamental causes associated with this "typical" approach:

1. The effect on the culture is ignored.
2. The full range of software engineering is not considered.

The positive-to-negative swing in perception is very natural and even expected in a change of this magnitude. Thus, a primary key to success is with planning for resistance up front. This will help to minimize the effect of the discovery point and to put the perception back into a positive light. This process involves identifying where and when the swings will occur, identifying potential roadblocks, and putting a proactive organizational change management strategy into place. These cultural aspects will be developed later in chapters 4 and 5 of this book and integrated into the recommended SE/CASE selection and implementation process in the last chapter.

For most initial CASE initiatives only one or two parts of the software engineering spectrum are automated. The internal CASE selection committee's objective is to select the best tool, be it an analysis tool, a management tool, or whatever. This is referred to as the "best of breed" approach. Given the general concepts outlined by IBM with their AD/Cycle vision, this strategy has merit. This concept maintains that IBM's repository will integrate all of the CASE tools, thus diminishing the use of integration as a selection criterion.

Reality, however, says differently. Even if IBM's repository concepts become a reality, there's much more to integration than just tool connectivity. Before selecting the appropriate techniques, methodologies, and tools, an organization needs to consider its development approach(es) (e.g., IE, RAD), management philosophies, and organizational culture. All of these aspects are part of the software engineering (SE)/CASE infrastructure. We'll develop these infrastructure concepts in chapter 3.

In addition, there are many other pitfalls that contributed to this "typical" implementation cycle. The following are a few of the more common pitfalls. A full model of potential pitfalls mapped to critical success factors will be developed in chapter 6.

Taking on too much at once. Many corporations want to build the full environment right from the start—taking on five to ten different technology implementations simultaneously (e.g., an SDM, a metrics program, an estimating tool). This dilutes managements attention, energy, and funds. Remember, the real work of MIS still has to get done.

Too narrow a focus, usually at a project level.   SE/CASE is a global issue. Many people look only at a specific project. A major project is a good catalyst, but should not be the driving force. Do not look at CASE from the project impact/implication level, but from the organizational level.

Using SE/CASE technology to rescue a failing project.   Bringing in a new technology serves as a divergence from the real problems (e.g., project management, missed specs). SE/CASE can get management's attention and buy the project team a little time. The problem is that new technology will generally slow down a project due to the learning curve, further compounding the project's problems. Even when an experienced consultant is assisting, there's usually so much retrofitting needed that whatever time is saved, it's lost in this activity. The project generally fails and the technology is blamed, putting a "black mark" on it for any subsequent implementation attempts.

Using technology vendors to obtain your SE/CASE education.   SE/CASE contains a variety of concepts and ideas. It's very easy to allow your prospective technology vendors to train you in SE concepts and technology. After all, it doesn't cost you anything and the training/presentations are convenient, usually held at your site or at a local training center. This arrangement is enticing. After all, what harm will it do? Most of this education, however, is simply too biased. Remember, whatever they're telling you is leading to one, and only one place—a product purchase. This is not necessarily bad, especially if it's a solid product and you're well informed. We all need a little prodding once in a while to get us off our duffs and to make a purchase. The problem is that the education is usually too shallow, focusing mainly on the tools and not the concepts and methods. There's much to be learned before diving into an implementation. This information is usually best acquired from books (like this one) and from general SE seminars.

No clear definition of success or failure.   How do you know when you're successful? When the tool is used for a pilot? Whenever the MIS director declares it successful? Whenever all of the implementation problem discussions go away? The problem is that most people usually leave this area open for the imagination. This results in subjective judgments, which tend to feed the political process. Measurements are rarely used to define success or failures.

Unclear as to why you're perusing SE/CASE.   Sometimes the momentum gets moving so fast that people forget why the organization is pursuing SE/CASE in the first place. The organization's "visionary" might have had great reasons, but never bothered to write them down or to communicate them to anybody else. This allows the selection person or committee to go astray. In addition, MIS organizations are very dynamic, with constant reorganizations and leadership changes. This can result in loss of continuity and understanding of the rationale of implementing the technology. Many times the selection process takes on a life of its own. Usually the best reason that people will provide in these situations is that everyone else is doing it.

Getting enamored with the technology. Investigating SE/CASE technology can be fun for a technician. If you're not careful, you can get into too much detail too quickly and force yourself into an early, miscalculated decision. This is analogous to buying a house. If you're not careful, you might start looking at rug color (to match your blue sofa), landscaping (you love Japanese maples), etc., before looking at items like location, number of bedrooms, and the local school system. Contrary to popular belief, whenever you look at details, you can tend to get overly emotional about a decision. For SE/CASE, if you find that a particular tool has a unique windowing navigation feature or that it runs on your personal laptop PC, you might overlook (either on purpose or subconsciously) the fact that the data model and process model are not well integrated.

Not treating SE/CASE implementation as a project. Implementing SE/CASE is very similar to implementing a package for a user. You need a user team to specify requirements, a selection committee to select the appropriate software tool, and an implementation group to make it all happen. Each of these activities needs to be planned well and executed according to plan. All too often, organizations treat SE/CASE implementation as something to do in spare time, often without a clear plan as to what to do next. This leads to missed steps (e.g., specifying SE objectives), lack of continuity (because whoever is available works on the project), and confusion (which can cause lack of confidence later).

"Trying out" any technology and hoping that it will evolve into the "right stuff." How would you react if your users simply went out and purchased the first MRP product they found and then announced that they're just going to try out the product. SE/CASE technology will change the way the MIS staff do their jobs. It's no small step. It can't be evolved to. This is the easy way out. Sometimes it works, but usually it ends in shelfware and disgruntled staff and management. There simply was no infrastructure to support the tool.

Leaving users out of the selection process. The user community doesn't normally care which specific CASE tool you select, but they will be indirectly concerned with which software engineering approach the tool supports. If the approach is information engineering (IE) or rapid application development (RAD), their project involvement and responsibilities increase dramatically—occasionally to the point where the users are actually using the tools. Many times, the selection team simply assumes that the users will naturally increase their project contribution to whatever MIS asks for. Whenever a person is involved in helping to select a technology, they're usually more apt to support the technology later in the implementation phase. It never hurts to have a few extra supporters, especially from the community that's ultimately footing the bill for the technology.

Leaving MIS staff out of the selection process.   The MIS staff will be the ones actually using the technology. It will be up to them to make or break the implementation. Anything that can be done early on will pay back nicely as time goes on.

Tying the success of SE/CASE solely to productivity gains.   Make no mistake about it—SE/CASE is about improving productivity. However, tying the technology directly to productivity improvements forces the selection team to think short-term. There are true productivity gains through quality improvements, but these gains will take years to show up. If productivity was the prime motivation and main selling theme for selecting SE/CASE, then the team is pressured to produce these gains. This strategy affords no intermediate steps that say you're making progress. It's an all or nothing proposition.

Lack of SE education surrounding CASE.   Most organizations do a good job training the staff on how to use a specific CASE tool. They bring the vendor in for a few days, make reference manuals available, and show examples of how the produced deliverables are to look. What's normally missing is the high-level education that supports the tool. Structured techniques (e.g., data modeling), engineering principles, teamwork concepts, and other softer concepts are sometimes missed. In the military, you can't train a soldier how to fire an artillery piece without educating him or her in the concepts of discipline, warfare, and handling gunpowder.

Using staff members who happen to be available.   Sometimes you can get lucky with the timing of resources. Your best analyst might be between projects and available to work on the SE/CASE initiative. Usually, however, it's staffed with the few who are typically hard to place on real projects because their skills are never quite right, the current project is just too important, or they would not blend in personality-wise with the rest of the project team members. Be forewarned—these individuals don't belong on this type of effort. Perhaps one, but only as a behind-the-scenes support person.

Allowing the selection of SE/CASE technology to be used to justify a specific hardware platform.   Politics can have interesting effects on the SE/CASE selections. CASE technology is very related to DBMSs, PCs, LANs, operating systems, and other platform-related technologies. There's a certain synergy achieved when selecting these technologies in unison. The key is to determine which technology is driving which. All too often, the supporting technology drives the SE/CASE selection, resulting is a less-than-desirable technology-to-culture fit.

Inherent Risk Factors

Implementation of SE/CASE is inherently risky. Not to scare you from attempting a project of this nature, but it's important that you understand the risks that lie ahead. If it were an easy process with little risk, many more organizations would have made the conversion to SE/CASE long ago. However, MIS is a very conservative profession, one that goes out of its way to avoid any hint of risk. At least by knowing the potential risks that lie ahead, you can proactively plan for them. Remember, however, the worse risk is doing nothing at all. In this case, ignorance is not bliss.

SE/CASE has a long payback schedule. At its best, expect to take about two years for SE/CASE to begin to pay for itself. If a long-term strategy is selected, expect a five- to six-year payback scenario. Within these time scales, management can begin to get very antsy, threatening to cut the financial cord if improvements are not made faster.

Priorities within MIS are constantly changing. What was important last year is out of vogue this year. Witness the constantly changing top ten MIS issues as surveyed by a few major MIS publications. SE/CASE is close to the top of the list today, but give it a few years. Within that time frame, other priorities like client-server architectures and AI will steal the spotlight. With the spotlight will go money, energy, and support, without which you can't expect to be successful.

Instability of MIS departments. MIS departments are like professional sports teams. If you have a bad season, the most likely corrective action is to replace the manager. This change in leadership is also accompanied by a major change in ideology. For example, if it's a football team, then the new coach installs a new attacking defense system or a "run and shoot" offense. For MIS, the new manager wants to shake things up as well, many times focusing on the development ideology. The new manager will undoubtedly affect any ongoing SE/CASE initiative. It's just human nature to want to put your own personal stamp on the initiative.

Hot projects will pull the best. As business competition intensifies, your best and brightest will be pulled from SE/CASE initiatives to address "real" needs. This will tend to slow down and potentially kill SE/CASE momentum.

Better tools will become available. The last three to four years of CASE development have been focused towards perfecting the tool type popularized by Excelerator and IEF. Advances have been evolutionary and relatively slow. As organizations compared competing technology with the one they selected, they saw nice features unavailable to them, but not enough to jump ship. The next few years, however, will provide some interesting and different options. There will be better mousetraps to come as application generators, reverse engineering, and OOD-driven technologies come of age. The temptations to switch will be greater than ever.

Large financial investment will attract many layers of management. Faced with dwindling profits and international competition, corporate management is now looking much closer at capital investments in the price range of SE/CASE technology. With this scrutiny comes a reluctance of MIS management to support such long-term efforts.

Inability to prove value of SE/CASE. With modern measurement techniques and tools, MIS's improvements in both quality and productivity can be measured. The problem is that few companies have metric programs in place. In addition, once the program is established, it usually takes two to three years to build up the data to where it can support and validate the proof. Without such proof, it's getting increasingly harder to convince upper management to spend capital dollars on improvements.

Relative complexity of SE/CASE might reduce management commitment. True commitment for a technology like CASE can only be cemented through comprehension of the concepts supporting it. When times get tough and push comes to shove, if management doesn't fully understand SE/CASE, they will very quickly pull away from the technology. It's at this time when management is least likely to listen to arguments for the technology. If they were not prepared beforehand, they will unlikely support it in the long term.

Inability of MIS departments to make major decisions. Many major decisions within MIS are only made with full concurrence. Also, many times technological decisions (e.g., which CPU to go with) can be thought through and each person is convinced of the decision. SE/CASE and the ideology it brings along, however, presents a more complex situation. With a group of five or more, you might never get full concurrence (even though consensus is what's really needed).

Failed similar efforts. If MIS has attempted to implement similar efforts (e.g., 4GLs, leaderless teams), then this puts a black mark against the SE/CASE initiative from the very start.

"Flavor of the month" syndromes. MIS staffs are very much in tune with the cyclical fever over specific technologies set out to change their world. Many staff members lived through the 4GL, JAD, prototyping, and other related technological wonders with very little changing. This conditions them to expect very little change with future initiatives.

2

A Structured Approach to SE/CASE Implementation

The IC/VISION Approach

Elements of a transition project

As mentioned in the previous chapter, a common pitfall of SE/CASE selection and implementation includes not treating the effort as a real project. A successful application project usually has objectives, a strategy, a work plan, predefined deliverables, and a project structure. An SE/CASE transition project should be no different. After all, SE/CASE technology is about providing structure and discipline to the development and maintenance processes. Why, then, shouldn't you provide structure to the process that sets up the development and maintenance processes? It goes back to the old adage, "Do as I say, not as I do." You need to apply the same (if not more) energy, enthusiasm, and structure to a transition project as you do to an application project.

Identifying the objectives of a transition project is the most crucial step. Just as with the package selection process, all selections and decisions should be based on clear, written objectives, not "gut feeling." Sometimes these objectives are simple and direct. With unsuccessful projects, however, the objectives are vague and unclear. A few examples of SE/CASE transition objectives include:

- Position MIS to be used for competitive advantage.
- Consistently produce quality systems.

- Improve responsiveness to the user community.
- Reduce/contain MIS costs.
- Improve MIS productivity.
- Ensure effectiveness of user involvement.
- Gain better control of projects.
- Improve predictability of the processes.
- Improve the maintainability/adaptability of software.
- Meet user requirements.
- Satisfy user expectations.

These objectives need to directly support the business objectives of the organization, for there needs to be a business basis for the expenditure of the time and money needed to implement SE/CASE successfully. In addition, these objectives should be brought forward for each and every major decision made during the course of the transition project. As such, these objectives need to be dynamic and flexible.

For example, if in the course of selecting a systems development methodology the objectives don't quite fit the technology that appears to be right, then reconsider the objectives. Not that you should simply change your objectives to match the technology of the hour, but that objectives are hard to get right the first time. Often, as many as ten objectives are identified up front as key and important. Some people take the list provided above and say they want it all. However, when push comes to shove and its time to make a decision based on these objectives, the true objectives come forward in striking simplicity. Be conscious of these key objectives and make sure they squarely support the overall business objectives (if in fact they're known to you). Be flexible enough to allow yourself to make the right decisions. The key is that decisions need to be made with objectives in mind.

The definition of transition strategies is another crucial element to success. Every organization has sightly different needs. These differences are handled with distinct selection and implementation strategies. For instance, an organization that's strapped for cash might initially focus on the soft side of SE/CASE, implementing concepts like empowerment, teamwork, and discipline. For automation is not an essential prerequisite for many software engineering concepts, although the ultimate goal of automation with these concepts is very effective. Another organization that has a reputation to improve with the user community might elect to focus on the project management aspects of SE/CASE. Speed, budget, specific needs, politics, glitz, and internal marketing all play a part in defining the organization's transition strategies.

These strategies don't need to be elaborate. In fact, the simpler the better. If you can explain your strategies and the reason for their importance in three to five minutes, you've hit the mark. What's important is that the strategies are well thought out and written down. We have no cookbook advice to give you for developing a SE/CASE transition strategy. Each set of strategies is unique for your situation. However, we will later provide more examples of strategies as a guide to getting you started.

Once these strategies are established, a project work plan needs to be developed. Considering that a full transition can typically run for three to five years and cost a larger MIS organization well over a million dollars, (including tool costs, training, consulting, etc.) a work plan is a must. It's needed to control and monitor costs, reduce inherent risks, and ensure continuity as staff members working on the transition project get reassigned to other areas of MIS. Like any other work plan, a transition project work plan should be detailed enough to assign specific tasks to individuals and to identify specific deliverables to be completed. Since the ultimate goal of a full SE/CASE environment is many years away, a work plan also provides the team with intermediate goals to obtain and show that progress is being made—thereby maintaining momentum for the transition project. Without these intermediate goals, management might get itchy for results and rush the process.

In chapter 7, we'll provide a template of potential phases, activities, and tasks from which to craft your work plan. This template needs to be customized to your specific organization, in the same manner as a systems development methodology (SDM) is customized to an application project. This template, called IC/VISION, is for selecting and implementing methodologies, techniques, tools, and culture. In essence, it's a "meta-methodology."

The team responsible for delivering SE/CASE is part of the project structure. A project of this magnitude (both cost and cultural impact) needs to have representation from all internal MIS groups, the user community, and MIS management. In addition, it must have a sponsor with authority and political muscle. This sponsor needs to control the budget, resources, and direction. The work plan will pull the activities of these different groups together to achieve the desired results.

IC/VISION concepts and principles

IC/VISION stands for Infrastructure, Culture, and Vision. These are the three fundamental components of a full SE/CASE environment. These three components are shown in Figure 2.1, which was adapted from Tom Peters and Bob Waterman's 7S Model.

IC/VISION has evolved from CGA's original approach/methodology for selecting and implementing SE/CASE. This approach was called SYS*CASE. SYS*CASE, and its recent derivative, has been used successfully by CGA at seven different U.S. organizations, ranging from a major airline with more than 1,000 MIS professionals, to a regional bank with 175 MIS professionals, to a smaller manufacturer with 20 MIS profession-

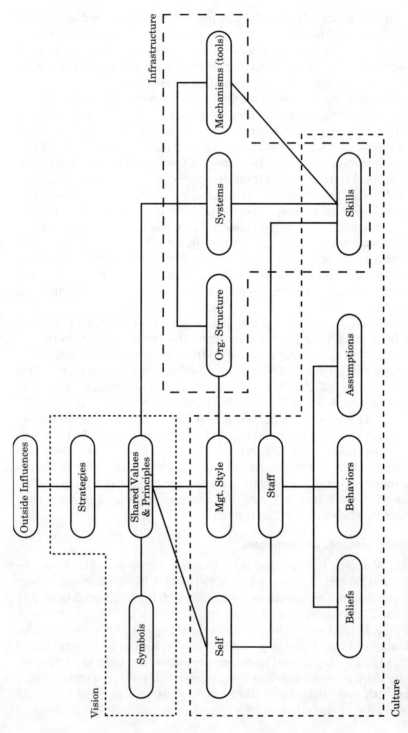

Figure 2.1 The SE paradigm. (*Copyright CGA, 1991.*)

als. In each case, the basic structure of the approach stayed consistent; only the amount of assessment, research, detail, and documentation varied with MIS department size.

In this book, we're making CGA's previously proprietary approach publicly available as a small but important effort to improve America's overall competitiveness. As consultants, we can only do so much; we have limited resources. However, by writing this book, a broader circle of MIS organizations will be better able to participate in the important revolution of quality, process improvement, and structure.

In order to present IC/VISION within the context of a book of this nature, we restructured and simplified the approach. We felt that it was important to highlight the essence of the approach, as opposed to the activities. Each organization is different, and we can't presuppose each of your situations. We've also simplified the approach. Sometimes too much detail can get in the way of the good stuff, so we practiced the 80 percent-20 percent rule— 80 percent of the meat is in 20 percent of the tasks. The objectives for both SYS*CASE and IC/VISION are identical. They're listed in the following

Reduce the SE/CASE implementation risk. As mentioned in an earlier section of this book, SE/CASE is inherently risky. It's not an easy process; there are many roadblocks already built into the way things are naturally. Our approach will help you to identify these risks and to proactively plan around them. As a result, you should be able to reduce the probability of stagnating the SE/CASE initiative and of "backsliding" into the old approach.

Deliver the appropriate technology. This involves selecting what's right for you and your MIS culture, not what the latest issue of a DP magazine says to do. Each organization is different, and each of the tools and methodologies are different. The combinations of these differences is impossible to capture in a five-page technology assessment article. However, these assessments are important sources of up-to-date information that can help you make your decision. IC/CASE will properly position these sources.

Shorten the implementation cycle. This objective seems impossible whenever you look at the IC/VISION work plan template in chapter 7. Within this template there are more than 25 different tasks to be accomplished, a seemingly overwhelming number for the relatively simple selection of a piece of software (i.e., CASE tools.) You'll need to customize this work plan to your organization's needs and crisply complete each of the tasks. If these selected tasks are followed, the total elapsed time will most likely be shorter. You'll find yourself much better prepared to make consensus decisions, thereby reducing the amount of seemingly endless searches for "one more" piece of data. The key is doing the task selection right the first time.

Remove internal and vendor bias from the decisions. SE/CASE decisions can become very emotional at times. With emotions come a natural tendency to be biased without even knowing it. In addition, the selection of the wrong consultant to help you select the technology can also produce a bias. If that consultant also represents an SDM or CASE tool, the chances are nine out of ten that their tool set is the "ultimate one for you." IC/CASE will provide you a forum for dealing with these internal and external biases.

Consider a broad perspective. Too many times, SE/CASE decisions are suboptimized around a given technology like code generation or project management without consideration for how they fit and support other technologies.

The base principles behind IC/VISION are relatively simple. First, SE/CASE decisions need to be directed from a top-down perspective. They should not be made from the top, just directed. If they're made and then dictated from the top, support among the project managers is very suspect and implementation will be very difficult. If decisions are made from the middle/bottom of the organization without the top perspective, long-term funding and support from top management is virtually impossible. Thus, the best approach is to blend top management goals, objectives, and aspirations with project manager and staff selections and implementation planning.

Management direction is best supported via a graphics-based vision. Typically, this vision paints a long-term view of where the MIS organization is headed in the next three to five years with regard to SE/CASE. This vision helps to sell the overall concepts to staff, users, and top management and to help channel the individual activities towards building the eventual environment.

Second, the SE principles of quality, process improvement, and effectiveness need to be at the center of every SE/CASE decision. This is what we call principle centered analysis. Your ultimate goals might be increased productivity and responsiveness, but without understanding the rationale of the underlying principles, you're playing Russian roulette with your organization. There's very little magic that works today. Most of the long-term, significant productivity and responsiveness gains made by companies today are made the hard way—by earning them through attention to SE principles.

Third, consensus needs to be reached for major decisions. Please note— consensus is not full concurrence. Not everyone needs to agree in total with every decision. As mentioned earlier, in a larger organization it's virtually impossible to achieve full concurrence. In addition, a broader range of involvement and participation in selecting and implementing SE/CASE is needed, further compounding the full concurrence dream.

Consensus is built from a full understanding of the decision. A person might not agree with a decision, but at least that person understands the rationale for the decision, had a say in making the decision, and thus can support the decision. Even though consensus is easier than concurrence, it should not be used as a shield to hide a dictate from management. A JAD-like session mixed with specialized education classes is a very powerful combination for achieving an informed consensus.

Fourth, SE/CASE selection and implementation needs to be treated like a real project, with objectives, deliverables, and work plans. This is very similar to package selection for the user community. You're simply selecting a package for development and maintenance processes.

Fifth, the new SE/CASE environment can't ignore existing strengths within the current environment. These strengths need to be identified and built upon.

Finally, the resultant environment needs to take into consideration the environment situation (e.g., why you need SE/CASE), the available technology, and the cultural impact. The integration of these three components will provide a solid, long-term solution to today's software crisis.

Overview of the IC/VISION process

IC/VISION is a collection of activities that should be performed at given stages of the SE/CASE evaluation and implementation process. These activities are meant to be methodology-like, providing checklists and guidance, but not providing a sequence of activities or strict deliverable requirements. We want to avoid many of the inherent problems found with traditional systems development methodologies. These problems include: too large and complex, not flexible enough, and not appropriate for the environment.

IC/VISION, on the other hand, is delivered to you via this book. We cannot provide direct training or coaching to those who will read and use this book. Therefore, IC/VISION needs to stand on its own and address these problems directly. For this reason, we have described IC/VISION based on stages of implementation, as opposed to by phase. These stages are:

1. Considering SE/CASE. What is SE/CASE? Are you ready for SE/CASE? Is it right for you at this time?

2. Creating the SE/CASE vision. What are your strengths to build on, weaknesses to prop up, opportunities to exploit, and threats to guard for? What vision are you aiming for? How far out should you look? Which technologies are appropriate?

3. Selecting anchor technology. Where do you start? What do you build around? What's your nucleus for the SE/CASE environment?

4. Planning for the transition. How should you change the MIS culture? How do you get there? Who needs to do what?

5. Implementing/using technology. How can you monitor resistance and success? How and when do you tweak the SE/CASE environment?

These stages make it easy for you to identify your position in the implementation process and to quickly pick out the activities from IC/VISION that apply. The simplicity of the stages also makes it easier to sell the concept to management.

Within these stages, however, runs a more sophisticated theme. Each task within IC/VISION supports one or more dimensions of study. These study dimensions are used to help you select and drive the appropriate tasks. These study dimensions include:

- SE work practices—planning, development, maintenance, and project management activities. Addressing the processes of MIS.

- SE/CASE tools—automation of the MIS processes.

- SE skills—technical skills (e.g., data flow diagramming, testing) and business skills (e.g., interpersonal skills, facilitation, leadership).

- MIS culture/concepts—the beliefs, behaviors, and assumptions of the MIS staff towards the concepts and practices of software engineering.

- User/MIS relationship—the ability and effectiveness of the user/MIS working relationship.

- Organizational structure—the formal and informal people/power structure within MIS.

For each of these study dimensions, IC/VISION recommends an assessment, definition, and implementation set of activities. You might not want or need each of these dimensions addressed. Perhaps they're someone else's responsibility or you might simply not have the time or authority to address all of them at the same time. In any event, we've provided a quick reference mechanism to allow you to quickly identify those activities that are not appropriate. However, we strongly recommend that the activities related to the MIS culture/concepts study dimension be kept within your study. As previously mentioned, ignoring the cultural aspects of SE/CASE is a major reason for many companies to experience shelfware and "backsliding." As evidenced by the title of this book and its middle chapters, we also recognize the major importance of this dimension of study.

The strategic planning relationship

The IC/VISION approach, as outlined and developed in this book, is really part of a larger strategic planning process. The scope and deliverables of this approach fit in nicely along with other IS planning architectures, those being data, process, and technology. Figure 2.2 shows a simple yet powerful view of where IC/VISION fits in.

The information architecture represents the structure of the organization's present and future data files and databases. It's usually represented

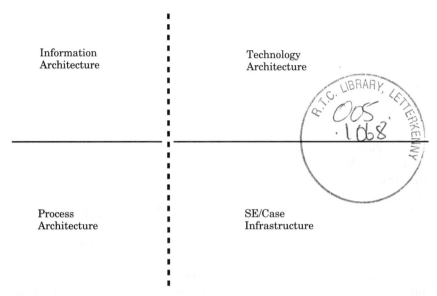

Figure 2.2 IS planning architectures.

via a logical entity relationship diagram that identifies the major data entities and the relationships between them. The focus of this planning effort is
to surface the information that's needed for the organization to make decisions and to keep the business running. With the advent and implementation of relational DBMSs, many organizations are now in the process of
documenting the current architecture via data dictionaries and related diagramming techniques and tools. A few organizations are also proactively
planning their future data structures via a coordinated planning effort (e.g.,
an information engineering approach.)

The process architecture represents the organization's present and future functions, programs, and systems. It identifies the major corporate
functions (via decomposition diagrams) and defines boundaries of future
applications. In many organizations, this architecture is usually the most
advanced of the four, for without it, there would only be a hodgepodge of
programs floating around. At a minimum, most organizations have flow diagrams that depict the interfaces and major functions of their legacy systems. In addition, many organizations also plan this architecture out for a
few years. It's traditionally used to define their backlog and to help prioritize upcoming projects.

Another more advanced architecture is the technology quadrant. The
technology architecture represents the organization's hardware, software,
telecommunications, protocol, and other technology-related concepts and
products. This area is solely the responsibility of MIS and is usually de-
picted in grandiose network-like diagrams depicting a wide array of hard-

ware and communications lines. Because of the tangible, visible dollars spent in this area, the technology architecture is usually planned out for five or more years.

The last of the four related architectures is the software engineering architecture. This architecture represents the organization's reporting structure, work practices, methodologies, CASE tools, culture, and skills. It's usually the most overlooked of the four architectures. It's often treated in a tactical manner—usually, whenever a major system needs to be built and the organization realizes a weakness in this area.

However, how often does an organization run out and acquire a new mainframe computer or reorganize its complete data structure because of a single project? These decisions are usually treated in a top-down manner. True, a major project might have precipitated these changes, but that was not the only reason for them. SE/CASE technology is often selected primarily for a given project, then left to languish in a tactical, short-term-oriented environment. No wonder there's so much CASE shelfware today!

IC/VISION is designed to proactively define and implement this planning architecture in congruence with the other three architectures. In an ideal world, all four architectures need to be considered and built in unison. There are many interrelationships. For instance, the choice of a particular RDBMS will have a major impact on the data modeling and code generation technology selected. The condition of the current portfolio and the types of future systems to be built will have a major impact on the inclusion/exclusion of reverse engineering and the selection of the SE approach. In addition, SE infrastructure situations can and do affect the other architectures. For instance, the culture and skill set of an organization should be an important determining factor for AI and object-oriented languages and databases that might be needed to support future process architecture requirements.

If at all possible, IC/VISION should be executed along with a formalized planning approach that usually focuses on the data, process, and technology architectures. If the timing and political situation allows, you have found the best possible scenario for using IC/VISION.

However, most organizations will not find this an ideal situation or will need to move much faster than a four-pronged architecture study will allow. IC/VISION is still very valuable, and is, in fact, designed for just such an occurrence. The other three architectures are referenced within the activities of IC/VISION, but they're not the central theme. If you're lucky enough to find yourself in the ideal situation, you'll need to extract the essence of IC/VISION and integrate it into your formal planning approach. This is not a difficult task, but a very important one.

In either event, you'll need to identify where your organization is the strongest and from which planning architecture to lead. Some organizations are very dynamic and provide the users a very flexible environment from which to drive systems development. These organizations typically drive from the technology architecture, usually building a client/server-like environment and developing a strong data architecture from which to evolve systems. Other organizations tend to be application oriented and focused on the process architecture, building systems that integrate well and build on one another.

The key is to understand where you stand in each architecture and to ascertain the organization's strategies for building systems. Please note—just because you're weak in a particular area, that doesn't mean it's bad. One organization we know of has at best a six-month window of future projects and an undefined process architecture. The business is simply so dynamic and changeable that no one can pin down future activities with any certainty. However, their technology and SE infrastructure architectures were very well defined and thus the organization was able to quickly respond to and support the user needs. This, by the way, is more of a wave of the future with international competition on our heels. We'll still have the large utilities and banking institutions that need firm data and process architectures, but for many other organizations, the technology and SE infrastructure architectures will become more important, and flexibility and responsiveness will be the primary SE objectives.

All of the four architectures need to be developed in unison and balanced for ultimate results. This is similar to balancing the career, family, spiritual, and physical aspects of our own lives. We can't afford to be one- or two-dimensional over the long run in order to live a successful and satisfying life. We need a vision for each of these areas and a plan for achieving our personal goals.

Just as each person has different objectives to reach these goals, so too does an organization. What's right for company X might not be right for you. Thus, we can't tell you in this book what's right for you. Nor can you decide what's right for your organization within the SE infrastructure area without considering the other three architectures. If you don't consider these other three, you'll undoubtedly overanalyze and overspecify this area. You'll tend to shoot for the moon—just as people can overemphasize career if they're not reminded of the other aspects of life. There's only so much organizational money, energy, attention, and patience. Your job is to help optimize the overall situation, not to simply suboptimize the SE/CASE environment.

The Transition Project

Elements of a transition project

The decisions made and technology acquired during this IV/VISION process will impact the MIS organization for years to come. With this level of importance comes a willingness and an appreciation by an organization to structure the process. This structuring should result in a work plan, (complete with milestones, deliverables, and assignments), a project team (called the transition team throughout the remainder of this book), occasionally a steering committee, project objectives, and a project charter outlining the team's responsibilities and authorities.

The work plan needs to be based on the IC/VISION template presented in chapter 7 of this book. It needs to be a step-by-step plan that results in specific, defined deliverables. Like any application project, the work plan needs a quality control function. This is usually provided by the steering committee. This degree of structure will allow you to assign resources to accomplish specific tasks. Without these specific assignments, the transition team will languish in countless meetings trying to sort through all the details.

Don't get me wrong. There will be many joint meetings for consensus gaining and decision making, but there are just as many preparation activities that are not suited for meetings. These activities will not be dynamic, fun, decision-making work. There's a lot of groundwork that needs to be accomplished in order to efficiently and effectively get to the decisions.

This is an area where a lot of organizations get bogged down. Usually a committee is established with a loose game plan. Members usually volunteer or are selected as a perk for doing a good job. Most of the participants are project managers with a large ego and/or a very tight schedule.

These committee members are all excited about moving forward quickly, and they don't view participation on the committee as work. They look at it as fun, dynamic stuff. Thus, few people volunteer for doing the grunt work to prepare for the meetings. What preparation work that's performed is usually performed in a lackluster, cursory way, or is performed with a particular biased agenda in mind. This results in decisions that never get made or decisions that are just not well supported or well founded.

Treating this initiative as a real project, with a work plan, deliverables, assignments, and milestones helps to eliminate the majority of these problems. Keep in mind, however, that a transition project properly staffed will require a significant time and resource commitment—two commodities that most MIS organizations have in short supply these days. Depending on your organization's size and needs, it might take as long as three to six months before any technology is acquired, and the project might consume three to five people (each participating about one-third to one-half time). Thus, taking resources away from the real work to participate on a planning project like this can be politically upsetting. So, two conflicting dimensions to consider when scoping this effort include:

1. Keep it realistic.

2. Pay me now or pay me later.

Keep it realistic means don't go too far. I've seen a few organizations put 10 to 12 people on the transition team. Sure, it helps to get full representation, but with this large team, every half-day meeting expends more than a full work week (40 hours). In addition, these organizations tend to over-re-search and over-define everything. These organizations usually start out with great intentions only to realize that the real work is suffering and the elapsed time is moving past quickly. In an effort to jump-start the stalled ef-fort, many times the important decisions are quickly made and technology acquired. This scenario is better than doing nothing up front, but the money, energy, and time was not effectively spent. The results could and should have been better.

Pay me now or pay me later refers to not doing enough up front. Many or-ganizations feel that they can jump right into a CASE tool and its related techniques/skills/methods and that everything will eventually evolve into place. Many times it does, but with many casualties, much aggravation, and a very long elapsed time. If the money, energy, and time were calculated in this scenario, you'd find that a top-down planning approach (as espoused with IC/VISION) would have cost less overall.

Compare these scenarios with selecting a computer. How many times have you seen a company agonize over their computer decision and finally select one that's soon obsolete because their decision took years to make— or the organization that jumped quickly and has been spending dearly to make the equipment work right ever since.

As with any important decision, there's a fine edge to walk. This decision is no different. Walk the edge carefully!

The transition team roles

A transition project is typically staffed with two different groups: a transition team and a steering committee. The transition team is responsible for re-searching alternatives, preparing for JAD-style meetings, documenting deci-sions, creating straw-man recommendations, and managing/coordinating the entire effort. The team is typically a group of three or four staff members.

A steering committee is responsible for making the final recommendations (and approval if granted complete authority) for many of the important SE/CASE decisions. The steering committee consists of broad representation from all groups affected by the new technology, including users, operations, and management.

There are two sometimes conflicting strategies towards staffing the tran-sition team. The usual approach is to select members from a wide and com-plete representation of all groups, teams, or divisions. Another approach is to select based on skills, experiences, and abilities. MIS usually staffs appli-cation projects via this second method, and it seems to work, so why switch?

The main reason to choose a broad representation is for political support. In addition, this broad membership seems fair (especially if membership is considered a perk) and is the easiest way to ensure fair representation.

Please note: representation is an extremely important dimension, especially whenever it comes to implementing the selected technology. However, broad representation should not be the only criteria used to select membership. The following characteristics also need to be considered for membership to the transition team:

- Leadership—IC/VISION is a planning exercise. Major change might come about as a result of it. There's potential for revolutionary recommendations for the development and maintenance environments. Without true leaders, the transition team will stay conservative and recommend only evolutionary solutions. In addition, the transition project itself is involving and potentially very dynamic. A project manager type is needed to keep things under control.

- Interpersonal skills—There will be a significant amount of interviewing (within MIS and the user community) and many meetings. Without the ability to communicate and relate to one another, there's potential for political wars to start and specifications to be missed.

- Coaching/educating—During the activities of the transition project, the transition team will be immersed in the concepts and technologies of SE/CASE. They will become relative experts in the mechanics, benefits, and underpinnings of the technologies. In order for the steering committee to be in a position to make the appropriate decisions, the transition team members need to act as educators and customize and present an explanation of the technology to the steering committee. In addition, during implementation, these same people will help to roll out this new technology, again using their training skills.

- An understanding of the current development/maintenance ideologies— The transition process can't start from a completely blank page. Just as you select team members with a business understanding of a new application, you need to select people who already have an understanding of the domain of SE/CASE. There's a potential risk that these people might not see beyond their understanding, but if all of the other characteristics have been met, this is a small risk.

- Being respected—Don't overlook this characteristic. The majority of the transition team members need to have the respect of the project managers. The project managers are the ones who will make or break the implementation. They control the majority of the decisions as to how systems are built and maintained. If these people don't respect the transition team members (e.g., they're all young/new or are utility staff with nothing else to do) then the transition project will go nowhere.

- Facilitation experience—At least one person on the transition team has to be experienced driving joint consensus-building sessions (e.g., JAD leaders). There will be many such meetings throughout the project, usually with management, users, and key staff present. This will be the primary interface mechanism between the transition team and the steering committee. Lack of this talent will kill the project. This is one of the primary principles upon which IC/VISION is based.

- Presentation skills/marketing presence—There will be many opportunities for each transition team member to sell the initiative, both formally and informally. Possessing the innate ability to sell to a person's perceived need is much more important than memorizing the 20 prepackaged benefits of the full environment.

The transition team itself needs to be relatively small, consisting of three to five people. These staff members need to possess the characteristics previously listed, in addition to a hands-on, energetic, and supportive attitude. They will be responsible for the majority of the grunt work and for making the key recommendations for the steering committee. It's also valuable to include a consultant experienced with helping clients implement SE/CASE. A consultant who has only used one tool/technique, however, does more harm than good. These consultants come in with a very strong bias towards the approach/methods/tools that they know. Their main intent (conscious or subconscious) is in securing additional revenues after you select their pet technologies. A broadly experienced consultant, however, should be able to support your global objectives.

The transition team also needs an identified project leader/manager. This leader will become the point person, keep control of the process, and have the responsibility of meeting budgets and schedule. Without such a person, the transition team can get caught in a never-ending cycle of investigation. There will always be something better out there to choose from. He or she will also have the difficult job of balancing theory with practicality.

Representation can be easily and more effectively handled via a steering committee mechanism that's used to review progress and to finalize decisions. In addition, since this mechanism requires less time per individual, you can also get many of the better yet busier staff members involved. This is also an excellent place to get user representation. Many of the decisions will affect the amount, nature, and types of work that the users will be expected to perform, especially if RAD, JAD, and/or prototyping are implemented. Without their participation, you might run right into a brick wall upon implementation. Representation from computer operations can also be accommodated by this mechanism.

Steering committee

Membership on the steering committee should be seriously considered. This committee will be responsible for setting the direction of the transition team and for approving their recommendations. The characteristics needed for each member include:

- Recognized representation—Just because a person is from a particular group or team doesn't mean that they fully understand the problem, concerns, and aspirations of the group's constituencies. A "face member" might satisfy political protocol but will do little good (and even potential harm) if he or she doesn't truly represent the unit.

- Open-mindedness—There are many different ways to skin a cat (poor cat!) and the member needs to be willing to at least hear them out. If a person goes in with a political agenda of selecting a particular tool or technique, they can't really be open.

- Visionaries—The committee members need to be able to view the world beyond their current set of problems. Yet they should not be so far removed that the practical application of the technology is missing.

- Ideology drivers—These are the folks in an MIS organization who really call the shots, many times the project managers. These people are not always the formal seats of powers, but they have the ability to shake things up a bit. Many times they're the department's rising stars.

The key to the steering committee is that it should not become a "rubber stamp" committee. The transition team might have a technological advantage over the steering committee because of their intense study with the details of SE/CASE. However, the steering committee should insist on down-to-earth explanations and strategies before moving on. If the steering committee doesn't fully understand these recommendations yet approves them, then this puts the entire initiative at risk. Beyond their stated duties, the steering committee members will also become informal marketers of the SE/CASE infrastructure. Underinformed or misinformed messengers are the worse kind!

If you're having a tough time properly filling the transition team and steering committee roles, then wait. The timing is probably not right. You might need to do a little marketing to prime the pump in order to get the right membership. Sometimes the right person needs to be convinced that their efforts don't go to waste. Also, pressing problems can keep the right people from participating. If your organization is in such disarray that the right mix might never become available, then its probably time to leave. Without SE/CASE technologies and culture, the situation will only get worse.

Positioning for a Transition Project

In the early days of SE/CASE selection and implementation, the most-asked question was, "Am I ready?" To answer this question, there have been several models (e.g., Howard Ruben's footprints) put forward. A key factor in each of these models was motivation. Sure, SE skills, investment, and timing are all issues to contend with, but without motivation, nothing happens. With genuine motivation, almost anything can happen. Funds can appear, attitudes can be changed, and talent can be found.

Motivation

Just what is motivation? Motivation in this case has two major components: pain and the level in the organizational where the pain is felt the most. Pain is aggravation and agitation—aggravation and agitation to the point where the status quo is no longer acceptable. Potential sources of pain include:

- Outsourcing pressure.
- Diminishing credibility with users.
- Missed estimates.
- Unable to prove value to user community.
- Quality inconsistencies.
- Maintenance burden.
- Loss of control over development.
- Attrition of key staff members.
- Pressure to do more with less.

The level is the person or persons in the organization who feel the effect of the pain the most. Sometimes it's within the staff, sometimes within the user community, and sometimes within upper management. As would stand to reason, the higher the organizational level, the greater the relative pain.

The change agent's role in this process is to identify and highlight the pain—not to start fires, but to pull together the different instances of pain to magnify and document the "heat." It's also his or her role to find the pain threshold—that point where it's time to address the root causes and not to soothe over the symptoms.

As previously listed, within MIS there are a number of standard pain items. One of the most crucial, visible, and potentially dangerous is outsourcing pressure by the user community. This is an interesting story to unfold. See if any aspects of this story match your organization.

In the XYZ company, MIS has generally been unresponsive to the user community due to staff head-count restrictions. MIS tries hard, but "you can only push so hard." As a result, many users started to do their own programming. This seemed harmless enough. However, as these users developed systems, the systems began to get more complex and needed to be integrated. After a certain complexity point, these systems became the property of MIS to maintain. This maintenance burden further reduced MIS's ability to deliver new systems. This then lead the users to select a vendor package of software and contract directly with third parties to build software. Of course, MIS was again left with the maintenance, further overburdening the department. Finally, as a last course, the users contracted out for all MIS activities: development, maintenance, and operations—eliminating an internal MIS organization.

Sound far fetched? Well, it is a bit. However, look at the print shops of yesteryear. There was a time when most organizations had their own print shops in house. It was always difficult to get your copying and duplication work done because some big shot had to get the annual report through before the board meeting, and the print shop had a head-count restriction to live under. A good excuse, but you were still left holding the bag. Even when you did get the print shop to do your job, they printed your material two-sided and three-hole punched and you wanted to bind the pages together. It was a job-shop mentality, with little emphasis on customer service. There might have even been a sign on the wall stating:

You want it quick?
You want it right?
You want it cheap?
Pick any two and call me.

After all, where could you go? There was a company policy about going outside the organization.

However, as we all know, times change. The policy was initially modified to allow you to go outside of the organization for those "crucial" jobs. However, what happened was that the print shop around the corner could get it done faster, cheaper, and better! Before you knew it, most people were using outside services. Well, this made the cost of internal work even more expensive, so head count was restricted even further, and the new machinery (e.g., highspeed copier/sorter) was postponed indefinitely. This situation only made matters worse. If the print shop culture didn't change to meet this new competition and management didn't give one last investment in the print shop infrastructure (e.g., machinery, tactics), then the department was doomed.

In order to have the motivation to properly respond to this external type of competition, the print shop needed to feel the pain of the present situation (e.g., not meeting schedules) and future conditions (e.g., loss of a job). They could not be smug with the policy of no external work. Policies are only temporary.

MIS is not much different. There are a lot of hungry consulting firms just waiting for the opportunity to take over MIS operations. Many of the larger consulting firms can deliver "soup-to-nuts" services—from strategic planning and development through operations. In addition, these firms have the advantage of an aggressive culture, with the proper methods and tools, and the capital funding. Very much like the corner print shops.

An additional factor to consider is "offshore" contracting. Programming skills are not indigenous only to U.S. shores. Armed with an acceptable command of the English language and a good COBOL class, there are plenty of foreigners who are willing to work for one-fourth of what an American professional with a degree demands.

Not only do you need to be concerned with the type of pain, but also the level at which it's felt. Typically, the type of pain that brings on outsourcing is felt outside of MIS, making it harder to gauge. If it were felt inside MIS, then the gradual buildup would make a case for change long before a drastic outsourcing decision.

Related to the previous story is MIS's lack of credibility with the user community. After countless missed estimates and an inconsistent process, the user community might no longer trust MIS. In addition,, sometimes we just don't appear professional. Sure, our profession has only been around for some 30 years and is much newer than most other business areas (e.g., accounting), however, the fact that our profession is more than 30 years old says that most of the early pioneers are long since retired. The majority of the MIS staff in many organizations are college educated in the discipline. We truly have no excuse to be disorganized and unprofessional. For the most part, the realities of this situation are changing for the better, but the perception lingers on. This significantly hampers our ability to prove our value to the user community.

We can also lack the ability to consistently deliver quality systems. MIS can deliver systems and upgrades left and right, a few of them quite good. The good ones tend to be our legacy systems, the base of our functional architecture. However, the majority of the systems that come in direct contact with the users, the periphery and special-needs systems, stink. They fall apart, can't be modified, and look awful. We know how to deliver decent quality, we just can't do it consistently.

The growing maintenance burden is another pain-causing situation. As we build systems, we need to maintain them. As mentioned earlier, this reduces our ability to build new systems. As a result, the range of maintenance activities for some organizations is 90 percent or more. This long-term focus on maintenance reduces the organization's ability to develop systems. They just don't have the experience or confidence to develop systems any longer. However, some of the systems might now be 20 to 30 years old, desperate for replacement. Even with the newer reverse engineering tools, you still need to know forward engineering concepts and tools to be successful. This situation can spur turnover and reduce service to the user community.

In addition, the organization might want to move aggressively towards newer production technologies such as expert systems, object-oriented databases, and executive support systems. However, the organization realizes that it doesn't have the appropriate infrastructure in place. Without the firm structured base, many of these newer types of systems are very difficult to deliver.

At a lot of organizations, nobody knows the true status of the system. They have no idea of what's to be delivered, what resources are needed, and what the final budget is. To make up for this loss of project control, numbers are sometimes made up and, of course, held to. This situation causes many late nights and hard feelings that can in turn cause communication breakdowns, infighting, and unnecessary political maneuvering.

The prioritization process that drives this situation makes the matters even worse. Many times, whoever shouts the loudest gets the most. Not exactly effective management of resources.

Another cause of pain is the loss of staff, especially the good ones. Everyone knows that a little attrition of the "misfits" and "slouches" is healthy. However, when the key developers, maintainers, and managers begin to go, you have a major problem. First of all, the work load is intensified for everyone. Its amazing how much a talented individual can do. Next, because of this increased workload and the exodus momentum, other solid performers begin to leave. This then causes a hiring blitz, usually attracting "opportunists" from other companies. You know them—the ones that look good on paper, but never seem to get anything accomplished. They're usually distinguished by a string of jobs, one to two years in length.

Morale suffers, productivity drops, service is nonexistent, and finally, management is axed and the department is rebuilt. This scenario doesn't need to happen if management can anticipate it. Again, future pain is tough to see, but it's just as motivating if properly identified. In this case, the pain is felt initially inside MIS, then, as the situation intensifies, outside MIS. Once felt outside of MIS, drastic actions can occur.

Some organizations are plagued with the inability to attract top recruits, even though they might pay well. Many times an organization gets a reputation as a "sweatshop" or as an archaic place to work. These reputations can live long after the reality of the situation.

The pressure to do more with less is a major cause of pain, but rarely the primary motivating factor. This pressure usually causes small adjustments, but never major initiatives. The time to do the initiatives is generally perceived as taking away from the ultimate goal.

On the positive side is upper management's drive to improve quality and responsiveness. There's a genuine movement in American business today to truly improve operations, not just to squeeze additional productivity out of an already overworked staff. SE/CASE fills in nicely with this new business focus.

Each of those causes of pain is focused at the organizational level. However, personal pain also plays a large part in a SE/CASE initiative. Like many of us, the decision makers are also driven by pain. For many, it doesn't matter where the pain originates.

The following are a few of the personal pain items to consider:

- Pressure from the department's "up-and-coming" hotshots who know about SE/CASE.
- Peer pressure from other managers inside and outside the organization.
- Realization that management (as well as staff) need SE/CASE in their resumes.
- Realization that if the top guys walk out, you can't effectively run the MIS department.
- The desire to control outsourcing by putting formal structures in place. In essence, if you can't beat them, manage them.
- Personal credibility and potential upward mobility.

Moving to an SE/CASE infrastructure complete with a corresponding shift in the MIS culture is a major undertaking. It will not be easy, cheap, or quick. This type of change needs big-time support. You don't do it because it's "neat" or the latest thing to do; you do it because you need to. If you don't have a strong case for deployment of SE/CASE at this time, then abort this process. Either continue to build a stronger case or wait. It's better to wait a year or two than to start and fail in an initiative like this one. For most individuals, SE/CASE implementation is a once-a-career opportunity (at least within the same organization).

If you do have a strong case based on pain and motivation, then move on to the other factors identified and developed in the following paragraphs. These are not so much readiness factors (like motivation), but mitigating factors. They will provide input into your selection and implementation strategy later in the IC/VISION process. Unless extreme (e.g., the company is going bankrupt), they will not affect your go/no go decision. It's amazing what can happen given a strong motivation to make things happen.

Timing

Being at the right place at the right time takes more than just luck; it takes planning. This is never more true than with the implementation of SE/CASE. There are so many timing issues to coordinate that they could never align naturally. If you wait for just the right time, you'll be waiting for years. There's always a manager with a "chip" on their shoulder, a project that went poorly, a morale problem to deal with, a key staff member who left, or a reorganization to weather through. Each of these situations could be potential reasons to delay the SE/CASE initiative. However, they could also be reasons to proceed more quickly as previously discussed in the section on pain. These issues need to be worked though. Don't allow them to become roadblocks.

There are, however, a few very important events that can figure nicely into the timing of an initiative of this nature. These include a corporate-wide quality initiative, recent IS and business strategic planning efforts, new departmental leadership, and large mission-critical development efforts.

Around 15 percent to 20 percent of American corporations today are planning to or are currently implementing a corporate-wide Total Quality Management (TQM). These initiatives are usually based on the continuous improvement process outlined by Edward Demming, Philip Crosby, Bill Conway, and others. Riding the coattails of this type of initiative can be very beneficial. These initiatives presell the concepts of: implementing a process (i.e., an SDM), focusing on quality, and satisfying user (i.e., internal customer) expectations. In addition, these programs help to expand the organization's investment horizon. Where before, management was looking to reap the harvest of the technology investment within a year or two, now management is willing to wait up to five years for the fruits to become apparent. If you need to wait six to twelve months to properly synchronize your initiative with the corporate-wide program, it's probably a wise wait. We've found that the second year of the corporate-wide program is the best time to start a SE/CASE initiative. This provides a little time for the concepts to work their way into the business culture. However, remember, every organization is different.

As mentioned previously, this book focuses on the SE/CASE infrastructure component of the MIS strategic planning process. However, each of the other three architectures (i.e., data, process, and technology) provide valuable input into this process. For example, it will be difficult to select a SE approach if the type of systems needed in the future (e.g., decision support versus transaction processing) are not known. In addition, without knowing the nature of the database, it's difficult to select a code generator that can generate the appropriate SQL DML statements. You can proceed without a clear knowledge of the future from an information, process, or technology perspective, but the potential rewards might be muted. For this reason, if there's a strategic planning process underway or under consideration, you should try to integrate your process with the planning process.

New MIS leadership is often more open to implementing SE/CASE than their predecessors. Perhaps this is due to a wider exposure to these concepts from outside the organization. Or perhaps they simply have more leverage due to being new with a fresh start. In either event, it's not an opportunity to waste. If you're faced with this situation, give the new manager a little time to get their feet wet (three to six months) before starting your move.

One of the most common reasons for SE/CASE implementation is the advent of a large, mission-critical system. Many times, a major, mission-critical system can act as the catalyst for getting an MIS organization moving towards SE/CASE. The project gets management's attention and concern and also provides a little extra capital for purchases of tools and methodologies.

Funding

Money is an important element in the SE/CASE selection and implementation process. For a larger organization (500 to 1,000 MIS professionals), out-of-pocket expenses for SE/CASE can be well into the million dollar plus range. The real cost, of course is much higher. Even for smaller organizations, the expenses can extend into the hundreds of thousands.

However, if funds are really tight, there are plenty of short-term activities that can be used to improve quality and productivity. For instance, the proper implementation of the JAD process can significantly improve MIS's ability to meet the users expectations, and data modeling techniques (even without the CASE support) can be used to better select software packages.

The key, however, is motivation and pain. Where there's a will, there's a way. However, it never hurts to have a few dollars allocated to prime the pump.

Applicability

CASE, narrowly defined as analysis/design support and code generation, is not for every MIS organization—especially for those organizations who are primarily package shops. The principles and concepts of software engineering, however, are for everyone. Many of the techniques and supporting tools can be applied to package and nonpackage shops alike.

Maintenance is another area where the principles apply very well. Even though the original systems might be a spaghetti mess, the concepts and tools of SE can really help.

3

Overview of
Software Engineering (SE)

A Software Engineering Framework

Software engineering (SE) is a very broad discipline. By many accounts, SE refers to an integrated set of methods, procedures, and tools for specifying, designing, developing, and maintaining software. However, we've been referring to software engineering within the text of this book as SE/CASE. Based on this definition, the SE/CASE term we use is somewhat redundant, for CASE is already a part of SE. The problem is that many people consider software engineering to be just the methods/techniques, and CASE to be just the tools. Thus, the SE/CASE term brings both halves together. We also include the culture for SE/CASE as part of our definition. Why not? Since we're coining a new term with SE/CASE, we might as well be unique. Together, our definition for SE/CASE supports the top-down orientation objective of the IC/VISION process.

Our official definition for SE/CASE comes in the form of a soccer-ball-like diagram. The SE/CASE framework diagram in Figure 3.1 highlights the different components of SE/CASE. Each of these components will be described in this chapter.

To help explain the components of SE/CASE, we develop two analogies: "making a meal" and "getting fit." These analogies are unrelated to SE/CASE in terms of end deliverables, but the components of each match very closely. These analogies are also very helpful when explaining SE/CASE to management and the user community.

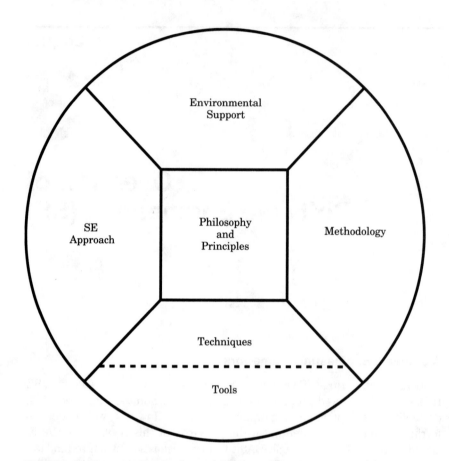

Figure 3.1 A software engineering framework.

SE principles

SE principles are at the heart of making SE/CASE happen. These principles are the most important and, unfortunately, the most overlooked component of SE/CASE. SE principles are the driving and controlling force behind a successful SE/CASE environment. You can select the best tools, techniques, and methodologies and still fail if the SE principles are ignored. The primary SE principles are: effectiveness, quality, rigor, process improvement, and automation.

- Effectiveness is building the right system, the right way, right from the start. You only have to build one unnecessary application or redo a major phase of a project to realize the true time-and-cost impact of ineffectiveness.

- Quality is a very difficult term to define. Is quality meeting specifications (i.e., defendable quality)? Is quality meeting expectations? Is it producing error-free code? The easy answer to each of these questions is that it depends on who is defining quality. Quality should be defined by the users, the maintainers, and management. By the way, "you'll know it whenever you see it" is no longer a valid response.

- Rigor has been succinctly defined by Vaughn Merlyn, industry expert, as correctness, consistency, coherency, and completeness of a process and the resultant deliverables.

- Process improvement implies continuously improving your processes in order to improve quality and effectiveness. It's a focus on the process, not the product. The new adage behind process improvement is "if ain't broke, you haven't looked hard enough."

- Automation includes two basic components:

  1. The mechanization of existing tasks.
  2. The leverage or ability to do tasks differently.

These principles are esoterically pleasing, but are they practical in the real world? Producing quality for quality's sake is really of little value. We can produce perfect code, but if it doesn't help to improve productivity or responsiveness, we haven't accomplished much. This was the early knock on many CASE tools; they drew pretty pictures, but so what? In addition, implementing rigor and automation without focusing on effectiveness might simply mean doing the wrong things faster.

Thus, when viewed individually, these principles are somewhat valueless to management with a job to do. Their true value, however, can be understood by focusing on the interactions between these principles as well as their resultant effect on management's goals. Figure 3.2 details the interactions between the SE principles. Figure 3.3 completes the picture by pulling in management goals and supporting principles.

At the center of both of these diagrams is rigor. Rigor is embodied within SE/CASE as a process (or a method). A rigorous process is used to correctly, consistently, coherently, and completely develop and maintain systems. The result of this process, when rigor is applied properly, will be high-quality system components (e.g., code, documentation, test cases). Rigor also ensures the effective application of time, energy, and resources to the appropriate problems and needs, allowing you to do the right things the right way.

This rigorous process can be fine-tuned (thus further improving the resultant quality and effectiveness) via the process improvement principle of continuously trying to make things better. However, rigor is not easy. There are many checks, balances, and details that need to be adhered to. Automation (i.e., CASE) enables rigor to happen. Automation can perform many of the mechanical details to keep things straight. Automation can also

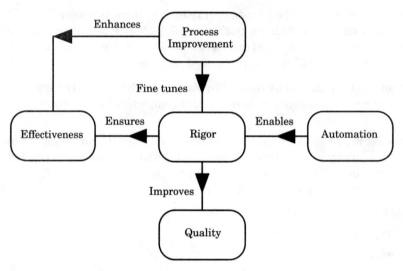

Figure 3.2 Software engineering principles.

help to support a few aspects of the thinking processes, thereby leveraging key staff members.

Together, these principles form the nucleus of an engine, affectionately called the "rigor mill." It's from this platform that SE/CASE is driven. Most people, when implementing SE/CASE, recognize the existence and necessity of these SE principles, but do little or nothing to support them. These principles should be used to form the appropriate culture for SE/CASE. For example, the cultural dimensions of discipline and standardization directly support the rigor principle. Each of the SE principles can be mapped to these cultural dimensions. Culture dimensions will be explored in more depth in chapter 4.

These SE principles map very closely to the philosophies of the corporate-wide Total Quality Management (TQM). TQM philosophies are based on the work of Edward Demming and others. Demming espoused 14 principles of process improvement and quality aimed at changing an organization's culture. It's because of this close relationship that we recommend implementing a SE/CASE environment in conjunction with a TQM if at all possible. This connection will help you buy enough time with management to see the long-term benefits of SE/CASE. It will also help to justify the funds needed for methodologies, tools, and training.

The aim of this "rigor mill" and related TQM influence should be focused on improving the fundamental goals of systems development and maintenance. These goals include:

1. Increasing productivity.
2. Improving responsiveness.

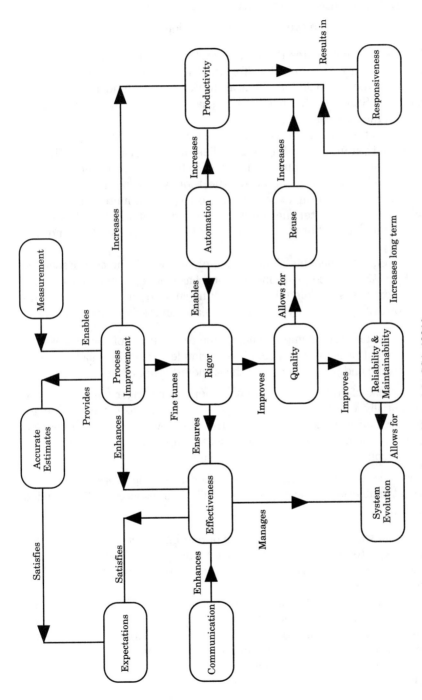

Figure 3.3 Software engineering principles and goals. (*Copyright CGA, 1991.*)

3. Satisfying end-user expectations.

4. Allowing systems to evolve over time (i.e., longer system life).

Figure 3.3 incorporates these goals and other supporting SE concepts with the primary SE principles. Together, they represent the essence of SE/CASE—the rationale for why it all works. It's this fundamental understanding of SE/CASE that needs to be shared between MIS management, staff, and the user community.

A description of Figure 3.3 needs to start with productivity, management's "holy grail." According to this diagram, increasing productivity is possible through direct automation. CASE tools can and do directly increase productivity. Depending on the tool type (upper CASE versus code generator), you can expect from 5 to 15 percent increases in the development process after the traditional learning curve. There have been larger claims made, but those are usually for one specific phase, not the full life cycle.

However, these benefits alone are simply not worth the cost associated with SE/CASE. These costs include purchase price, maintenance costs, training expenses, learning time, consulting support, and general aggravation. However, productivity is further increased in the following three ways:

1. Incremental process improvements due to the fruits of the process improvement principle. This could be as simple as identifying a task that's not useful and removing it from the standard process.

2. The reuse of code and design components. The "rigor mill" will create potentially reusable components of manageable size, measurable integrity, and increased visibility. In the next few years, techniques and tools will be developed to exploit these components. As a result, reuse will become the MIS watchword of the 90s.

3. Easier software maintenance. As systems become more reliable and maintainable as a result of the "rigor mill," less resources will be needed to support these systems.

Together with direct automation, the proper implementation of SE/CASE can be expected to improve productivity from 30 to 50 percent over the course of 3 to 5 years. This type of savings is worth the cost and effort of implementing the technology.

Improved productivity, of course, helps to reduce and/or maintain costs—a very important business objective. However, if MIS is to be used for a competitive advantage, responsiveness is an even greater benefit. Improved productivity will result in improved responsiveness. In essence, we'll be able to produce systems much faster and ones that can change quickly with changing business times.

Satisfying user expectations is another goal of most MIS managers. After all, the user community is ultimately paying the MIS bill and deserves satisfaction. Expectations are satisfied in two ways: through more accurate estimates and through greater effectiveness.

You can do a great job on a project, be very creative, manage it smoothly, and produce great quality, but if the estimate is missed, the users are usually unsatisfied. We're not saying to sacrifice quality in order to meet schedules. The following quotation from the Quality Assurance Institute (QAI) is still very appropriate:

> "The bitterness of poor quality remains long after the sweetness of meeting the schedule has been forgotten."

The key is to produce accurate estimates to start with. Accurate estimates are provided through the process improvement principle. Process improvement relies on measurement in order to review the process. Measurement will provide the history upon which accurate estimates are made.

Improved effectiveness also helps to satisfy the users' expectations of what the system should do. We're not saying to do everything the users want, but to provide what they need and to allow them to see the difference. Effectiveness is generally enhanced through better communications with the user community and within project teams. Communications can be improved through diagramming techniques, JAD-style meetings, joint working relationships, and other people-related activities.

Together, the principles of effectiveness and quality help an MIS organization to evolve their systems over time. Systems of quality and vision should be able to withstand the winds of change. This will help to extend the useful service life of many systems many more years. This is a direct cost savings for the years to come.

Now that you have been exposed to these SE principles, do you feel like Dorothy from Kansas? As if a whirlwind has just uprooted your secure development perspective (picket fences and all) and plopped you into a strange, new land? One that you need to find a way out of?

However, think about it. These principles have been there all along. Somewhere along the way, each of these principles was ingrained in each one of us. The challenge is learning how to use and trust in them again. Like Dorothy from Kansas, she had her ruby slippers all along. She just needed someone to point them out to her.

Our analogies of "making a meal" and "getting fit" also have a center core of interrelated principles. When making a meal, cleanliness, presentation, and quality ingredients all interrelate to bring about the goals of eating healthier, satisfying the family, and surviving. In the process of getting fit, diet, exercise, discipline, and a long-term focus all interrelate to bring about the goals of feeling better, improving longevity, looking better, and perhaps even running a marathon. The key to achieving each of these goals is incorporating these basic principles into your everyday life—not for grasping at the latest fad for quick improvement.

Support environment

SE principles can't work in a vacuum. Management can't just pronounce that from this day forward all systems shall be produced with quality and effectiveness. However, it's an easy thing to do. Many organizations have great posters on the wall like "think quality" and "do it right the first time." With no support, these types of posters do more harm than good. They antagonize people. It's just another empty management initiative. The staff is conditioned to know that whenever push comes to shove, it's back to the old ways. "Damn the posters, just do it" becomes the battle cry.

The "getting fit" analogy does an especially good job at describing this support component. During the process of getting fit, you can put messages on the refrigerator and declare a daily exercise regime, all of which supports the basic principles of getting fit. However, without support from the family and society, many of us would not hold to these principles. We're constantly reminded by the government through commercials and other sources not to smoke, not to drink and drive, to eat less fat, and to exercise. Our incremental efforts are praised and supported by our families. Without this support, we would all tend to lapse into unhealthy habits whenever temptation arises.

The same holds true for making a meal. The support systems in this analogy include your mother, grandmother, ethnic tradition, and cooking shows, each of which helps us to drive through the basic principles.

The support environment for SE/CASE needs to be driven by management. It involves concepts like empowerment, enablement, trust, and teamwork. Each of these concepts is within management's control and can't be left open and unaddressed. Doing so would only confuse the staff and dilute the SE principles. Each of these will be discussed in further detail in chapter 4, the culture for SE/CASE.

These concepts need to be backed up with teeth. The old adage of "what you measure is what you get" holds very true within SE/CASE. The key is in being able to measure and thus receive quality, effectiveness, process improvement, and rigor. Many organizations take the easy way out and measure visible activity and results. Results need to be measured, but should not be the only thing measured. By not measuring the process along with results, you're encouraging the staff to take shortcuts.

Measuring and rewarding effectiveness is very hard and many times very subjective. The importance of measuring and rewarding effectiveness is seen in an often-told fable. At a major corporation there were two project teams starting at the same time. The projects were somewhat equal subsystems of a major system. Project team A worked hard and diligently at the start of the project, putting plans and strategies in place before starting. Project team B quickly threw together a plan of attack and dove right into the meat of the project. The project manager of the second project felt that the challenge of the system was in the complexity of the code and he wanted to get right to it.

In the early months of the project, project team B was clearly ahead of schedule. The users felt that they were getting their money's worth. They had seen a prototype of the finished system and the project team was already talking about testing and conversion plans. The A team was still doing interviews and drawing pictures—not a lot of valuable actions.

As the months went by, team B began to falter. They had forgotten an important database component and needed to rewrite a core section of code. The team was making a serious effort to keep on track and began to work later and on weekends. The users and management were still very happy. The user's needs were being addressed and the project team was really working hard. Users could see the strain on the collective faces of the team. The users were getting their money's worth.

Well, team A finished a few weeks before the scheduled installation date. Team B was a little later, but still a day or two early. The system went in with a few problems, mostly caused by team B, but the overall project was deemed a success.

The project leader for team B got a promotion. He had clearly shown how he could motivate people in the face of adversity and still get a project in on time. A few of his team members left the corporation shortly after completion of the project. However, if these people couldn't handle the strain of systems development, they should not be part of the group anyway. The rest of the team was treated to a CASE conference in Orlando for their display of effort. They were the organization's top SWAT team, and they knew it. They were proud. They could do anything. They were heroes.

Team A only got a letter from the user V.P. thanking them for a job well done. Well, what was rewarded, activity or effectiveness? What was most visible? What do you think will happen the next time? Remember—what gets rewarded gets done.

Other elements of this support environment will be discussed in later chapters. In short, the support environment is the culture in which we work. This culture needs to be fine-tuned to support the SE principles and SE objectives and to integrate the other SE/CASE components.

SE approaches

Software engineering approaches are the integrated assertions, theories, concepts, and strategies that constitute a way of developing systems. In short, they're the ideology behind getting the job done. The different approaches are shown in Table 3.1.

TABLE 3.1 SE Approaches

SE approach	Year started
"Seat of the pants"	1955
Structured Coding	1965
Structured Analysis & Design	1970
Package Software Acquisition	1977
Information Engineering	1985
Rapid Application Development	1988
Reengineering	~1993
Object-oriented Analysis & Design	~1995

These approaches are not a true evolution of the way to do systems. So, you shouldn't simply go down to the bottom of the list and order the most advanced SE approach. Nor should you really consider the earliest two approaches: "seat of the pants" or structured coding. There are much better ways to achieve the desired results today.

Each of the remaining approaches has its individual strengths and weaknesses. Not every approach is right for an organization's culture, skill set, and type of systems to be built. The right SE approach for you needs to be selected as you would a tool, with a full understanding, selection criteria, and concrete reasons.

On occasion, multiple approaches might be selected, especially for larger MIS organizations. Keep in mind, however, that multiple approaches cost extra money in terms of tools, SDM, training, and support. These costs need to be weighed against the added benefits.

Each of these SE approaches shares a number of techniques. Data flow diagrams (DFDs), entity relationship diagrams (ERDs), and structure charts are all commonly used across the approaches. What makes the approaches different is how and when these techniques are used in conjunction with other techniques and tools. It's not the use of a technique that distinguishes a particular approach. For example, the information engineering approach places a strong and early emphasis on producing data models (i.e., ERDs). Structured analysis and design also uses ERDs, but not until after the process model is somewhat complete. ERDs are used primarily to document the data flow, not to analyze business rules.

Next to the SE principles, the SE approach is the most important and the most overlooked aspect in establishing SE/CASE. They're definitely the most debated aspects. Too many times, an organization will quickly select a CASE tool and accompanying methodology without finalizing their SE approach. As the CASE/SDM implementation unfolds, the project teams will begin to realize the relative merits and disadvantages of the inherent approach within the SDM. However, at this time it might be too late to do anything about it. The ideology might have created a momentum for itself, leaving the organization in a constant battle over ideology. How many times have you heard people arguing over the relative merits of a data-driven versus a process-driven approach long after the tools and techniques are in place. This argument needs to be put to bed early in the cycle.

For this component, the "making a meal" analogy works the best in describing the concept. Within my extended family, there's a constant battle over how to make a meal. On the one hand, there's my mother's way—cooking from scratch. She starts with flour, sugar, spices, and many other basic ingredients. She uses a job-shop ideology, focusing on building to specifications. My mother-in-law, however, uses an "assemble from parts off the shelf" approach. She uses canned gravy, instant rice, bouillon cubes, and frozen dough. She assembles these parts, along with a few of the basic food ingredients, to form her finished product. My wife, however, has a more direct approach. She likes to order out.

All three get the job done. I get fed. Also, quite frankly, it's all quite good. The differences are in the approach, not the end product. The order-out approach is the quickest and sometimes the best. However, it's definitely the most expensive. The "assemble from parts off the shelf" approach is also relatively quick, less expensive, and easy for the chef to master. However, the taste is sometimes suspect (this might be mostly mental) and the nutritional content is usually lower. Cooking from scratch is emotionally the best way to go. You know the ingredients and can customize to your taste and nutritional needs (i.e., low salt). However, it takes a long time, is sometimes rather expensive, and usually requires a greater skill level to achieve the desired results.

Each family needs to find the approach or approach(es) that are right for them. Once this is established, then the appropriate tools (e.g., mixer, can opener, credit card) and methodologies (e.g., cookbook, restaurant guide) can be purchased. This might cut down on the method argument for years to come.

Within the "getting fit" analogy, you can choose from a diet-driven approach, an exercise-driven approach, or a holistic approach. Each approach might get you to your desired goals, but one approach might do a quicker, better, less expensive job getting you there. In addition, each approach uses many of the same techniques (e.g., aerobic exercises, meditation) but with a different sequence, emphasis, and orientation. Like the SE approaches, the getting fit approaches need to be appropriate for the individual, and the latest approach might not be the best.

Methodology

A *methodology* is a systematic series of actions integrating a set of complementary techniques to build and maintain systems. In short, methodology is the physical manifestation of the SE approach. It's that 13-volume set of manuals that tends to sit on the shelf collecting dust. It's usually known as a systems development methodology (SDM), but many commercially available SDMs are now covering the planning, maintenance, and project management aspect of MIS.

A methodology consists of the following components:

- Work Breakdown Structure (WBS)—a set of phases, activities, tasks, and worksteps for getting the work done. Some commercially SDM have WBSs numbering in the thousands of tasks/worksteps.

- WBS level descriptions—each with recommended techniques and tools, design tips, sample forms and examples of completed deliverables.

- Roles/responsibilities matrix—clearly defined responsibilities for each task and associated deliverable.

- Supporting project procedures—integrated tasks/activities to address quality assurance/control, project management, and change management.

Figure 3.4 presents a model of an SDM showing the relationships of these components. This diagram was adapted from one used by ASG to describe their SDM, firstCASE. The diagram uses the entity relationship diagram notation.

Within the cooking analogy, the methodology is easily definable. It's the cookbook the chef uses to create the meal. This cookbook includes step-by-step guidance, recommended techniques, how-to advice, suggested tools, and pictures of the interim and finished product. However, a few cookbooks don't stop there; they also address how to set the table, what wine to serve, and how to sequence the events so that everything is warm for the serving. This added advice is similar to the project management and quality assurance aspects of an SDM.

For "getting fit" there are many methodologies to follow. These include Weight Watchers and Nutri-system type programs as well as fitness books. Each has a step-by-step way to look and feel your best.

SDMs have in the past been referred to as "cookbooks." This description, however, has left a bad impression with most people. It implies that an SDM is an all-or-nothing approach. With more than a thousand tasks/activities, the all approach doesn't sound appealing. This is the prime reason for an SDM to collect dust.

It's true; too much SDM is just as bad, if not worse, than no SDM. Government workers from Australia and Great Britain know this all too well. Whenever they go on strike, they don't leave their jobs; they simply follow every rule and regulation to the "T." Like MIS, they also have their own version of the 13 volumes on the shelf to turn to. This, in turn, dramat-

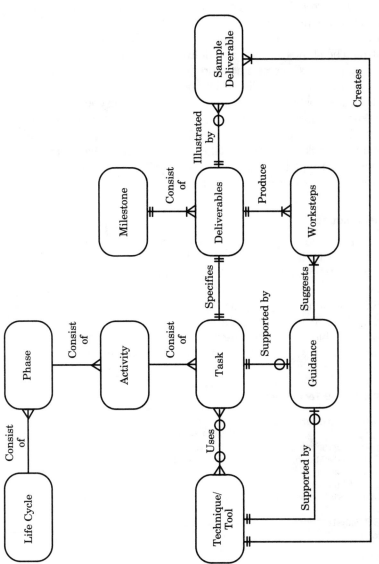

Figure 3.4   An ERD for an SDM. (*Copyright CGA, 1991.*)

ically slows down their function, thereby crippling their agency. Another popular term for this is "malicious compliance."

The key to the successful use of an SMD is in understanding it. Only through a full understanding can the real benefit be unleashed. There's a lot of good stuff in an SDM. Why reinvent the wheel for each project? An informed project manager needs to be able to quickly find and apply this good stuff.

An SDM also helps to improve quality by standardizing deliverables and integrating the mechanics of QA/QC into the development and maintenance process. Another important benefit of an SDM is with improving project control. The standard tasks and deliverables provide a predictable way to estimate projects, assess status/progress, achieve interchangeability of resources, and highlight individual responsibilities.

SDMs are most valuable on large projects, but the concepts, terminology, and flow also work well for smaller efforts. This is where the understanding of the SDM is crucial. Without a full understanding, a person would tend to overspecify tasks/worksteps, ballooning an estimate beyond acceptability. With a proper understanding, the essence of the SDM is left in, and many of the overall benefits are maintained.

SE techniques

A *SE technique* is a proven, detailed, specific set of actions to accomplish a given activity. It's usually finite, with a physical deliverable. Many people look at the techniques of SE/CASE as if they were the ideology or methodology. However, a technique is only a small part of SE/CASE. As described, an SE approach is a collection of integrated techniques, and a methodology is the physical implementation of the approach. The list of techniques shown in Table 3.2 is only a representative sample of some of the more familiar techniques. The full list would be three to four times longer.

TABLE 3.2 SE Techniques

Decomposition diagramming	Data Structuring
	Wariner-Orr
Data flow diagramming	
Yourdon, DeMarco,	Process control modeling
Gane & Sarson	Ward-Mellor, Hatley
Consensus building	
JAD, FAST, The Method	Object-oriented design
	Booch, Joboson,
Matrix analysis	Codd, Yourdon
Prototyping	Data normalization
	Structured programming
Entity life cycle modelling	
	Structured testing

TABLE 3.2 *Continued.*

Structured walkthroughs	White/black box testing
Structure charting	Critical path scheduling
Jackson, Constantine	
Entity Relationship Diagramming	
Chen, Bachman, Merise	

Techniques for making a meal include kneading dough, parboiling, and deep-fat frying. Techniques for getting fit include aerobic exercises, plastic surgery, hypnosis, and acupuncture. None of these techniques by themselves can produce the desired results. However, used with other techniques, they will be very productive.

In the same vein, overusing techniques or using a technique to do more than it was designed for will give less-than-optimum results. Remember, if all you have is a hammer, everything looks like a nail.

There are three type of techniques used within SE/CASE:

- Diagramming techniques (e.g., DFD, ERD, GANTT Charts).

- Procedural techniques (e.g., normalization, white box testing).

- People/meeting-oriented technique (e.g., JAD, walk-through techniques).

The majority of time, energy, money, and attention over the last few years has been paid to the diagramming techniques. This has been the backbone and focus of many of the CASE vendors and also was the main focus of the structured analysis and design revolution in the late 1970s. The reason for this emphasis is because of the communication and clarification value of these techniques—a picture is worth a thousand words. It's also because diagramming-based tools sell better than nondiagramming support tools and techniques. In this case, a picture is worth a thousand bucks.

The properties of a good diagramming technique include:

- Richness—able to depict many different aspects of a situation within the constructs of the diagramming convention.

- Rigor—directly supports completeness, correctness, and consistency.

- An aid to clear thinking—a simple, yet powerful message enabling you to get to the heart of the issues. Many times switching from left-brain to right-brain processing.

- An aid to communications—users are able to read, critique, and draw the diagrams.

- Supports stepwise refinement (i.e., decomposition).

- Automatable—able to easily create/maintain/reshuffle constructs.

Tools

Computer Aided Software Engineering (CASE) tools are the most widely discussed aspect of the SE/CASE environment because the tools are the most visible, most costly, and definitely the most glitzy part of the environment. Along with this attention, however, comes much of the blame if an implementation goes poorly. As mentioned in an earlier chapter, it's much easier to blame a technology than to blame ourselves. It's just a natural human response.

However, CASE plays a crucial role with implementing SE/CASE. CASE is the catalyst for getting serious about SE/CASE. Software engineering approaches, techniques, and methodologies have been with us now for more than 15 to 20 years. SE has been proven by many to be the way to go. Why then, hasn't SE caught on in a big way? The reason is part technical and part political.

Technically, CASE enables the earlier-mentioned "rigor mill" to get into gear. It lets a person do it right without an undue amount of behind-the-scenes, administrative activities. However, this alone is not enough. CASE tools are also expensive and are typically considered a capital cost. Capital costs need the approval of VPs and other high-ranking authorities within an organization. This approval necessitates a clear business plan and justification. In the process of making the CASE case, the other elements of SE/CASE are discovered, planned for, and implemented. In addition, IBM, with their September 19, 1989 announcement of AD/Cycle, legitimized SE/CASE. This removed a major political stumbling block for SE/CASE.

We consider CASE tools to include project management, configuration management, testing, reverse engineering, and other related tools and tool sets. The usual definition for CASE, however, only includes the tools that support the planning, analysis, design, and construction phases. These tools can be further categorized into:

- Component CASE (C-CASE)—tools designed for one specific technique or activity. These are also called point tools.

- Integrate CASE (I-CASE)—a series of point tools for specific techniques and phases all integrated together by one vendor.

There are many other aspects of CASE tools that need to be considered during the selection process. These will be explored within the details of the IC/VISION approach outlined in chapter 7.

There are many tools for "making a meal" and for "getting fit." Some of these include garlic presses, mixers, and food processors, as well as exercise equipment, food scales, and blood pressure gauges. However, our two favorite tools for getting fit really help to put CASE into perspective.

An advertisement in a May, 1990 magazine touted the wonders of a new type of exercise device. The ad pictured a muscular man attached by wires from his abdomen to a briefcase-sized machine, complete with electronic gauges and controls. The ad stated:

> "This is the **safe and effortless** workout system that guarantees results. See **immediate improvement** as thousands have worldwide. This is **the most effective electronic exercise unit available**."

Now, we haven't researched this product as for its effectiveness, and it might in fact work. However, really now, would you buy one?

Yet, this is how some people look at CASE tools. Just hook up the wires and plug it in. Somehow it will perform a "Vulcan mind meld" and extract requirements and produce code safely and effortlessly—no hard work and guaranteed results. Now, CASE might get farther towards this vision than many of us currently envision, but let's get realistic. CASE is not there yet.

A closer analogy is shown in another advertisement, this one for an automatic bread maker. With this product:

> "Every step of bread making, including kneading and baking, is performed automatically."

The unit mixes the basic ingredients, raises and kneads the dough, and bakes the loaf over a three- to four-hour cycle. I've seen this unit in action and it does work. The problem is, you can only make a round loaf of bread and, of course, it doesn't work for cookies or pies. It works great within the limits of the tool. It's a special-purpose tool, much like many of the code generators of today. They work great for online, database-related applications, but they stumble over the batch and complex logic of some systems. In summary, most all tools work; you just need to properly position them.

Scope of SE/CASE

SE/CASE covers much more than just the development aspects of systems. In our view, it also encompasses strategic planning, project management, and maintenance. This broader view allows an organization to see the gaps and overlaps when planning for and building an SE/CASE environment. This is very important, especially whenever another part of the organization is building its own environment from their own myopic viewpoint.

For example, we've seen a few organizations implement a development-only SE/CASE environment while at the same time implementing an unconnected, strategic planning-only environment. The suboptimization of these two environments tends to lead to different methodologies (with different terminology and deliverables), different data modeling techniques and tools, and at times, even different cultures. Each of these differences are, of course, well supported to meet the individual objectives of the two different groups. However, the planning group will eventually need to pass to the development group the deliverables of their efforts. Many times these deliverables are looked at and then ignored by the development group(s), since it would take too much time to retrofit them into the development group's tools and techniques and no one has extra time to do this job.

Another common situation is when an organization optimizes a particular aspect without consideration for future growth or change of mission. For example, an organization might purchase methods, tools, and training in order to get a handle on the maintenance area, focusing on the existing portfolio of COBOL-based applications. This investment might prove very valuable for the first year or two, but whenever 4GL programs written by the user community, C-based PC packages, and new code-generated systems need to be maintained, the investment in the maintenance technology appears wasted. In addition, the existing environment has no features to help reverse engineer the existing COBOL into a higher level of abstraction in order to reengineer the applications, an opportunity brought on by the acquisition of a code generator.

In each of these situations, the organizations didn't consider the full range of SE/CASE, but only a narrowly focused part of it. Keep in mind that you don't have to build the entire SE/CASE environment at once; you can create an integrated vision and build to this vision.

This is similar to landscaping a home. Perhaps all you want to do is build a deck and plant a few shrubs around it. You can bring in an expert on building decks, design it with him or her, build the deck, pick out shrubs, and then plan them. If all goes well, the work can be complete within two to three months. Then, however, a couple of years later you decide to add a gazebo or a brick patio. Well, now there are a whole host of limitations you need to work within because of the installed deck. There's no longer a clean slate to work with. The sleek, ultra-modern design of the existing deck doesn't easily allow access to the area where the gazebo or patio would go. A person would now have to walk twice as far to get to a gazebo or patio and, in addition, a few expensive oak trees might have to be moved, potentially killing them.

By starting with a landscaper and developing a five-year plan, your requirement for a gazebo or patio might have been identified before the deck was designed. This requirement could have been incorporated into the deck design, saving you money and time and producing a more aesthetically pleasing and effective space whenever the total project is complete.

All too often, MIS organizations want to find an expert in their current hot technology and move quickly. They have a picture of the "deck" (i.e., CASE tool) they want, and they already have a large "party" (i.e., project) planned, and thus they need the deck finished as soon as possible. Occasionally, the expert has the vision to see beyond the hot technology and into the other areas, but the phrase "we'll take care of that area whenever we get to it" has a way of killing any long-term vision. It's this lack of a plan or vision that gets most organizations into the previously mentioned situations.

The SE/CASE vision needs to be succinct and focused. It needs to look forward a number of years (usually five to seven) and define the functional and technological needs of the organization. The full set of functions and technologies represents the scope of SE/CASE. Figure 3.5 categorizes these functions and technologies into four overlapping SE/CASE environments.

For any given organization, all of the functions and technologies might not be appropriate. To simply say I want one of each is wrong. Each individual function and technology needs to be examined for appropriateness to your organization. For example, an organization who uses package solutions might not be legally allowed to or want to reverse engineer the existing package code. Or an organization whose business is dynamically changing might not be able to model the enterprise to any level of detail.

This SE/CASE scope model is provided as a starting point for creating your customized SE/CASE vision. Your SE/CASE vision needs to be succinct and crisp. It needs to clearly delineate the boundaries of the different SE/CASE environments and to specify the interfaces between them. Simply

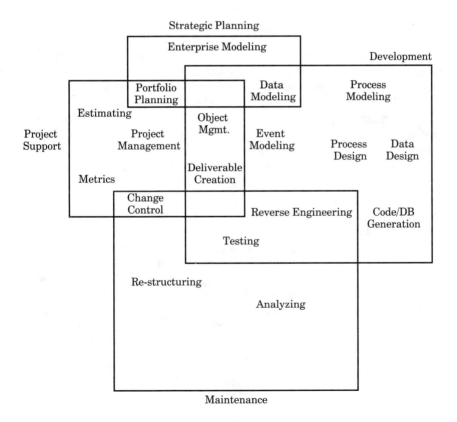

Figure 3.5 The scope of SE/CASE. (*Copyright CGA, 1991.*)

to say that the IBM repository will solve all of your interface problems and cover the full range of SE/CASE is being very naive. You need to plan this area very carefully, like you would a new WAN/LAN setup. Simply to rely on one vendor to solve future communications problems or to ignore them altogether will many times get you in trouble. At its best, this strategy will at least restrict valuable future options. The following sections describe the details of each of the environments.

IS strategic planning environment

This SE/CASE environment supports the IS department's need to view systems from a global perspective, beyond the requirements of any one application. As mentioned earlier, IS strategic planning focuses on the creation and maintenance of the primary planning architectures:

- Information—data files, databases.
- Process—functions, programs, systems.
- Technology—hardware, software, telecommunications.
- Software engineering—methodologies, CASE tools, culture, skills.

The functions and technologies listed for the IS strategic planning area all support the creation, analysis, and maintenance of these planning architectures, the key function of which is enterprise modeling. This function uses the techniques of decomposition diagramming, entity relationship diagramming, data flow diagramming, and matrix analysis to model and analyze the different planning architectures. Once these architectures are created, a strategy is developed to implement the architectures.

Two key interface functions are portfolio/resource planning and data modeling. These functions serve as the bridge from the data and process architectures created in IS planning to the actual development and enhancement projects. When building your overall SE/CASE vision, pay particular attention to the requirements of these functions.

Another key SE/CASE vision perspective is whether or not the planning architectures are static or dynamic. Within a static environment, the four planning architectures are re-created every two to five years with planning task forces or committees. The earlier planning architectures might be used to "kick-start" the effort; however, the intent is not to improve the old, but to replace it—usually because major business change or other similar event occurred.

With a dynamic I/S strategic planning function, the architectures are created and maintained by a permanent planning group. As systems are developed, enhanced, and purchased, the appropriate information and process architecture are updated to reflect the changes. In addition, as the business changes, the architectures are used to analyze and plan for these changes.

Depending on your current political, staffing, and skills situation, either of these two perspectives might be appropriate. From a SE/CASE scope perspective, the determination of a static versus a dynamic situation will have a major impact on the type of development and project management tools and techniques selected. In addition, it will even have an impact on the basic SE approach. For a dynamic environment, Information Engineering has proven to work well in larger organizations. The static perspective will work for many of the remaining SE approaches.

Development environment

For most individuals seeking CASE, the development environment is usually the most well-known and the most comfortable. For this reason, it tends to get overemphasized and, as a result, suboptimized. Make no mistake about it; this environment is the one that gets the work done. Without the development piece, everything else is purely academic.

However, a focus on the development environment alone has resulted in many IS organizations spending the majority of their discretionary funding and time on what typically is only 20 percent to 40 percent of their primary activities. (Maintenance and enhancements are typically in the 60 percent or higher range.) For optimal results, expenditure of these funds and resources needs to be spread out over the entire scope of SE/CASE (i.e. IS planning and maintenance), not just development.

The functions and technologies of the development environment are incorporated into the traditional waterfall functions of analysis, design, code, and test. These functions include data, process, and event modeling; process and data design; code generation; and testing. You'll need to decide which of these functions are needed within your scope of study and to what extent. Event modeling and code generation are the two that are most often left out—event modeling because many people don't understand it and code generation because of the use of 4GLs, package selection, outsourcing, and other coding alternatives.

A technology that will have an interesting and potentially valuable future is reverse engineering. When fully matured, the tools of this function should be able to take existing code (usually COBOL) and migrate the encapsulated business rules and data structures into the other development technologies. This will then allow a project team to forward engineer the systems, incorporating any additional requirements. Even though reverse engineering technology is not yet fully available, the inclusion of this technology into your long-term SE/CASE vision will have a significant impact on the selection of the other development tools and techniques. This is a major SE/CASE scope decision.

Not only does reverse engineering affect the development environment, it also affects the maintenance environment. Reverse engineering has far-reaching effects, technologically and culturally. When fully available and implemented, reverse engineering should be able to allow a person to maintain/enhance the code from a higher level of abstraction—from a business level. Many of our best, "hot shot" maintainers might not be able and/or willing to allow that to happen.

Testing tools and techniques also affects both the development and the maintenance environments. Many of these tools exist today, but are only used for development purposes because their selection was suboptimized from the development side. The selection and implementation process for this technology needs to consider both.

Maintenance environment

MIS traditionally expends from 60 percent to 90 percent of its resources maintaining and enhancing systems. Yet, very little is spent on tools and techniques to improve this process. The strategy expressed by many is to improve their new development process so that later maintenance of new systems is easier. This is true, but it takes a long time for the applications to turn over. If only 10 to 40 percent of your efforts are on new systems, it will take many years (even decades) to rewrite all of the existing systems in order to revolutionize the maintenance function. By that time, the expanding maintenance burden coupled with the need to maintain/reduce costs might push the maintenance percentage even higher, further elongating the timeframe.

There are many new "toolettes" on the maintenance side that can help you maintain nonstructured programs. Various code analyzing and restructuring technologies have been proven by many organizations to quickly improve productivity while simultaneously increasing the quality and reliability of the systems. True, these technologies are not valuable for those new systems created with the CASE tools, but until the percentage of new systems gets to be significant, investment into a maintenance environment can prove very worthwhile.

We view these tools as tactical technologies. By incorporating these technologies into your SE/CASE vision and implementing them early, you'll be able to quickly show productivity and quality improvements (usually within six months). These improvements will allow you to pull people from maintenance for development, thereby quickening the pace for rewriting the major legacy systems into the new SE/CASE approach.

Another important dimension of the maintenance environment is how the new SE/CASE approach-developed systems will be maintained. Many of the CASE vendors have also focused on the development aspects of the tools. The maintenance of these systems needs to be addressed within your SE/CASE vision.

Work management environment

The functions and technologies of the work management environment tie together all of the tasks and deliverables of the other environments. These are also known as cross-life cycle technologies.

At the center of this environment is object management. Otherwise known as a repository or an encyclopedia, this function involves the collection, organization, and interconnections of all of the planning, development, and maintenance objects. An object is anything created as a result of an activity in one of the environments. For example, data flow diagrams, test cases, project memos, and code modules are all objects.

Object management is synonymous to the database (e.g., relational, object-oriented) of an application. Object management is a very important component of the SE/CASE vision. Even though the technology to support this function is not yet fully available (e.g., IBM's Repository), don't overlook the importance of this aspect. There are quite a few alternatives becoming available, some with different meta-model standards and interface protocol. Selection of the wrong object management technology could have major implications as the vision is pieced together.

Work group support technologies are other central functions that cross into the different environments. These include many of the traditionally non-CASE technologies of LAN support, word processing, desktop publishing, and messaging/E-mail. The integration of each of these technologies needs to be considered a part of the complete SE/CASE vision.

The traditional project management functions of work plan creation, estimating, scheduling, and monitoring should also be considered part of the complete SE/CASE vision. These functions, along with change control, manage the processes and deliverables of I/S.

A new breed of tool, the Integrated Project Support Environment (IPSE) tool is starting to get popular in this area. An IPSE tool can be thought of as an umbrella structure that pulls many of the work management aspects together. It's also considered the next generation of traditional project management tools. Not only do IPSE tools contain the traditional GANTT and PERT capabilities, they also incorporate deliverable management, tool-coordination, work-group-support, and object-management-interface functions.

You'll need to make a conscious decision to include IPSE-like technologies or stick with traditional project management technologies. The two technologies can be integrated into the SE/CASE environment, but the high degree of feature overlap is sometimes more trouble (in terms of coordination of deliverables) than it's worth. Again, it's not a technology that you can implement immediately, but it might need to be on your long-term SE/CASE vision. However, a few organizations that we've consulted with chose to start with this area first.

Metric technologies look at the quality and productivity of all other IS functions. Primarily using function point counting techniques, productivity and quality baseline marks can be established, and future developments can then be measured from a relative perspective. A few organizations we know started the implementation of their SE/CASE vision from this area. They felt that without a clear set of baseline measurements, implementation of the remaining functions was like trying to improve the speed of a car without a speedometer to let you know how you were doing.

Rationale for SE/CASE

Our software dilemma

In almost every IS organization that we've consulted with over the years, we've seen an honest attempt to produce a quality product for a reasonable cost. Few organizations are simply going through the motions. Each organization is expending time, money, and energy towards improving itself.

However, in the vast majority of these organizations, the improvement efforts are fruitless and even counterproductive. Many of the following situations still exist:

- Software costs are spiraling upward.
- Quality is inconsistent.
- The systems don't integrate well.
- IS can never seem to satisfy the user community.
- Project estimates are inconsistent, sometimes in orders of magnitude.
- The maintenance burden is continuously growing.
- Past mistakes are repeated over and over.

We want to improve these situations, but rarely do we have the time, energy, and political clout to attack these problems head on. Instead, we concentrate on quickly soothing over the symptoms of the problems. This quick-hit, patchwork improvement strategy usually causes more problems down the road, thereby further worsening the situation. For example, to satisfy a user, we sometimes rush a new system into production before it's ready. This quick-fix strategy tends to reduce quality, thereby dramatically affecting the maintenance effort.

We seem to have gotten ourselves into a sticky dilemma with no apparent way out. We're like a frog being cooked in boiling water. Put the frog directly in boiling hot water, and it will instinctively jump out. However, put it in cold water and slowly raise the heat until boil and it will stay in until cooked. IS organizations instinctively know it's getting hotter, but we can take it.

The key to solving our dilemma might lie in how we got ourselves into this mess in the first place. When you analyze the situation, there are many different groups responsible. IS management, the IS staff, and the user community have all played a part. Each group needs to be analyzed and addressed.

For years, IS management has been inattentive towards the development and maintenance processes, especially the maintenance process. The decree has been "I don't care how you do it, just get it done by the scheduled date." Management assumes that the project team follows an appropriate process and that it's up to the project manager to make sure the process is followed. In addition, IS management is simply not interested in how the job gets done. They paid their dues in the early days of IS; now it's time to forget the details and concentrate on the important management issues of staffing and equipment acquisition.

IS management also tends to look the other way on quality issues if the completion dates are met on time. They talk a good line on quality, but this is only lip service. Quality is rarely rewarded, and, honestly, most IS managers wouldn't know quality if they saw it.

IS management usually empowers the project manager. He or she was given the authority and responsibility to get the job done. The problem is that the project team is rarely properly enabled to do the job. Training is often seen as unproductive and usually given after a successful project as a reward, not before as a preparation step.

The IS staff also is to blame for this software dilemma. Over the years, an "assembly worker" mentality has evolved. Within many of the organizations we've been in, the IS staff simply will not extend themselves, either in hours worked or in roles played. They have a job and they do it 8:00 to 5:00—a very predictable, comfortable life.

This situation is much like the auto workers of the 1970s and the government workers of the early 1990s. Each had a union to protect wages and to clearly delineate their jobs. It was a comfortable and safe living. They knew what they had to do and they performed their jobs with predictability and sameness. Neither situation warranted any changes from the staff perspective. They relied on management to look out for them. If they needed to be retrained, management would see to it. If the process/procedures needed to be changed, management would tell them. After all, that's why management gets the big bucks.

We all know about competition from the Japanese in the auto industry. Many of those auto workers are now making about one-half of their previous salaries in other occupations. Government workers are now faced with declining federal, state, and local budgets and the accompanying trend towards privatization where productivity is much higher. Many long-time government workers are being forced to look for other, less financially rewarding employment.

In each case, the secure, comfortable mentality kept the workers from wanting to improve their individual skills and value. Why rock the boat? Neither group noticed the temperature rising in their "pot" until it was too late.

Within IS we also tend to feel very secure. We learned to program in college or trade school and feel that, coupled with our many experiences, this is enough to maintain our relatively high salaries. If we should need to stretch and acquire another skill, management will tell us and direct us. The problem is that the dilemma discussed previously keeps management from making the right decisions. The IS staff is needed to maintain the existing systems. Pulling them off to learn a new skill takes too much time, not to mention the accompanying political hit from the user community. However, more importantly, IS management has nothing to start with. The IS staff doesn't appear eager to learn a new technology or approach. The staff has not prepared by keeping up-to-date on the latest technological developments. About the only thing they read in *Computerworld* are the want ads! There are very few self-education efforts. As a result, the IS staff slowly slips into technological obsolescence, a frightening "disease."

Technological obsolescence has a way of sneaking up on you. It's very contagious. It's usually caused by the inertia of the status quo. It's best treated with preventive medicine (i.e., training), but training dollars are usually the first things cut in lean times. In the final analysis, technological obsolescence costs the company a lot, but it can recover by hiring new staff. Technological obsolescence costs the professional dearly; many might never fully recover.

Thus, consultants are usually brought in for the higher-skill jobs. This leaves the existing IS staff where they were, comfortable with maintaining the old systems and developing new systems with old technologies. However, how long can this go on? Like the auto and government workers, something has got to give.

Another major contributing factor for the dilemma is the IS staff's distaste for formalization and rigor. Documentation is traditionally created after the fact, if it's done at all. Those project plans that are in place are usually ignored. The staff cherishes creativity and spontaneity and will instantly fight any attempt to organize or structure their processes. They're craftspeople. They will resist becoming "programming robots."

IS management and staff are not the only ones to blame for the dilemma. The user community also plays a major part. They're the ultimate customer and, as such, they hold the purse strings, either directly or indirectly. If the user community were not involved, IS management and staff could probably find their way out of the dilemma sooner or later. However, the user community is where the short-term pressure for meeting schedules and improving productivity ultimately comes from.

The user community deserves service and quality for their money. After all, there are plenty of consulting organizations eager to vie for funds from

users. However, even these outside organizations will have problems satisfying this group.

The user community feels that it doesn't need to understand our development and maintenance processes. This is why we get paid—to understand the complexities of the technologies. To an extent, they're right, but
they still play a major role in projects and on maintenance enhancements.
They can't be completely disassociated if they're involved. The result of the
user community disassociation is the imposition of arbitrary time scales and
budgets, playing corporate politics with MIS, and not always providing sufficient and timely assistance on projects. Each contributes to our current
dilemma.

Well, the solution to our dilemma is straightforward, yet difficult. True, the
techniques, methodologies, and tools of SE/CASE will provide a lot of the
structure, quality, and effectiveness that's needed to right this downward cycle, the benefits of which are addressed in the next section of this book.
However, it should be clearly evident that the cultural aspects are equally
important. It's the belief and assumptions of IS management, IS staff, and the
user community that need to be realigned to match the new SE/CASE technologies. These cultural aspects will be covered later in chapter 4.

The benefits of SE/CASE

The benefits of SE/CASE are widespread and real. Many of the causes of the
situations identified in the previous sections concerning our software dilemma
can be successfully addressed through the proper implementation of SE/CASE.
SE/CASE has been proven to work for organizations large and small, centralized and decentralized, custom and package oriented. SE/CASE can work for
you.

The main problem with achieving these benefits, however, is that the
benefits are almost too widespread and interconnected. In some ways,
SE/CASE is like a shotgun. Both provide plenty of power, allow for some
margin of error (versus a single projectile gun), are seen as the ultimate
tool to the untrained eye, and produce a wide pattern of benefits. A shotgun will give you a wide circle of pellets. SE/CASE will provide a wide circle of benefits.

Like a shotgun, the SE/CASE benefits are an all-or-nothing proposition. It's
very difficult to selectively achieve a subset of the benefits. For instance, it's
very difficult to sustain long-term productivity gains without achieving long-
term quality improvements. Before you fire, you need to understand the full
ramifications of the powerful instrument (either shotgun or SE/CASE) that
you possess. SE/CASE is a package deal.

In addition, you need to know what you're going to do with the instrument (shotgun or SE/CASE) before you purchase one. Are you going to
shoot skeet, hunt deer, or scare off burglars? Each function needs a differ-

ent type of gun with a different size, weight, gauge, and pellet. A multipurpose gun will work for each, providing valuable benefits, but the true professional needs a honed selection. SE/CASE is no different.

There's one other similarity between SE/CASE and a shotgun. You can shoot your foot off if you're not properly trained and prepared in proper use. With both, you need to know how and where to ready, aim, and fire. By the way, neither the shotgun nor SE/CASE is an area where Tom Peters' ready, fire, aim strategy works very well.

There's one important difference. The shotgun will provide you with instantaneous results. Ready, aim, fire, and there you have it. You either hit your mark or you didn't. If you missed, you either practice more or reset the gun sites and try again. With SE/CASE you can ready, aim, fire, and wait years to reap the benefits. However, if you're constantly changing the "gun sites" of SE/CASE before you truly know the results, you'll never be able to properly adjust the instrument.

Also, if you're not watching for and measuring the results, how do you really know the type and value of the benefits achieved? Without measurements, you'll need to rely solely on word-of-mouth evidence. However, simply asking the project team how the project went is not enough. Politics, short-term selective memory, personal preferences, recent problems, and cultural impact all represent filters for this important information. We need to be able to see clearly and as quickly as possible the real results of our actions. We need a measurement "target" that we can use to adjust our sites and training.

To be honest, a few organizations have already abandoned SE/CASE. They took the ready, fire, aim approach. They bought a tool thinking they had a shotgun. They shot it a few times. They shot themselves in the foot and then declared the technology a failure. Well, if you're in an organization where ready, fire, aim is your culture and you're looking for quick results, then we have some valuable advice for you. Don't implement SE/CASE. You'll simply waste your money and time, and you'll spoil any future hope of ever properly implementing the technologies.

SE/CASE is like a shotgun. To get the wide benefits, you need to select the proper instrument, receive the appropriate education (e.g., safety education), get hands-on training, fire, check the target, adjust the sites, fire, check the target, adjust the sites, fire, . . .

The benefits of SE/CASE are not just for the MIS department. They also affect the user community and the MIS staff. All too often, an organization will focus only on the MIS department benefits. However, the user community is ultimately paying for the technology, and the MIS staff members are charged with making the technology work. For successful implementation, the benefits that address each group need to be considered and marketed. The following paragraphs discuss these individual benefits.

MIS benefits. Over the long term, SE/CASE will provide the MIS department with improved productivity. According to the Gartner Group, a properly implemented, integrated CASE environment can be expected to improve development productivity by 20 to 40 percent, depending on the nature of the project. In addition, the environment will also be expected to improve the maintenance of the developed application by more than 100 percent, effectively slashing the maintenance by half. However, these benefits will not be fully realized until four to six years after initial implementation. These are impressive numbers, but a long time to wait between fire and adjust the sites.

Improved quality, however, is a benefit that will begin to show up much faster than productivity. It shows up as fewer change requests, less production reruns, little schedule slippage, and fewer testing defects. Each of these areas is measurable. SE/CASE can dramatically improve these types of quality measurements in a one- to two-year time frame. Adjustments to the SE/CASE "gun" can then be made based on the quality measurements. If you believe the premise that as quality is improved, productivity will follow, you can then feel confident that you're aiming in the right direction and can "stay the course" or readjust as needed.

SE/CASE also allows an organization to develop large, complex applications with confidence. The segmentation of work allows you to focus on a task at a time; it improves project control, which reduces the risk of runaway scope; it promotes improved inter/intra-team communications, and it formalizes the user partnership arrangements.

This, surprisingly, is usually the main reason for many organizations to get serious about SE/CASE. These organizations somehow are able to get by through the years producing smaller, isolated systems with traditional, seat-of-the-pants methods. However, sooner or later they're faced with a mission-critical system that has to be done right the first time. SE/CASE is the first and probably the best solution to their situation. Whether this mission-critical system is the main reason for SE/CASE or simply a catalyst doesn't really matter. What does matter is that SE/CASE allows you to break the complexity barrier with confidence. This is an important benefit of SE/CASE. Many times, it represents the prime justification for the funds and time needed for implementation.

The decomposition and control aspects of methodologies within SE/CASE make it much easier to effectively use staffing resources. These aspects also make it easier to share work with less-experienced staff and users, in effect leveraging the skills of top professionals. Without these methodologies, a key resource might be assigned a particularly difficult subsystem. Since creating that subsystem was viewed as one chunk of work, the key resource did all the design, programming, testing, and administrative support tasks. With a methodology, the key resource now might only do the crucial design and programming work, leaving the other tasks for the less-experienced staff member. This key resource is now freed up to do other crucial and complex work. This is accomplished through standardized tasks, a focus on detailed work plans, and supporting project management tools.

The control aspects of the methodologies make it easier to manage a project. They use known processes that produce standard/predictable results; the segmentation of the work provides visibility and structure; the detail of the tasks makes it easier to estimate the total project, and many methodologies have integrated quality reviews.

The most important, yet overlooked, benefit of SE/CASE to the MIS department is that SE/CASE facilitates reuse. The decomposition and rigor principles of SE/CASE produce smaller, encapsulated system components. The quality principle provides a greater degree of trust in these components. Also, the automation of SE/CASE provides greater visibility of these components. Altogether, SE/CASE provides a platform on which to institute reuse.

Reuse has the potential to improve productivity by orders of magnitude. In addition, responsiveness will be greatly enhanced. Rather than building systems from scratch, we'll be able to build systems from components "off the shelf." This is a very alluring scenario, but it's not a given for SE/CASE. As mentioned above, SE/CASE facilitates reuse, it doesn't ensure reuse.

In order to achieve the full benefit of reuse, MIS needs to be committed to building a library of components for the shelf. We need to build and buy system components with reuse in mind up front. In addition, the techniques and tools of SE/CASE need to be enhanced to better support this process. The creation of this library will take years to accomplish, with little added benefits in the first few years. It's a noble goal, but one that needs staying power. The goal is not for everyone, but those who do achieve it will find themselves in a very enviable situation.

Another important and overlooked benefit is improved maintainability. Most organizations realize that this benefit is there and they rely on its value, but they don't proactively plan for it. True, SE/CASE will produce sound systems with few defects and standard code. These maintenance-related benefits will be there, regardless. However, the creation of flexible, repairable systems is a different matter. Enhancing and maintaining systems is a slightly different process than developing systems. Yet, the focus of selecting a SE/CASE environment is always on how well it produces systems. Little time is spent exploring how well these SE/CASE environments maintain the systems that they build.

User community benefits.   The main benefit of SE/CASE to the user community is somewhat surprising. SE/CASE is producing systems that users need, and SE/CASE truly supports the principle of effectiveness—doing the right things the right way, right from the start. Doing the right thing means delving deeply into a request to find out how best to resolve it. Doing the right thing doesn't mean jumping quickly into a solution. By focusing on the need, the users will be satisfied, even delighted in the end. SE/CASE supports this benefit by properly sequencing the activities, by improving communications, and by forcing added rigor into the analysis and design phases, where getting it right is to take place.

Doing things right the first time, right from the start, results in accelerated software delivery (i.e., improved responsiveness). Without SE/CASE, many of the activities of a development or enhancement project resulted from rework. Howard Ruben from Ruben and Associates has found that more than 30 percent of the activities of a typical development project are rework activities. Perhaps a requirement was missed up front, or a design component was wrong, or a test case missed a defect. Reduction in this 30 percent rework is direct savings, often resulting in significantly quicker delivery times.

Responsiveness can also be significantly improved by using some of the RAD and prototyping technologies. When used effectively and for the right types of systems, these technologies have resulted in orders-of-magnitude improvements. DuPont IEA consulting has reported 3:1 to 5:1 improvement for smaller, standalone systems. This has afforded their clients the luxury of installing their systems in a much quicker time frame. Also, in the fast-paced speed of today's global business environment, speed sometimes can mean real dollars.

Getting the systems right also means more accurate and reliable systems. With SE/CASE, quality systems are a given. This results in fewer system crashes, less time spent getting it right in the maintenance phase, and longer life of the systems.

With SE/CASE, the user community can begin to rely on our estimates of cost and schedule. They can begin to factor our numbers into their planning efforts. They will no longer have to double both estimates and pray that we come close.

MIS staff benefits. The benefits to the MIS staff members are almost always ignored until the implementation uprising starts. This is when the staff begins to resist the new changes and wonders why they're going through such disruption for these long-term MIS and user benefits. Benefits, by the way, that they might never personally reap. Since the "tour of duty" for the average MIS professional is relatively short (around three years), by the time these maintenance and quality benefits begin to show up, they might be at a different organization.

Since the benefits of SE/CASE attributed directly to MIS staff members are usually introduced to the staff under stressful situations, the benefits are rarely believed. However, these benefits are no less real. To be useful and believed, they need to be introduced up-front.

The most important benefit to the individual is to be able to maintain his or her professional value to the organization and to society. This is very crucial in order to maintain the relatively high salaries of MIS professionals. Without SE/CASE knowledge, understanding, and skills, they'll be competing with overseas contracting firms who pay their programmers and analysts only one-fourth to one-fifth of what we're paid in the United States. SE/CASE provides a temporary "leg up" on this competition—temporary because these overseas firms know about SE/CASE as well. They're a bit behind us, but not by much. Today, a successful MIS professional needs to get and stay very aggressive towards developing new skills.

SE/CASE also helps an individual to enhance their satisfaction with their job. SE/CASE promotes team synergy and gives staff the feeling that their actions are a valuable part of the overall goal. There's nothing more demoralizing than pouring your heart and soul into an activity only to find out later that it was wrong, redundant with another person's work, or simply not needed. It need happen only once before a person develops a cynical attitude towards expending that extra effort towards a goal.

In addition, SE/CASE leads to less finger pointing when things go wrong. First of all, because of SE/CASE, things will go wrong less often. Also, when things do go wrong, it's a lot clearer where the blame lies. A few staff members will not like this. However, it's these staff members who are bringing down the rest. By finding the weak links, the organization will be able to properly fix the problem through coaching and training. In the long run, everybody benefits.

Another benefit is a partial solution to a staff's worst nightmare—maintenance. With SE/CASE, systems are easier to maintain. The architecture is solid; documentation is up-to-date, standardized, and self-producing; all components are well tested; tools exist to help in understanding code, and tools exist to automate many of the mechanical/clerical tasks.

The problems with the proof.   Altogether, the MIS, user, and staff benefits are quite impressive. They provide a widespread circle of benefits, each interdependent on one another. However, for those who don't fully understand SE/CASE, these benefits appear elusive. There's a constant questioning of their reality. Many are asking if these benefits are simply a CASE vendor's dream. Quite frankly, the jury is still out, but there's strong case-by-case evidence emerging that many of the benefits are in fact real.

The problem, however, is that the deck is stacked against positive proof. At the time of publication of this book, there are few objective, long-term, ongoing studies to prove the value of SE/CASE. About the only one that holds any promise is Howard Ruben's work on productivity improvements for individual SE/CASE technologies. It's very hard to find objective sources with a long-term focus. Most of the other studies were usually commissioned by CASE vendors interested in promoting their products. Their studies usually separate SE from CASE and focus only on one particular phase of the life cycle (usually coding).

In addition, the industry lacks nonsubjective, standard measurements for productivity and quality. Function-point-related measurements are starting to show promise, but that's still too subjective for many hard-core "show me" folks.

However, even under ideal measurement conditions, people still will not believe the numbers. The cry that "we're different" will always be heard. Well, some organizations are different, and some aren't.

The solution of the proof lies in two areas: understanding and measurement.

- An understanding of how the benefits are achieved. A black-box understanding is not good enough. It hasn't been good enough for our user's understanding of what MIS does, and it's not good enough for our understanding of SE/CASE.

- Measurement of the interim quality and productivity improvements—improvements in the process as well as the results. Only through hard work can your organization come to believe in the benefits of SE/CASE.

The disadvantages of SE/CASE

A few disadvantages come with the advantages of SE/CASE. Like moving into a new home, nothing is perfect. Sure, you might get more interior space, a bigger lot, and better plumbing. However, the larger lot means more mowing and the roof might not be as good, but you're willing to put up with the new problems and inconveniences because of the benefits. SE/CASE is no different.

SE/CASE disrupts the culture of the organization. It changes the way that the organization works. That's the primary emphasis of this book. These soft issues will be addressed in chapters 5 and 6.

With SE/CASE, especially the CASE part, the old adage of "garbage in, gospel out" is never more appropriate. CASE, with all of its checks and balances, appears to produce error-free systems. Well, they're mechanically error free (or very close to it), but sometimes it's simply "clean garbage"—error-free modules that don't do what's needed. Clean garbage is sometime more dangerous than the old variety. With clean garbage, you begin to overrely on it.

CASE technology can also be a straightjacket, locking you into a given approach/tool. Some of the tool vendors are beginning to offer more flexible environments, but they still support a primary approach (e.g., information engineering). The disadvantage is not necessarily between known approaches (e.g., IE or RAD) but with unknown future approaches. Perhaps within a few years a new object-based approach involving reusable modules will be perfected and will be significantly different from information engineering.

The large amounts of money and political goodwill spent towards implementing information engineering might keep your organization from moving towards this new approach. Not to say that you want to jump on each new development, but at least keep your future options somewhat open. The glitz of the CASE tool can sometimes overshadow the underlying technique(s) of software engineering. This might keep the staff from fully understanding these underlying techniques, thereby putting the implementation at risk.

CASE technology has come a long way since the early days of DesignAid and Excelerator, but many of the early frustrations still exist. The staff can get frustrated over the "porthole view" of the project that CASE causes. By putting many of the system deliverables on the PC, the only access is through a 13-inch monitor. This is like looking at an ocean through a porthole window. We can only get a small snippet at a time. Then when we split the screen, the individual windows shrink in size. With the old way, we could clutter up our desks and walls with a sea of paper, allowing a much wider, contiguous view of what was going on. A few of the larger monitors available today now allow a few full-size pieces of paper to be shown on a screen at one time. This is a major improvement. However, I guess we won't be totally happy until the monitor is literally the desktop and we're able to move, turn, and rearrange the documents through touch or light-pen interfaces.

Another frustration is the relatively long learning curve for SE/CASE. This time it's not the CASE tool, but the techniques behind it. They're not easily learned and acquired. It takes many months, sometimes years, to totally internalize the process.

For many people, SE/CASE changes the way they think and draft. Before, the only limit to creativity was finding a pencil and a napkin; now they need a PC, monitor, and plenty of disk space. We've begun to rely on the power of the PC. As for me, I can no longer write without my laptop PC. Paper and pencil are simply too slow and limiting, although some of us still occasionally lapse and use napkins. For the analyst and programmer using SE/CASE, the same need exists. In addition, the imperfect CASE tools are filled with technical nuisances (e.g., having to click three or more times to perform a function) and are relatively slow for apparently simple activities (for real-time access tools). Also, limited departmental budgets have left the professional with sharing the tools.

4

The Culture
for SE/CASE

Organizational Culture—A Definition

An organization's culture is made up of a set of integrated beliefs, values, behaviors, and ingrained assumptions about how things are done within the department. All else being equal, when it's change versus culture, culture almost always wins. That's why it's so important that you pay attention to how the culture is going to be affected by the change caused by SE/CASE.

With SE/CASE, you have two choices: change the culture to look like the change, or change the change to have less impact on the culture. The second option is by far the more desirable if there's an ability and willingness to do it. Changing the culture can be time-consuming and expensive. To do it takes an awesome amount of commitment.

An IS Culture Model

Many people today tend to talk around the cultural issues related to implementing SE/CASE. Few seem to get down to specifics. The trade press gives clear messages that culture is a very important aspect of implementing SE/CASE, perhaps the most important aspect. However, for something so important, there's little in the way of advice and structure on how to deal with this important issue. Look at a recent article. The title might be enticing, but the substance will probably be lacking. You'll probably be left worse off than when you started. As a result of the article, the challenge has intensified, but you're still left with little to attack the problem.

Why is this? Why are we left to fend for ourselves when our jobs and perhaps our careers could be on the line if we fail? The primary reason for this gap is simple—technologists hate to play behaviorists, and behaviorists don't want to understand SE/CASE technology.

The folks writing articles on SE/CASE are mostly all hard-core, IS-raised professionals. They understand the fundamental SE principles of rigor and effectiveness, but they have no behavioral knowledge or experience on how to apply these principles. All they have are their own experiences with these new principles and a little knowledge from other IS professionals trying to implement SE/CASE. This is hardly a basis on which to create behavioral models and approaches to help an IS organization implement SE/CASE.

When we talk and write about these issues, we feel like we're playing psychiatrists. We're afraid of being wrong. We assume that unless we have a Ph.D. in behavioral psychology, we probably don't know what we're talking about. To a certain point, that's right. Many times, bad advice is worse than no advice. At least, as a profession, we know when we're out of our element.

On the other side of the coin, behaviorists really don't want to get close to SE/CASE. SE/CASE is not an easy set of concepts to internalize. Many behaviorists would like to stay at a higher level, removed from all the details.

Well, this is our primary reason for writing this book. We both have a wealth of experience implementing SE/CASE at a number of different companies—Tom from the technology perspective and Jim from the behavioral perspective. This book is a blending of these two perspectives into one common approach.

Another reason for the lack of advise from industry sources is that recommendations in the culture area are almost never absolute (as opposed to the technology selection side) and are almost always long-term. There are no quick fixes or easy solutions to changing a culture—except, of course, firing all the staff and starting from ground zero. Kind of like a "green fields" culture change. Doing this stunt, of course, sets up a negative culture for the future. For those coming in, how long will it be before the next wave of technologists replace them? This could seriously affect the cultural dimensions of trust, teamwork, leadership, and supportiveness.

Furthermore, culture doesn't lend itself to being visual. Culture is a very soft and tangled set of concepts and ideas. The very thought of trying to put order into this area is almost sacrilegious. Our first attempts to tie these components together ended up in a "birds nest" jumble of a diagram (see Figure 4.1). Unless you're a glutton for punishment, don't try to weave through this mess. It's very much like spaghetti code. There's a program there; it's just too hard to find.

However, culture does need to be visual. Without a picture, a common vision is almost impossible. As a result, 20 different people will have 20 different versions of what the culture should be like.

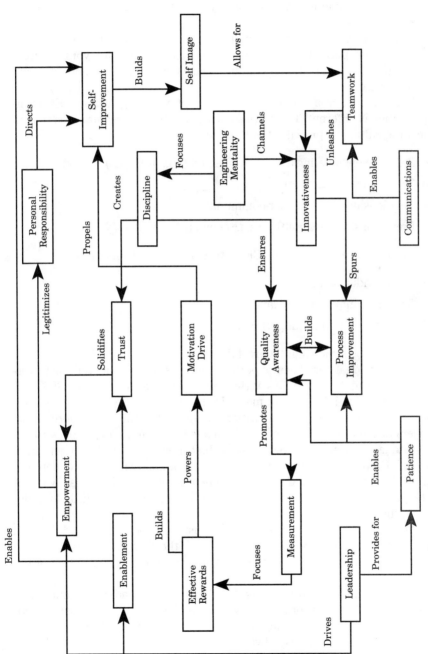

Figure 4.1 The culture "bird's nest."

Imagine if we developed systems without getting specific with words and pictures (i.e., models like DFDs.) Perhaps a team of 5 to 10 would simply talk around the new application and then management would come in and say "let's build it!" The probability of a clear, shared understanding is rather remote.

For this reason, we have developed a cultural model for SE/CASE. This model is not perfect. It's not complete. It's not ideal for your environment, but it is a start. It's a beginning place for you to start modeling your own culture.

We could not create a model that would fit every organization. Every organization is different. There are so many variables in organizations that affect the culture. A partial list of these variables includes:

- Software engineering approach selected (e.g., RAD, IE).
- Size of the IS organization.
- Relationship with the user community.
- Prevailing business culture (e.g., competitiveness).

Our model segments SE/CASE culture into three distinct layers:

1. An individual core layer.
2. The environmental core layer.
3. The environmental support layer.

This mapping is shown in Figure 4.2.

The individual core layer is perhaps the most important, yet most overlooked part of this model. It's at this fundamental layer that most SE/CASE implementation mistakes are made. In the rush to do well and get the ball moving quickly, most IS organizations jump right to the outer, more visible layers of the model. Many organizations feel that they can get back to the individual layer after the SE/CASE technical environment has been established. However, this strategy is difficult, if not impossible. For without the individual layer, the SE/CASE environment is simply a shell. Also, without the people to drive and sustain this shell, an initiative can quickly lose momentum and die.

At the individual core layer, mutual trust, self-confidence, and drive all interact to get the individual ready to take on the changes and challenges to come. This layer focuses on the individual and their interpretation of the changes.

The individual has to first trust the departmental leadership concerning the value and reasons for the changes. Switching to SE/CASE is asking a lot of an individual. You're asking them to completely change the way they do their jobs. Remember, this individual has lots of time invested in the old way

Figure 4.2 IS culture profile. (*Copyright CGA, 1992.*)

of working. They have invested years of college or trade school and even more time through learning by experience. They're not going to change simply because management asks them to change. They have to be able to trust that management has the employees' best interests in mind, not just management's own self-interest in mind.

This situation is similar to the change that secretaries felt in the early 1980s with the advent of word processors. As the new automation features became available, new ways of doing business emerged. Now their bosses were typing their own letters; spell and grammar checkers reduced the need to manually check documents, and letter and form templates were readily available for standard business documents. These secretaries had lots of time invested in basic typing and reviewing skills. Now it appeared that this new change would be eliminating jobs and drastically changing what jobs were left. Many felt that their existing skill base was now useless.

The key to successful implementation was that the secretaries had to trust that management had their best interests in mind. If they didn't feel that way, resistance ensued. No amount of training and education could overcome this basic fear.

Next, employees have to feel self-confident that they can make it in the new environment. In this area, training is an important component. However, so is security, patience, and self-image. People need the time to make the change. However, they also need to feel that they can successfully make it and will be able to contribute long-term.

Finally, the individual needs the drive to move forward. You need to make the new way of doing business more desirable than the old. The status quo should no longer be acceptable. Drive is enhanced through management direction, career advancements, and peer pressure.

Once the individual core layer is established, then you need to move outward to the environmental core layer. Again, many organizations tend to start further out in the third layer, environmental support. The dimensions in that layer are more physical and focused. However, at the second layer, the dimensions of teamwork, discipline, total quality, ownership, and leadership need to be established before the support dimensions are installed. For example, without the total quality and teamwork dimensions firmly entrenched, it's very difficult to establish the measurement or incentives dimensions. In addition, without leadership, the dimensions of empowerment, enablement, and patience are almost impossible.

The dimensions of the environmental core layer represent five overlapping philosophies. These five are at the heart of successful software engineering. Read a few current articles and books in this field. It's almost impossible to read something about software engineering without the piece discussing these dimensions as a framework. Each of these will be further explained in the next section.

Finally there's the environmental support layer. It's at this layer that programs and processes get implemented. However, behind each and every program (e.g., incentives) or process (e.g., continuous improvement) is a basic set of beliefs that, for success, need to be shared by the department.

Together, these layers form the culture for software engineering and CASE. This model is based on concepts from the Total Quality Management (TQM), leadership/effectiveness principles, and individual motivation theories. As mentioned above, these principles should be customized for your organization's needs and existing culture. Later in this chapter, each of these dimensions will be explored in detail.

Getting People to Make Coffee

Software engineering and CASE works best whenever the culture of an IS organization is fine-tuned to support the basic principles and philosophies of these new technologies. Using our culture model can help in this fine-tuning effort. The culture doesn't have to be in perfect alignment with the change, but the closer, the better. Whenever there's a major conflict between a new change and the ongoing culture, the culture almost always wins. Thus, aligning your culture to support SE/CASE will help to greatly reduce implementation risk.

This is an intriguing concept, but what does it mean in real life? How can the underlying beliefs, behaviors, and assumptions of an organization really affect what happens in that institution? After all, doesn't SE/CASE imply a certain amount of rigor and standardization that everyone needs to follow? Couldn't you simply acquire a complete, detailed systems development methodology and a very rigorous CASE tool and be assured that all will go well?

Well, many organizations have tried just this approach with dismal success. People have found ways to circumvent the SE/CASE environment. Others have performed only the visible, politically necessary steps, leaving the core architecture of the systems for the old way of developing systems.

The best way to understand this situation is to draw an analogy to a very common business situation. Surprisingly, getting people to make coffee is very similar to effectively using an SE/CASE environment (i.e., SDM and associated tools). This analogy is not on the same scale as software engineering, but the implementation issues are very similar.

Many of us, including myself, have a habit of drinking coffee, but we never seem to make it. This task gets left to a few individuals who make it for the rest of us. Why? Management has gone out and spent good money on an easy-to-use coffee maker, yet this situation persists in many IS organizations.

The automatic reflex action is for management and others who make coffee to put up signs around the coffee machine like "If you drain a pot, make a pot" or "Your mother doesn't work here; make your own coffee." These attempts rarely get more people to make coffee. The primary effect is for people to feel guilty about not making coffee. What's more, these signs could anger some staff members, further preventing them from making coffee.

This is very similar to management's futile attempts at getting people to improve quality by putting up slogans like "Quality first" and "Q-ALITY: It Doesn't Work Without 'U.'" Slogans and signs are useful artifacts of an environment, but they don't work by themselves. What's needed is an understanding of the underlying reasons behind a quality problem and a proactive plan to address these components of the culture.

The same is true for getting people to make coffee. The reasons for not making coffee or not producing quality lie in the culture of the department. Each individual is different, yet a common thread of sameness runs among all of us whenever it comes to making coffee or producing quality work.

The key to getting people to change their behavior is understanding these beliefs, behaviors, and assumptions and working at this level to resolve the situation. A quick analysis of the coffee situation might leave you with the belief that the staff is simply too lazy to make coffee—a simple rationale for a relatively straightforward problem.

However, upon further analysis, a more complicated set of beliefs, behaviors and assumptions emerge. At the value level, staff members might feel that they're too important to make coffee. They're well paid to do a very important job, and making coffee cuts into their ability to perform this job. They still might feel guilty about not making the coffee, but the importance they place on the job justifies this guilt in their minds. These people honestly feel that they're doing what's best and right for the company. Obviously, putting up signs will not change their behavior.

There are a whole host of individual beliefs that surround the making of coffee. Some people might honestly feel that they don't drink enough coffee to justify making it. After all, one or two cups a day is only a small percentage of the total pot. There most certainly are people who drink more, and they should be the ones who make it. Then there are those people who feel that they don't make it very well or that they will break the machine if they try. Remember, these are honest feelings, not excuses for the guilt.

My favorite assumption is that it's someone else's job to make the coffee. This was perhaps a valid rationale for not making coffee in the early days of setting up a coffee pot. However, if this is the excuse that's espoused today, this person could fall into the lazy category.

Behaviors also play an important part in defining the coffee-making culture. The mere fact that a person was never instructed in how to make coffee could keep a person from making it. Some people just need the self-confidence before they act. Pride also plays a part. If a person has never made coffee before or hasn't made it in a long time, then being seen fumbling over the making of the coffee is something to be avoided.

The key is to be able to identify and separate the real reasons from the excuses. Once this list is known, then the job of changing the prevailing culture can begin. In the case of making coffee, if the real reason was that people felt they were too important, then the management of the department might need to be seen making coffee. The message given to the staff: if management is not too important to make coffee, then I must not be too important either. If the reason was that people were afraid of breaking the unit or that they simply had never started making coffee, then a refresher demonstration might be in order. You might still put up posters to reinforce your strategy, but the emphasis is on a plan, not on shooting from the hip.

Automation is rarely a solution to cultural change. However, this is just what one of our Midwest consulting offices tried. They attempted to dramatically reduce the coffee-making steps all together. They purchased a new high-tech machine that only required an occasional full can of coffee grinds and one long roll of filters. The machine worked great, giving each person a freshly brewed and filtered cup of coffee each time. The problem was that no one really knew how it worked. They could do the simple steps of adding coffee and filters, but whenever the machine malfunctioned, which was often, no one knew how to fix the machine. The result was days without the life-sustaining liquid! At times, some of our code generators reach this dilemma. However, this book is about the culture, not the automation.

The Cultural Dimensions of SE/CASE

Now that we've defined an integrated model for the many dimensions of culture, we'd like to define each of these dimensions in greater detail. It's from this understanding that you can begin to analyze your organization's cultural situation—its beliefs, behaviors, and assumptions.

Individual core layer

Mutual trust. Trust is the most important cultural dimension with the implementation of SE/CASE. Without trust, almost all of the other dimensions are just words. Trust builds the foundation for the other cultural dimensions to take effect.

Trust goes both ways. From management towards staff and from staff towards management. Both sides have to feel that they can trust the other side during this important transition. IS departments have been too political in the past. This is not the environment in which SE/CASE can flourish. An SE/CASE implementation represents an opportunity to get back to basics and to do things right. It's an opportunity to build back the integrity and respect lost over the years of fighting to keep our head above water.

Trust needs to be built on tangible actions, not just words. Both sides need to make commitments and live up to them. Again, it can't be one-sided. Building trust is an incremental series of give-and-take iterations until both sides are no longer holding back.

For example, in one organization we worked with, the initial level of trust was very low. Off-the-record discussions with both the IS staff and the management team revealed a deep level of suspicion of the other sides. The situation was to the point where both sides were at war and plotting to derail the other side. There were constant swipes in public by management towards the staff and in confidence towards the management team. In short, the department was a battle zone.

In this situation, we started our work at rebuilding the trust with the staff. The level of mistrust was so high in this department that starting from the management side would have been met with too much suspicion. Once, twice, three times burned—forever shy!

Our initial efforts were relatively simple. We started by interviewing key staff members concerning the technical and cultural problems of the department. The first level of trust was for the staff to feel that their responses would not be used against them. Of the ten staff members interviewed, only three or four were openly honest. The rest just hemmed and hawed around superficial issues. Most were too afraid to speak out.

For management's part, the summarized issues list served as a good basis from which to reciprocate the trust. They published the list within the department, even though it was not especially flattering. This really started to show the staff that management was serious about healing the wounds from past fights.

From this base, more suggestions rolled in as the staff started to get used to speaking out. The politics of the department seemed to be diminishing. As the good suggestions started to get elevated, management began to act on these suggestions. This really floored the staff. Management had actually listened, not just asked.

This IS organization continued this iterative give-and-take cycle until both sides were united towards winning the war, not fighting themselves. It was from this foundation that the rest of the culture could be implemented.

Drive.   There have been many books written over the years on the subject of motivating employees. Most of these books focus on getting people to be more productive. The primary result of these approaches is to get the work out faster. Many of the approaches recommend some form of pressure that comes from management to keep production up. While this sort of drive/motivation is certainly needed for crucial situations, this is not the type of drive that's needed to make SE/CASE happen. In fact, this type of pressure could backfire if not properly handled.

As the authors of the culture model presented in this book, we debated long and hard over whether to put "drive" or "motivation" into the model. For by putting it into this very visual artifact, it could be used to legitimize increased pressure tactics. However, we felt that leaving it out would do more harm. As a compromise, we decided to leave it in, but to call it "drive." The following are characteristics of drive:

- Needs to be channeled.
- Commitment towards a common goal.
- Competitive (MIS folks tend to be competitive by nature).
- Make-it-happen/stick-to-it attitude.
- Positive morale.
- Energy/excitement.
- Inter-drive.
- Willingness to stay late.

- A positive tension caused by "creative dissatisfaction."
- Avoids a condition of "ease."
- Paced momentum.
  - *a.* Focus on steady action.
  - *b.* Staff endurance.

Self-confidence. The self-confidence dimension is the hardest to identify within an IS organization. As such, self-confidence often turns out to be the one factor that brings havoc into an SE/CASE implementation. It's like a bug in a program that only sporadically shows up, but in different circumstances each time.

An individual's level of self-confidence is very hard to determine, for we're dealing with an individual's ego—his or her pride. With many of our war veterans (not the military types, but the early IS types), lack of self-confidence is very tough to reveal. To admit that you possibly couldn't handle the new technologies of SE/CASE is a foreign concept.

However, without confidence, the best-laid plans will not work. People will disrupt your plans either consciously or subconsciously. Like the secretaries of the early 1980s, if employees are not made to feel confident that they can make this transition, resistance starts almost immediately.

With the advent of SE/CASE, you're threatening a person's livelihood. You're asking them to change how they make their living. There's a lot at stake. According to many psychiatrists, the loss of a job is the second most stressful period in a person's life, after the death of a relative. To even remotely put a person's livelihood at risk is a very dangerous situation. This is why it's easier for the new, young kids of the department to change. They don't have much invested in the old ways of IS. They have much more self-confidence than many of the longer-term staff. They haven't been burned enough in the past to fear change, thus they're much more willing to give a new approach a try.

Building self-confidence is a very touchy thing. If you overdo it, you run the risk of patronizing the individual. If you underdo it, you might lose an individual or two. In addition, you need to simultaneously build the self-confidence of an individual and of the team to which he/she belongs. To be effective, you need to be patient and clever.

It's not a simple matter of just training! All too often we concentrate on the training part of self-confidence, forgetting the ego part. Simply knowing what to do might not be enough. I remember early in my career I was assigned the responsibility of converting a hard-core COBOL programmer over to the concepts and techniques of structured design (i.e., structure charts). I had recently graduated from college, where I had been exposed to these techniques. This was in the days right before DFDs, IE, CASE, and all of the other new stuff. For this discussion, we'll call this individual Bob.

The initial weeks working with Bob were tough. At first he mistrusted me and the management team. He felt that management had little idea of what these structured concepts were all about and that I was only a young punk without battle scars. However, after we began to work together we produced a few nice pieces of work using the new technique. As a result, Bob began to trust us and he removed this crucial barrier. Next, management helped by reinstilling the drive in Bob to want to change. Through a creative incentive program and one-on-one talks, management was able to get Bob to a state where he truly wanted to make the switch to the structured concepts.

My job then was to train Bob on the techniques in order to get him to the point where he could "go it alone." I worked hard and long. I found books for him to read, which he read. We worked through exercises from my college studies. I even recommended that he facilitate walk-throughs of other people's structured deliverables. He truly understood what the technique was all about. I believed that Bob was ready to go it alone. He trusted management, me, and the concepts. He was driven to get it done, and he had the skills to do it.

Then one day, after he was using the techniques somewhat successfully for a month or so, he surprisingly requested a transfer to a group that was still using the old techniques. It was a shock. He had given up—but, why?

The answer was simple. He had heard rumors about all of the other related techniques (e.g., entity relationship diagrams, data flow diagrams, and data structure diagrams) that were sure to follow for our group. He felt that since the initial transition was so hard for him to make, that he would never be able to make the full transition to structured concepts. It was simply too overwhelming for him. We were never able to talk him out of taking the new position, and the transfer was made.

I had succeeded in training Bob on the specific technique, but I had not instilled a confidence within him that he could continue on his own for the complete approach. In the rush to keep moving, I had forgotten Bob's ego, his pride. Most of us don't wear our egos on our shoulder like a badge. We hide it from full view and put on a face that everyone thinks is needed. However, when push comes to shove, pride always takes over.

If I had properly prepared Bob for the full environment (i.e., education, not just training) and moved a bit slower, Bob might have been less intimidated by the change. As a result, his self-confidence would have had a chance to slowly grow with the full expectations, and a good resource would have been most effectively used.

Environmental core layer

Leadership.   The art of creating collective wisdom and energizing it is perhaps the most overlooked dimension in today's American business culture.

In many IS organizations, this cultural dimension is seriously missing. To implement the technologies of SE/CASE, we need a long-term focus with a short-term emphasis on practicality. Management needs to be able to engage the people, not just simply manage the numbers. We need a blending of technical, social, and business styles. We need to stand up beyond the politics and do what is right. Leadership doesn't always come from the top. The staff needs to be able to recognize this, senior management especially needs to allow this, and the lower echelons need to recognize this as well, so that leadership can be shared and the whole process can become more participative.

Quality awareness.   Quality has to be the primary focus for software engineering. There's no substitute for quality, and its enhancement precedes productivity improvements. Quality awareness mandates a customer focus, which means that the quality effort must be actively managed with quality assurance controls at all levels, including the departmental and individual. Quality awareness today must be built on sound Total Quality Management philosophies.

Discipline.   The need for discipline requires that there must be a respect for and adherence to certain policies and standards, as well as a respect for standardization and the efficiencies that it brings. Added to this must be the disciplines of consistency, correctness, completeness, and coherency, the 4 Cs. We urge the adoption of what we call flexible-rigor—the ability to be flexible within a framework. This would also suggest that employees be willing and able to make trade-offs that make sense for the success of the project.

Teamwork.   Synergy is the ability for the key players and the key constituencies to be able to work effectively together. Synergy occurs when there's a sense of shared responsibility and mutual goals, and when there's a clear understanding that success requires interdependence. Teamwork also means company loyalty and being a "team player." It's not a time for egos to get in the way; it's a time to foster the idea that individuals can make a difference as part of a team, especially when they feel valued.

Environmental support layer

Empowerment.   There's so much talk about empowerment these days, and there seems to be as many different definitions as there are people to ask. Each person decides if they're willing to act as an empowered person; an organization provides the environment within which a person can act as an empowered person. It's important that the organization do this, but it's also important to remember that all people don't want to be empowered. Some only want to do their job and go home. For the organization that's capable of managing, or rather leading, an empowered organization, there are some tremendous payoffs.

Enablement. Another part of the support layer is providing the tools and training necessary to be able to do the job. This also includes sufficient administrative staff support and adoption of a no-excuse policy with regard to providing what's necessary to get the job done.

Effective rewards. There must be an effective reward system in place. No matter what the rhetoric, people react to their reward systems. You need to pay attention to both the formal and informal reward systems. Some organizations' informal reward systems are more meaningful to its people than the formal system. The informal system includes truly listening and patting someone on the back when appropriate. Both the formal and informal reward systems need to be tied to both the corporate and IS objectives, and this needs to be timely.

Measurement. Measurement is a way of keeping score. For our purposes, measurement should include the measurement of both process and product. Process measurement means to keep a constant vigil on how you're doing things and its efficiency and viability for continuing. Product measurement is the amount of quality work produced against a known or established standard. Both measurements are mandatory as a way to keep track of progress.

Patience. There's a new understanding and learning curve associated with a CASE project. This has to be kept in mind by those who are leading the project. Ideas must be given time to mature, which will in turn raise the comfort level of those that the ideas are new to. It might mean providing stability in some areas a little longer than you would like to.

There's a tendency to want to get "results," which often translates into going into a crisis mode or "fire fighting." This constant drive for action might lead to a hurry up and wait problem while the system or people are trying to catch up. Finally, patience means a lasting commitment to the project, with a long-term focus.

Process improvement. Process improvement means continuous improvement. It's fed by a feedback mechanism such as metrics. Being wed to "the way we've always done it" gets in the way of process improvement. A way to assure this is to say "If it ain't broke, maybe I'm not looking hard enough." With a proactive emphasis tied to the TQM philosophy that we talked about earlier, process improvement will accommodate both process evolution and revolution.

Personal responsibility. All parties to the project have a responsibility for professionalism. This means a willingness to accept personal accountability, dressing the part, being professional in their actions, working with a consultant's attitude for the company or profession, and not operating with a maverick mentality.

Self-improvement. Self-improvement also means to be self-directing. There needs to be a willingness to teach and to learn, a willingness to lead and to follow, and a willingness to invest in oneself. It means taking control of your own career and fully using management-sponsored opportunities to use new capabilities.

Engineering mentality. An engineering mentality means an architectural philosophy with a segmentation of work. Some would call it *hierarchical decomposition*. It means close attention to graphical specifications, standardization, validation, traceability, and reusability.

Innovativeness. Innovation is new blood. It's important to be open to new ideas from both inside and outside influences. The ability to transcend old, preconceived notions and to be leading-edge gives a competitive edge. It requires becoming forward thinkers and using imagination, imagineering, and creativity. Being innovative means having a tolerance for the unstructured (which means being comfortable with ambiguity, special assignments, and constant change), and being willing to try things and having the encouragement and freedom to try them.

Supportiveness. Supportiveness means being willing to help others, being a mentor and coach while providing an environment for fairness, and being a good listener.

Communications. Good communication can only take place when there are safe forums in which to be heard. This means to be heard without fear. This is two-way and is done through both formal and informal channels. Good communications suggests that there must be an openness to differences and new ideas that are not hampered by a "not invented here" syndrome.

Environmental comfort. This is provided by good social relationships, in an empathic environment that's also esthetically pleasing. Environmental comfort requires relative freedom from executive noise and other interferences.

It might also provide the opportunity to work at home or in an equally safe and nonthreatening climate. Finally, there needs to be a place for humor and an environment where work can be fun.

Evolution of the MIS Culture

Today's MIS culture

Every MIS department is different in some way. Each puts their own individual stamp on how systems are built and maintained. Yet, through our many activities with MIS organizations, both big and small, we've noticed a common thread of sameness about MIS organizations. Maybe it's because of the high rate of movement between jobs among MIS types, or maybe it's because of the nature of the work we do, but there's a perceivable similarity between these organizations.

Much of this sameness we're attributing to the overall culture of MIS. It's this set of beliefs and behaviors that make us tick. However, these beliefs and behaviors need to change in order to properly support SE/CASE. In this section, we'll explore the MIS culture so you can better understand your own culture. From this foundation, you'll be in a much better position to affect your future.

The current culture of MIS in many ways grew out of the programming mentality of our early predecessors. This mentality placed a high degree of emphasis on technology, efficiency, elegance, and fit. This resulted in treating the process of MIS as more of an art than a science. We developed systems like an artist painting a picture. No one could estimate how long it would take; the process to achieve the masterpiece was vague at best, and the final result was a mystery until it was unveiled.

Like an old-world craftsperson, we also have a tendency to custom build each system by hand. This job-shop mentality assumes that all users are different and that we're able to provide the best of quality and fit for their needs. This image idealizes what we do, but it's rarely achieved. Schedules, system changes, system interfaces, budget restrictions, and other project impact components all have a way of ruining our dream. The result is that we usually deliver less than we originally intended. The system we developed works, but it's not the ideal system that we initially imagined. The user might be satisfied and delighted with the results, but we're less than ecstatic. Our initial reaction is usually, "We'll do it right the next time." Yet we never seem to be able to achieve this ideal goal. In essence, we're craftspeople without masterpieces. That leaves many of us endlessly searching for the perfect system.

Our art/craftsperson emphasis also fosters a cowboy/maverick mentality—one in which a staff member does the work alone (even if in a group setting), learns through experiences and war stories, and does whatever it takes to get the job done. The cowboy/maverick mentality grew out of the fact that in the early days of MIS (and to a lesser extent even today), there were few good training programs, internal or external. Interestingly enough, this maverick mentality didn't evolve because of a lack of structured techniques or methodologies. They have existed now for more than 20 years.

As a result of the lack of training, the staff learned on their own and thus developed individual styles. Then, as programming and analysis standards were developed to make MIS more of a science, the staff resisted them. What worked for them in the past is now their primary foundation for the future. Thus, staff members are open only to those techniques and approaches that build on their self-styled base of knowledge and experience.

As a profession, MIS is very "grass-roots" oriented. We like detail. We like to solve problems with tangible solutions. As a result, we tend to overanalyze a particular situation and to suboptimize the solution. We're not "big-picture" individuals. Sure, we have a few planning types in most every MIS organization, but these individuals never quite fit into the MIS organization or its culture. They're considered outsiders.

We're almost always fighting fires. There always seems to be a major problem to solve or situation to conquer. We never have the time to focus on the future; the present is more important. What's most interesting is that we seem to revel in this disarray! I guess the adrenalin of the constant reactions makes us feel important to the company. Reacting is often seen by staff and management alike as a badge of courage as opposed to a sign of a breakdown. As a result, we seem to be stuck in an emergency mode, even if it's not needed. We've become addicted to reacting. We're hooked.

We're very conservative. This comes as a shock to many in the profession, who feel that MIS is on the "bleeding edge" in many respects. Perhaps we venture out on a technology ledge occasionally with a new computer system or piece of support software, but the basic decisions we make and the directions we take tend to be evolutionary as opposed to revolutionary. We universally stick to the "show me" mentality and trust very few new ideas and innovations. There are very good reasons for this conservative stance. The most prevalent reason is that we've all been burned a few times in our careers. Perhaps it was a new 4GL in the early 1980s or experimenting with JAD on the large order-entry system that had problems. In either event, the trauma from the past keeps us from being bold and decisive.

Related to our conservative nature is our closed-mindedness. In many of the larger MIS organizations, we constantly exhibit a not-invented-here attitude. We've been somewhat successful doing our work, so why change things? Somehow, the systems get implemented and the users are somewhat satisfied, or at least pacified.

A very important, and very unique, aspect of the MIS culture is the heavy reliance on the project manager. This individual is truly empowered to get the job done. There's very little responsibility within a project that extends beyond this person. On many projects, this individual is truly the only one who understands what's really going on.

This cultural aspect is very important within the domain of implementing SE/CASE. It's the project manager who will ultimately make or break an SE/CASE implementation. For it's this person who decides how a project is to be run and whether or not to fully use methodologies and CASE tools. It's this person's neck that's on the line if the project fails. Your SE/CASE marketing activities need to address this group first.

MIS departments love action. In many organizations, visible activity equates to progress. The phrase "Why isn't Sam coding yet?" (or WISCY for short) is heard many times within MIS organizations in an effort to get things moving in a positive direction. Also, if that's not bad enough, it's usually followed up with a sarcastic "analysis paralysis" innuendo. At times the organization does need a jolt to get moving, and a call for action is very commendable. However, our overreliance on visible action is simply a sign of management not understanding the development and maintenance processes. I guess it's better to have too much action than not enough, but it has been overdone.

As a department charged with most all computer hardware and software, we tend to solve many of our problems with technology. We're living by the old adage that if all you have is a hammer, everything looks like nails.

In addition, we're very narrowly focused. When pushed to stretch a bit, many MIS types are heard to utter "That's not my job" or "That doesn't apply to MIS." We have a vision of what MIS is to do, and that's what we do. We're a static organization with a surprisingly dynamic set of goals and objectives. Every year our focus changes, yet we stay the same. Perhaps we're immune to the organizational changes.

Surprisingly, most MIS departments are very political. You'd think that a department set apart from the rest of the company and focusing on one aspect of the business could leave politics aside and concentrate on the work at hand. In a few organizations we've seen, this has happened. However, in the majority, defensiveness, empire building, and fiefdom protection are the predominate management themes. Why?

In the early days of MIS, the departments were small and the lead person knew a good bit about what was going on. As a result, the department could work as a real team and accomplish goals together. As the departments grew, the outside pressures grew. The original leads were still technical people, and upper management wanted to professionally manage the MIS department. At this point, non-MIS management began to run MIS departments. As you might assume, a non-MIS person knows little about the development and maintenance process except for what they could see, and this, of course, was the code. (By the way, this is how the WISCY mentality was formed.)

These non-MIS types did bring structure to MIS, but only to the organizational structure and its policies and procedures. What they in fact created was a bureaucracy that in turn brought us the politics that we now endure. This is now changing back to the early team-oriented philosophies. A few organizations that we've consulted with are again proving the value of the team-structured department. We'll address this issue much more when we discuss the culture needed for SE/CASE.

Quite frankly, MIS professionals are spoiled. On average, we make more money than other equally educated professions. We're generally left alone to do whatever it is that we do. For years, upper management has tended to worship our unseen talents, but this is now starting to change. We feel secure in our careers and tend to work fewer hours than other professionals. (By the way, the amount of time worked varies widely from organization to organization). In short, many MIS staff members feel that their technological security breeds a certain type of "entitlement." Like social security or welfare, it will always be there whenever times get difficult.

MIS as a department is very resistant to change. In fact, we hate to change. We've changed so many other folks that we understand the far-reaching implications of change. This dimension will be discussed more fully in the next few sections.

On the positive side, MIS departments like to have fun. We're real people, not stuffy and pompous about our profession. We can let our hair down and relax with one another and celebrate our individual uniqueness.

In addition, we know how to motivate our staffs. Surprisingly, it's not always with financial rewards. Many people like their jobs, their profession. This is not true of many other professions where Mondays are feared. When the work is interesting and intense, we're at our best. We know how to work under pressure.

Well, this is how we see ourselves, or at least how we see many MIS organizations. Perhaps your organization is a little different. You don't need to agree with our analysis; perform your own using our descriptions as a "straw man" profile. The key is understanding where your culture is today and where it needs to be tomorrow. Later in this chapter, we'll address the culture requirements of the future.

The MIS image

An important aspect of understanding our MIS culture is to see how others view us. Just like with our own personality, how the outside world sees us is a crucial aspect of who we are. We can't ignore our external image. For an MIS department, it's no different. With the implementation of SE/CASE, we'll be asking the user community to change the amount and nature of our interactions. Understanding what they currently think about MIS will allow us to better select and implement the tools, techniques, and methodologies of SE/CASE.

Table 4.1 shows two different perspectives on the same MIS characteristics. Who is right is not important. However, recognizing and understanding the differences is important. We can't stay within our cocoon and do our own thing any longer. We need to emerge and integrate into the rest of the company. By understanding our MIS image, we can begin this transformation.

TABLE 4.1   The MIS Image

MIS view of MIS	Non-MIS view of MIS
Technology exploiters	Technology mongers
	Toys-R-Us department
	State-of-the-art driven
Specialists	Mystics/voodoo chiefs
Long-range visionaries	"Star Wars" dreamers
Change agents	Rabble-rousers
Technically correct	Overbearing, know-it-all
Busy	Deaf, aloof
Different	Eccentric
Org can't survive without us	Necessary overhead
Technical	Foreigners
	Noncommunicators
	Different language/jargon

We view ourselves as exploiters of new technologies—the knights sent to rescue the company from certain collapse. The user community sometimes see us going a bit too far—running off and acquiring one of everything, buying one of every type of computer, database system, programming language, and even CASE tool. Study the CASE vendor literature closely. You'll find the same major corporations on almost every list. They simply purchase one of everything and are thus considered users of the technology. One user representative that we talked to refers to MIS as the "Toys-R-Us" department, implying that all MIS does is play around with new technology.

Where we see ourselves as specialists with a specific mission; the user community views us as mystics. They have little idea of how we do our job. It might as well be magic. However, this situation is changing. The users are starting to learn how to program with spreadsheets (a frightening thought) and with 4GLs. In addition, many of the newer user managers have taken computer classes in college and are no longer mystified by our talents. Our voodoo chief status is starting to wear thin, and this could expose us a bit more than we're ready for.

Even though we don't take long-range planning seriously, we see ourselves as long-range visionaries whenever it comes to computer-related advancements. Many an MIS department will boast of their plan for client-server architectures and distributed databases. The user community, however, sees MIS as "star wars" dreamers—out in a dream land far from reality.

Even though we ourselves hate to change, we love to change the user community. We see ourselves as change agents capable and ready to meet any challenge. The users fear this aspect of MIS. They see us as rabble-rousers looking to stir up their pot whenever we get a chance.

We know our technology. We've mastered the bits and the bytes and we let the user community know it. However, many times we tend to be over-bearing know-it-alls. We tend to push the new technologies on the users in an effort to prove that we're right.

As mentioned earlier, we're an action-oriented culture—one that likes to continuously move. This action, however, is usually perceived by the user community as being deaf and aloof. We never have the time or the patience to listen to what they really want and need.

We're different. We tend to dress differently and act differently than the user community. This is changing of late, but we still like to celebrate our uniqueness. The user, however, sometimes see us as eccentric, fringe people who they need around to run their operations. Be it real or past perceptions, the image is still there.

In the users minds, we've become a necessary part of overhead—a necessary evil to getting their job done. Finally, our technical jargon and introvertedness have gotten us the label of foreigners and noncommunicators. Well, many of us have known for years that we're different from the user community. Why worry about it now? We've persisted for years and are very comfortable with our somewhat strained yet stable relationship with the users.

However, what will happen whenever outsourcing alternatives become real and known to the users? There are many major consulting organizations who are quietly and actively building consulting groups able to outsource development, maintenance, and operations work. These organizations are also building relationships and partnerships directly with the user community, bypassing the traditional MIS management route.

The user community can feel more at home with these consulting organizations. These consulting organizations work on constantly enhancing their image, and they know their clients. There will come a time in the not-too-distant future when defecting away from the internal MIS department by outsourcing will become the vogue thing to do. Working on the MIS image then will be too late. It's now that the MIS image is crucial. Now is the time for action.

Why it is so hard to change this culture?

Why would an organization that brings about change almost daily in the lives of its user community be so afraid to change itself? It seems inconceivable, but it's true. Many organizations we've talked to are perplexed with this dilemma, especially whenever it comes to changing the IS culture and infrastructure.

Well, we're like dentists before the days of novocaine. We know how much pain we inflict with our work. We know how disruptive changing the way we work can be. We've seen the ripple effect in the user community go far beyond the surface.

We also have a high investment in our current situation. As mentioned earlier, most MIS staff learned through the school of hard knocks. We didn't learn about the development and maintenance process through the class-room. Our training was informal and on the job. With on-the-job training comes the pain of failure. As many like to say, we learned through our mis-takes. Thus, we paid dearly for our education. We're not about to throw away this high investment. As in the world of finance, this is a "sunk cost," and we need to proceed from this point on and not look at what we paid in the past. However, for many, as in finance, this is very difficult.

For the few who have achieved a masters degree in the school of hard knocks, there's a potential ego problem. These individuals are heroes. They have not only fought the wars—they have won many of them. To change the way the battle is now fought means starting over and becom-ing another foot soldier in boot camp. This is not a very exciting challenge to these individuals.

MIS staff members understand the long learning curve that new tech-nologies like SE/CASE will take. They've been through this learning curve with the early assembler-to-COBOL shift or learning a new DBMS. MIS man-agement, however, never seems to want to acknowledge that this learning curve exists. As a result, it makes the staff reluctant to try something new.

Because we created our job (through on-the-job training and the like), we've become our jobs. Our individual personalities are built into our jobs and processes. As a result, getting rid of the old processes is like throwing out part of ourselves. This is perhaps the most important yet overlooked aspect of changing a person's environment. It's very hard for a person to understand and articulate these feelings. As implementors of new technologies and associated changes, we just have to assume that these feelings are there.

MIS departments are generally very comfortable. Sure, we get rushed at times and have our political battles to fight. However, in general, the salaries are relatively high, we have a defined set of responsibilities, and the work is usually challenging. With all this going for us, why rock the boat? At the global level, "If it ain't broke, don't fix it."

Finally, the MIS department is simply too busy to change—like the re-cent cartoon of a salesman trying to sell a machine gun to a king fighting a war with bows and arrows. The king says, "Leave me alone. I've got a war to fight." We're simply too busy to change, no matter how good the change is. Some of our resistance is legitimate. There are pressures that need to take precedence. However, are they all crucial to the mission? It's a tough decision.

5

The Change Process

Effect of History

Why is it so hard to stick to a diet? Why is it so hard to stop smoking? The answer to these questions has a lot in common with why it's so hard to get organizations to change. You might call it addictive behavior, or you might say that people don't like being disrupted out of their "comfort zones," or it might be that human beings are just naturally control oriented, and change causes them to feel that they're losing control. Actually, the answer is a little bit of each.

You've surely heard the statement that people "don't like change." That's probably true to a certain extent, but in the 1990s people are becoming more and more conditioned to the fact that change is just a part of life. Because of that, we believe that there's a better way to describe reluctance to change, especially as it applies in the organizational setting. What we find is that people don't like poorly managed change!

In organizations that have a decent track record of starting things and finishing them, the trust in and credibility of the management around change is good. However, how about those companies who have a legacy of starting a lot of things that just seem to disappear over time and are never heard about again? We hear employees standing around the water coolers and the coffee pots, and what we hear sounds something like this; "Whatever happened to that change they announced a few months back?" A fellow employee replies, "I don't know. I guess they decided not to do it." Now, multiply this same conversation over several hundred or thousand employees, over numerous projects, and over several years. What do you get?

The answer is "not much." In fact, if this process is repeated often enough, what it effectively does is teach your organization to ignore you. Why would anybody get too excited about a change announcement that probably sounds an awfully lot like some announcement they've heard many times before, and from which very little or nothing ever came? Add to that the fact that there's very little price to be paid for ignoring the announcement or change, and you'll very definitely find an organization that changes very reluctantly, if at all. I hope we haven't just described your organization. However, just in case this sounds too familiar, let's talk first about how to get people's attention for an SE/CASE project.

Getting Started, Getting Involvement

There's a three-part answer to the problem of getting started and getting involvement. First, you must significantly increase the amount of ownership in the project over what you have probably done for other projects in the past. This gets all wrapped up in the empowerment and participative management issues that we described in the previous chapter. Organizations with the "legacy" problem inevitably also have the issue of lack of ownership.

Getting people involved on the front end of the project is going to be important, as well as helping people feel valued in the decision-making process. At the risk of sounding like a broken record, we still see a lot of SE/CASE projects fail because of lack of end-user involvement. If this is your project, or if you're on the line for the success or failure of an SE/CASE project and you have this previously mentioned history of projects that go nowhere, get people involved from the beginning.

Second, the organization needs to see that there's reason to have more faith and trust in management's ability to make change happen. Employees will start to understand that when they see management start things, they see management finish them. Or, if management starts something and decides to proceed differently than first announced, the sponsors of the change come back to the organization and tell the employees. Or, finally, if management starts something and then decides for good business reasons to stop it completely, or short of the expected outcome, again the management of the change comes back to the employees and tells them. Don't leave them guessing about what's happening.

You also have to give attention to whether your reward system matches your rhetoric. The new rhetoric has to be that we're going to get people involved, and that there's going to be good communication around what's going on, but it also needs to be clear that in light of these two previous things, there's no place in your organization for ignoring directives any longer, and that there's a price to be paid if you do. This might sound like "tough talk," but if you're on a project that you can't afford to fail, you're sometimes going to have to put a stake in the ground to deal with those that just aren't going to get with the program.

Education, Not Just Communication

We were with a client recently in a meeting that was supposed to allow people to share with the senior management how they were going to approach a particular change. After listening for a few minutes, the CEO stood up and said, "Are we all talking about the same thing here?" What he was referring to was the fact that what they had been listening to was not just a different approach for different parts of the company; people got the feeling that they were not talking about the same change.

The CEO asked each one in the room to take out a piece of paper and write down their definition of the change. After about 20 minutes, he collected them and suggested they take a short recess while he took a look at what he had. After the break, he restarted the meeting by saying that he was appalled at what he was reading. "We're not on the same wavelength," he said. "In fact, some of you aren't even on the same planet with the rest of us. What the _____ is going on?"

What we have here is not as unusual or unique a set of circumstances as you might think. We see too many projects where there are as many different definitions of what the project is as there are people in the room. That's why the first and certainly one of the most important tasks is getting involvement on deciding what to do and then making sure that everyone clearly understands what it is you're about to do. Don't leave this to chance. Check it out!

There are probably a lot of people who think that communication is an overused word. Well, that can't be true as it relates to the management of a change like the implementation of an SE/CASE project. Communication and the way it's handled will play an important part in the success of your project.

Still using the same assumption that you have used a good participative management process to reach the decision as to what you want to do, now the task becomes getting the message out to all those affected. A strong recommendation is that you don't make the announcement with a memo or video broadcast. The best communications that we've witnessed don't lend themselves very well to that approach.

A leading business publication takes a survey each year to see where most of America's employees look for the most reliable information about what's going on with their job and with the company. The 1991 survey results reported that 78 percent rely on their boss as the source of that information. So what does that tell us that will be helpful?

If 78 percent of our employees look to their boss for their information, it means that we need to use the management structure to "get the word out."

This will accomplish two things. First, by using the management structure, you're reinforcing the buy-in on their part, which was begun with the participative management process. Second, by making them part of the process, you help them gain ownership in what they're reporting. How many times have you heard a "boss" say, when telling people about something that was about to happen, "Well you know this comes from the old man in the corner office. I just carry out orders." What a cop out! This is the kind of help that you can do without. What they should be saying is what "we" are doing; they should share it as an "owner."

What happens when you announce that there's going to be a reorganization? The first thing people ask is, "How is it going to affect me?" What we've found is that until they get that question answered, the reorganization doesn't have much meaning. It's something that's happening "over there," wherever that is. It becomes very important in the planning process that you take into consideration how you're going to translate the announcement of "the" change into language that people at all levels can understand and that will enable them to realize how the change is going to affect them.

This means that management, project leaders, etc., are going to have to take the "main" message and translate it into how it will affect people at every level being impacted by the change. Sound like a lot of work? It is. However, who said this was going to be easy? You have to look at each and every unit in the organization that's being impacted and ask yourself, "How do we have to say it so they will hear it?" One of the common mistakes that we often see is that one message is sent to everybody. That's a little like giving everybody a copy of the *Bible* and expecting everyone to have the same interpretation. It doesn't work that way. You've got to know your audience and put it in language that's meaningful to them. If you don't, and you send one message, we can guarantee that you'll miss a large piece of your audience.

Readiness Assessment

We once met a marriage counselor who had a remarkable record of success with couples. When asked to what he attributed his great success, he replied, "I interview them first, and then I only take those who are ready to make a change and make their marriage work." Let's look at how this same psychology could be applied to your SE/CASE project.

When you decided that you had to do something, SE/CASE might or might not have been the only option that you had as an answer. Assuming that there was more than one possibility, one of the things that you should have considered was which option had the greatest "assimilate ability" factor. All things being equal, the option that stood the best chance of being implemented, when measured against certain criteria, should have been your first choice. So what are these criteria?

The best predictor of future behavior is past behavior. That being true, you should be interested in knowing how good you've been at implementing other changes, specifically technological changes. If you haven't been very good at that, ask yourself why not. Find out from those who have been around long enough to know how good or bad you've been. If your work is thorough enough, you'll probably get enough answers that will highlight areas of concern from past projects. One thing you have to be careful of is whether this backward look is uncovering things that are attributable to certain people or things that are tied to processes or structure.

Problems that are tied to people might have gone away when they did, assuming they did. Concerns tied to processes or structure are more likely to still be around whether certain people are or not. So, you need to be careful to differentiate between the two different problems as you're doing this investigation and getting these answers.

Next is what we call the "ripple effect"—where and how much effect is this project going to have on parts of the company outside of MIS? In order to be able to get adequate input from the affected areas and do your planning, it's very important that you get as clear an idea as possible concerning where the effects of the SE/CASE project are going to be felt. You can't do this sort of planning in isolation; you need the buy-in and ownership of CASE to be as wide as possible.

How much commitment do you have from those that will be sponsoring this change? Is it enough commitment to see the change through when the going gets tough, as it inevitably will? Is the person or are the persons who are driving this change dissatisfied enough with the way things are today— enough to sponsor the effort for change? Our experience suggests that unless the "right" people are dissatisfied enough with what's going on currently, your project stands a good chance of suddenly losing its support if the effort starts to look like or feel like more cost than what the sponsors bargained for.

This train of thought raises another very important item to remember. If you've been the advocate for this change, and your successful advocacy got you an agent's job, don't sell the "bells and whistles of the change; sell the real cost of change." Now, some of you will argue that if you tell your "champion" everything, you stand the chance of scaring them off before you can even get started. That might be true, but it's better to be scared off before you get started instead of six months into the project, when your sponsors find that this is way more than what they bargained for based on what you told them, and then, because of poorly managed expectations, you lose your sponsorship. Take on the tough battles with the sponsors and with those that are going to have to make the change on the front end. It will save you a lot of grief later on.

Something else to remember is that sponsorship for change is often only as good as the last person asking the sponsor for help. You have to keep after sponsors and remind them of the reasons they agreed to get behind the change in the first place. The minute you walk out their door, someone else walks in looking for the same kind of help that you were. Sponsors only have so much time, and some have a tendency to get "overextended" in their zeal to be helpful.

Sponsoring a change carries a lot of work with it. You need to be sure that your sponsor understands what's expected of him, her, or them, and be sure you educate them as to what their sponsorship means to the success of your project. The zeal we talked about earlier is often the result of a lack of understanding. Some sponsors believe that sponsorship means signing a memo or making an announcement or video tape. You have to establish what the parameters are and be sure that the sponsor understands them also.

In some situations you might have the luxury of having several people to choose from to select your "champion." In that case, you can look at their current "load," their past track record, and other criteria that you establish, and figure out which sponsor will be best. However, in most cases, you have only one option, the "boss." That option is not only limiting but also underscores the importance of paying close attention to the boss because if he or she doesn't do the sponsoring job, your project will probably be dead.

Since we've raised the issue of "zeal," it might be good for us to talk about that as it applies, not to the sponsor, but to the agent. Often in organizations we see people who believe so strongly in what they're doing that they believe they can get the job done without the help of a sponsor. They think their own enthusiasm can make up for any shortfalls on the part of the sponsor, so they don't see the sponsor as important to the process.

If you're part of an organization that pushes accountability and responsibility downward and allows for mistakes without making them a career ender, you might be in one of the few companies where you or your group's momentum might get you the success you seek. However, we have to tell you that, in our experience, there's always a sponsor "lurking" somewhere, and if you count on "benign neglect" to get this project done, at some point you'll be in for a surprise call, visit, etc., from someone who all of a sudden gets "interested" in what you're doing. Unless you have total control over the money you need, the resources you rely on, and the leverage to get people to do what want, there's a sponsor somewhere who has one or all of those who can spoil your party.

Sponsors of change can also be terminators of change, but they're only one of several key roles in the change process. You'll also have those who are the agents of change. This will no doubt include the originator, but will also include others in the management structure acting as agents for their particular part of the organization.

There will also be nonmanagement people such as project managers, project leaders, etc., who will also have a big part in the daily tasks of CASE implementation. You might have an implementation team, drawn from various areas, that will also fall into this category. Think of the change agent as the "go-between" that bridges the gap between the sponsor and those that must change.

Change agents are chosen for a variety of reasons, and sometimes not the right ones. We see change agents who were chosen because they walked by someone's open door and were recognized. We also hear about calls to Human Resources to see who has some extra time or not enough to do. This is not very solid criteria for choosing those that will be effectively handling the day-to-day tactical implementation of your SE/CASE project. Change agents must be people who are respected for both their professionalism and their technical abilities. In today's environment, the technician must be a facilitator as well as technically correct.

Recently, the president of a sales software company came to us complaining that his people were taking a bad rap from their clients about their work. They're technically very good at what they do, but the problem seemed to be that once the software was developed, which is what they were contracted to do, they left. The problems arose when the client company was then left with the job of getting their people to successfully use the software. When they couldn't, they put the blame back on the software developer for not doing their job. The problem is now resolved because their technical people now have a good base in implementation skills.

Change agents must also have the discipline to stay with the change they have been sanctioned to be a change agent for, and not go off to work on other things. Sometimes we find people who will "volunteer" to be a change agent not because they're particularly fond of a change, but because they have their own agenda and seek legitimization to act in that capacity, but not to especially help the change. Agents also need to be recognized as credible and trustworthy within the organization. You can't afford to have, even with the best of projects, agents whose word or reputation in the organization puts them and you behind the curve.

Your agents must understand the concepts surrounding peoples' frames of reference and how that impacts how people react to change, how people communicate and receive communication in order to ensure that the message sent is the message heard, and how people will be impacted by the change.

The relationship between the agent and the sponsor of the change needs to be clearly defined, understood, and agreed to on the front end of your SE/CASE project. Sponsors of change in some places operate under misunderstandings about how much of their originating power can be delegated to agents. There should only be one or a group of sponsors of change, and they should operate from a position of power that cannot be delegated. If agents believe they have more power than they actually do, and they try to use it, they will certainly not get the results they want, and they will probably cause a great deal of antagonism in the process.

If you're in an organization that doesn't yet operate in the mode of participative management and empowerment, you know how frustrating it can be to be an agent without power, or to watch agents who think they have power, but don't, and watch good projects go down the tubes because the sponsor won't get actively involved and help the agent.

Sponsors of change who will not assume an active role in the change process might need to be educated or replaced, if that's possible. Tom Peters called it "management by walking around," which in our terms means that sponsors must also establish their direct relationship with those being impacted. This serves two purposes. It helps to establish the commitment of the sponsor, and it will get some things done in half the time it would take the agent. If agents come from staff positions, and today a lot of them do, staff positions typically don't carry a lot of power. So what happens when you have a person who generally doesn't have any power, who all of a sudden believes that now they do? They want to use it! Also, how do people being impacted by the change react to people trying to act like what they're not? Negatively!

Change agents have to be planners. They must be able to assist in the diagnosis, planning, and execution of the project implementation. This is not the role for a "hail fellow, well met" kind of person who relies on their personality and energy to get things done. There will be way too many things to manage for that, and it will be very important that they be able to devise and execute a tracking mechanism in the plan that will allow you to follow your progress.

The synergy that's so important to this process is very much the province of the agent. They stand in between the change recipient and the sponsor and will have a lot to do with how well the group works together. There are two kinds of synergy; one is between the key players in the change project, and the other is between groups that have to work together in order for the project to produce the maximum result.

Most companies build reward systems that have payoffs for results by functional area. Even if one department's goals are in conflict with others, as long as that department hits their "numbers," that seems to be all that's important. Some companies even go so far as to build in competition by having competing goals within the company. That's all right as long as the success of one department doesn't help or cause the failure of another.

One of the keys to this success was developed a number of years ago by Dr. Henry Weiman and further developed by a pupil of his, Dr. Charles Palmgren, an Atlanta-based consultant. Weyman saw that there were two key prerequisites to synergy being present in the organization: common goals and interdependence. We'll develop that whole idea of synergy in the organization later in the chapter. However, for our purposes now, it's important to know that the internal reward system of the organization must reflect a commitment to those two things.

The next role in the change process is the change recipient or receiver. This is the person or persons who must actually change how they're doing things or their behavior. The big question for them is the "why" question. "Why must I do this? What's the advantage in the change? What's in it for me?" This last question is crucial because we see a lot of companies announce change but never translate it down through the organization so that people understand how the change affects them and what they're supposed to be doing differently. We see a lot of change that doesn't take place because management is not willing to pay the price to do it, and people are not willing to change until management does. In some quarters it's called a "standoff."

The more you've had the end user involved in this process, the better off you're going to be. We worked in a bank where four people got together in a room and made all the decisions around the tools and methodology. When it came time to roll the change out to 1,500 end users, it was met with massive resistance. The leaders were dumbfounded; they couldn't understand it. Why, after all, the company was doing this for "their" benefit.

The key here is "ownership." You've got to give them a sense of being valued in this process. The bank spent four years trying to install an SE/CASE system and never got the job done. When they called us in to help them find out why, they felt they had two options. One, to continue trying to implement the one they had, or two, to start from scratch. Can you guess what the decision was? You guessed wrong if you said start from scratch, which, by the way, was the right decision. However, they had so much "ego investment" in the project that they couldn't let go, even after we told them we thought they had no choice. At the time we're writing this, they're still trying to make it work, without much success.

Another thing is that if you're going to use an implementation process to install the CASE project, you need to educate the receivers about the process. If you don't, you're doing a number of things that might not make any sense to them because they don't understand your implementation "methodology." Part of getting them to buy in is also in helping them understand how you're going about installing the tools and methodology.

Another very important but much overlooked role in this process is the advocate. What's an advocate? Well, the advocate wants the change to happen; it's just that they lack the position and power to make it happen. The thing that's usually not taken into consideration, though, is that they have "influence power." They're key people in your organization who might not be management; they might not even be a part of the implementation team for your SE/CASE project, yet they could be powerful allies if you only made them a part of the process.

Identify all the advocates who will be in the affected part of the organization. Find an "army" of advocates if you can. Bring them into your planning meeting, give them a role in the decisions you make, and then turn them loose to help you, and help you they will. We've seen some projects that were successful only because of the tremendous influence provided by some very powerful advocates in the organization. Think of the advocates as the influencers in the process, and let them do what they do best.

Advocacy happens at two levels in the organization. The first level is what we call the originator. That's the person or persons who saw the need and got the whole process started. The originator might or might not be the sponsor for the change. Many times, the originator is a person or group in the organization who sees the need for change but are not in a position to make it happen, only to suggest that it should. In some companies nothing much happens unless the originator somehow comes from a leveraged or respected position, or there becomes a "critical mass" of originators.

Sometimes even a critical mass of originators is not enough if the sponsor is too far away from where the need is. So long as the sponsor is not uncomfortable with the way things are, it's not likely that you're going to get the support you need. That's why it's a mistake if you and your advocate look for a sponsor high up in the organization because you think that higher position of power brings something to the process.

We believe that a better idea is to look for sponsorship as close as possible to where the change needs to take place. The rationale behind that is that the farther away the sponsor is from where the "heat" is, the more insulation you provide. If you can find someone who can write the check, commit the resources, and can cause the necessary changes to take place close to the needed change site, that's who you want to get for the sponsor. One of the best ways to keep up sponsor commitment is to keep them close to the "heat," so they're reminded often why they signed on for this project in the first place. This will make the life of the agent and the advocate a lot easier.

The other level of advocacy is when the originator is also the sponsor. This would seem to make it all a lot easier, and sometimes that's true. What you have to be careful of is the sponsor who is originating all over the place because they don't understand the role of the sponsor and in fact think that in most cases it's ceremonial. Its not, and they have to clearly understand what their role is and isn't.

So as you look to your plan, you need to be able to identify the sponsor/s, agents, receivers, and originators. As mentioned earlier, the importance of synergy between those that will have major responsibility for the CASE implementation across functional lines cannot be overstated. Some combinations of people, for whatever reasons, just cannot get things done together. It's certainly better to find that out earlier than later. With common goals and interdependence being the two forerunners of synergy in the organization, let's take a look at what Weiman and Palmgren suggest as the process for building synergy in the organization.

The first step is that you have to get all of the key players to "the table." Although this sounds easy, we've not always found it so in all organizations. Why? Well, a lot of times they don't come because the culture reinforces the fact that if they just do their job, that's all that counts. So they don't feel the need to "schmooze" with anybody else about the project as long as they get their part done.

Another factor in this first step is that if you're in a highly political environment, the reason a lot of those people would come to the table at all is to protect their turf and defend their own position, and that's not going to work! They have to be there because they see the interdependence need, and it will take a combination of the agent/s and the sponsor to get that across.

The second step is that those who come to the table must come with the idea that they're also there to hear and have respect for the differing opinions and views that will be represented about how the project should be approached or implemented. Those differing views can be a learning process if people will only let them.

This is also the point at which everyone is going to start to get some clear ideas about how other parts of the organization, other than their own, are being affected by the project. In these circumstances, it's possible to make adjustments to the implementation process that will be helpful to everyone. With all the give and take that there will hopefully be in this process, the final product should have a lot of ownership from the group.

The third step is the give and take. There will no doubt have to be a lot of compromises before a plan can be put together, but it's important that everyone at the table be able to feel valued in the process and dedicated to putting something together that they can take ownership of. Every person who is part of this process is going to have to be an advocate for the result out in the organization, so the more they feel they have influenced the final product, the better advocate they will be.

The last piece of this third step is to build the plan. After the give and take, after all the compromises, and after giving everyone a chance to feel and see their contribution, you have to take all that's now on the table and build a plan. You need to have clearly decided who has what responsibilities, and the time frames for carrying them out. All of the potential barriers that you have identified are going to have to be prioritized to deal first with those that are going to give you the most impetus for success in the early going.

The plan certainly has to have some flexibility in it, but don't be afraid of the details. It's when the details are left out and someone thinks someone else is "doing it" that things fall between the cracks. There are too many things to be orchestrated in the process to leave them to somebody's memory.

The final step is going out and making it happen. People will often ask us where along this process do we see it fall apart the most. The easy answer is "it depends," but in reality we see people come to the table, "say" they respect and value the opinions of the others involved, help to build a compromise and a plan, and then walk out the door and do as they darn well please. Why? Because there's no incentive to be any other way.

In the synergistic environment, the reward has to be for what "we" accomplish, and there must be a price for not following through by any part of the team. The reason a lot of change doesn't get accomplished in organizations is that there's no price to be paid for ignoring strategic directives. So, no matter what gets announced, people can pick and choose for themselves what they want to do. If your CASE project is one that you can't afford to fail at, then there has to be a mechanism for ensuring that follow through takes place.

Dealing with Resistance

One of the early lessons we learned was that there was no such thing as change without resistance. So one of the things we've to accept on the front end is that there are some people in this SE/CASE project who just simply aren't going to want to do it. The difference between success and failure might well be determined by how you react to this resistance.

Resistance literally means "to exert force in opposition." In opposition to what? Well, in opposition to the way things are being done now, or in opposition to the way people think things should be done. There are two ways people demonstrate a force in opposition to something: one is overtly, the other covertly.

Overt resistance is up where you can see it. It's visible. In companies where you have a lot of participation on the part of all concerned in the process, the likelihood is that you're going to be able to see and hear the resistance. It also means you have "ventilator" shafts in the organization—conduits by which people can express upward their concerns, fears, and frustration without fear of being cut off at the knees or making a career-limiting statement.

Overt resistance is what you want. You should even encourage it. We've found that hidden within resistance many times are nuggets of pure gold that will help your project more often than not, and many times help to eliminate problems down the road. A lot of companies don't have much tolerance for this kind of resistance and spend a lot of time and money trying to get resistance to go away. It won't!

The other kind, covert resistance, is underground. Many times, when people can't see it they think it doesn't exist. Wrong! Its not only there, but it's also being very destructive in the process. One of us got a real lesson in this in another life before we started our consulting practice.

As a young supervisor in a large corporation, Jim, as a part of his training, was put out in the shop in charge of a section on the line. After about three months, it was obvious the line on the error board, which kept track of mistakes made on the product, was headed in the wrong direction—up.

One day, one of the guys who worked for Jim asked him if he was aware of what was going on. Jim replied that he figured the problem was that he just had a bunch of guys who couldn't build the product. "Not true," the worker replied, "You're the problem!"

"What do you mean, I'm the problem" Jim shot back. "Well," said Tony, who, by the way, was one of the oldest and best workers, "You came in here like a hotshot thinking you were going to show us how to build trucks. As hard as we were trying to show you that we wanted to work with you, you made sure we understood that we worked "for" you. You shut us down, and what you haven't realized yet is that we know more about building this product than you'll ever know."

Jim wasn't quite sure how to react, but at least at this point he didn't overreact. What Tony was saying was that Jim had blocked the "ventilator shafts." By doing so, what he had effectively done was to drive underground the resistance to some of the changes that he had tried to make.

After a couple of days, Jim realized that Tony was right, and Jim made a lot of effort to open up the "ventilator" shaft. As fast as the line on the error board had gone up, it came down twice as fast. A young management trainee had learned a valuable lesson about covert resistance. When you drive resistance underground, you had better remember one thing: They have more ways to get you than you have to get them. It was a good lesson to learn early in a career.

So, overt and covert resistance are attempts to exert a force in opposition to what you're doing. However, there's another way to resist, and that's to simply do nothing. You might call it passive resistance. Nobody is actively working against the CASE project, either overtly or covertly; instead, they just do nothing. If there's no consequence for doing nothing, then that simple act has the effect of being resistant.

There's another form of resistance that we see, and that's what we call "malicious compliance." Here, people do what you say all right; in fact, they do "exactly" what you say, dotting all the Is and crossing all the Ts. There are no judgment calls here, or even using common sense. What you ask for is what you get. This specific issue is another important example of why it's so important to get as much "ownership" as you possibly can on the part of the end user.

When during the project can you expect resistance? Probably from the day you start until the day you're done. You'll have it at the beginning because it's new, and you'll have it during the project because people are always learning something new or different about the project, which gives them another reason to resist.

A key distinction between those who are successful at CASE implementation and those who aren't is that the successful understand that resistance is inevitable. That resistance is not a sign that something is wrong, but that something is happening. You need to remember that, so we're going to say it one more time. Resistance is not a sign that something is wrong; it's a sign that something is happening.

Resistance is more of a positive than a negative. In fact, when we hear someone tell us that they're not expecting any resistance, we can conclude one of several things. One, that the people being affected by the change don't understand it well enough to know whether to resist or not. Two, that those in charge of the project have, either purposefully or by neglect, not communicated well with the Receivers. Three, that those in charge of the project have sold the receivers "the bells and whistles of the change, and not the real cost of the change."

Managers will often tell us that if they tell what they know about some of the "cost" or obstacles that lie ahead, they'll never get the buy-in on the front end to get the project off the ground. We don't believe that's true. In fact, our experience has been that you run a greater risk by withholding information up front because, inevitably, it's found out later. When it's discovered later on in the project, a common response by those affected is, "Didn't they know about this, or were they deceiving us by not telling us about it?"

This approach can easily backfire on you because if the receivers conclude either of the two reasons we just mentioned, then your credibility and trust, especially if they think you withheld things from them, becomes a serious issue. So now you not only have a major project on your hands, but you're seriously hampered by people not having faith in the fact that you can pull it off, or that you lied to them. This kind of grief you don't need!

Take on the tough battles up front, both with the sponsor (if you're an advocate) and with the receivers (if you're an agent or sponsor). Resistance dealt with up front and ongoing will be less expensive than if you just "cram" it down the organizational gullet. In organizations that consistently "cram" or drive change through the organization, management ends up paying the price for this project's and other project's resistance for a long, long time. The cost of resistance is a direct hit to the bottom line, so the better you are at surfacing it and managing it, the better off you're going to be financially. That's language any sponsor can relate to.

The Impact of Culture

Webster's Ninth New Collegiate Dictionary says that an organization is "an administrative and functional structure." It also says that culture is "the integrated pattern of human knowledge, belief, and behavior that depends upon man's capacity for learning and transmitting knowledge to succeeding generations." So, an organization's culture is its integrated pattern of human knowledge, belief, and behavior, dependent on human capacity to learn and pass on this administrative and functional structure. Sounds pretty complicated, doesn't it? Well, it is.

However, for our purposes, let's think of culture as "the way we do things around here." A little easier to say, but no less difficult to change. Why is it so difficult to change? Part of the answer lies in how long it has been around. The longer the culture has been in existence and remained relatively the same, the longer it's going to take to change it. This applies to departments, divisions, and companies.

The reason that we must consider the organization's culture as we look at implementing SE/CASE, is because "Culture eats change for breakfast." We've seen a number of organizations try to implement CASE without the corresponding shift in culture to support it, and this approach failed. That's because, all things being relatively equal, when you pit change versus culture, culture wins!

If you were in a meeting and during the discussion a person new to the group and the company made a statement about how things were done in the place they had just come from, most likely an "old-timer" in the group would be quick to point out that they were no longer in their old company, and this is the way "we do things around here."

The culture is a part of the heritage, and people hang onto it with tenacity. A comment we hear very often in our discussions with people from a mature work force, where 20 years seniority is not unusual, is, "You're trying to change what got us where we're today. If it ain't broke, don't fix it." A recent article in a national business periodical suggests that in today's fast-paced business world, if it ain't broke or obsolete, you're probably not looking hard enough.

When posing the question of what kind of a culture do you need to support an SE/CASE environment, the common response is, "Well, let's implement CASE, and the culture we get is the culture we need." As much as that answer might appeal to your common sense, we've found that it's the wrong answer. The correct answer is that you must first determine the culture you need in order to support the project long-term, and then compare it to the culture you have and see what the difference is. Once you know that, you can plan for building the culture you need.

When you take on a project that's going to also significantly impact the culture, you in essence end up with two projects: one—to implement the change; two—to change the culture. Changing a culture can be a very long, time-consuming, and expensive process. In most instances of large-scale change that we've seen, this means years!

It's extremely important that whoever is writing the checks for this project clearly understands this. We've seen projects disappear when the check writer starts having to put out a lot more money than he or she had anticipated. I wish we could give you some good guidelines or rules of thumb about how long it will take to change your culture. We can't! Suffice it to say that it will probably be longer than you have or want. So what can you do?

Part of the answer lies in understanding exactly what it is we're talking about when we talk about changing the culture. When asked to describe the culture of their organization, most people can make some rough stabs at characterizing what it is. One of the reasons that we see cultural change as such a tough issue is because to a lot of people, senior management included, "the culture" is such an amorphous thing that it's tough to put your arms around it and deal with it.

When you start to break down what we mean by "the" culture, all of a sudden it starts to become more manageable. What we're talking about is the cultures within the culture or subcultures. What distinguishes the subculture from the culture is what makes it a subculture. It still has the characteristic patterns we talked about earlier, but they're sufficiently different from the embracing culture that you can distinguish them; yet, hopefully, the subculture is in alignment with and supportive of the overall culture.

Once you've decided on the culture you need, and you try to match those characteristics to "the" culture, it will prove to be an overwhelming task. If you do the same thing with the subcultures, you can begin to get a handle on just how much work you have to do. Chances are, if you approach it this way, you'll now have a culture change project that feels feasible, not overwhelming.

When you check the subcultures against your desired culture, what you'll find is that some subcultures will need more or less work. What this allows you to do is to better target your resources in the places where the most cultural shift needs to take place and not end up spending endless amounts of money trying to shift "the" culture. This is going to be a big enough task without spending money where you don't have to.

The key here is knowing what you have to have. This book and this chapter are talking about results oriented change (ROC). It's easy enough to talk about the process of change, but where the rubber meets the road is where you tie the process to a result and build a mechanism to follow your progress. As much of your result as possible should be measurable or observable (M&O). It will save you a lot of grief when you're trying to explain how the project is going and what you're getting for the money.

Vision

A company's vision is like a road map. It should give everyone in the organization a picture of where the organization is headed so that all parts of the organization can make decisions in alignment with and supportive of that vision. The reason we raise the subject here is that we're often surprised by how many places either don't have a vision statement or, if one exists, no one can tell you what it is.

In some places the vision statement is framed and put up on the walls. In other organizations, the vision statement is a catchy little reminder phrase on the company letterhead or memorandums. In still others, you can walk down the corridors and have it explained to you by almost anyone you meet. That's when it becomes real and "living," when people are relating to it everyday in making decisions.

If you haven't already done so, you need to place your SE/CASE project in line with its relative importance to your organization being able to accomplish its vision. The more viable the vision statement is, and the more you can tie your CASE project to the success of that vision, the more ownership you'll have throughout the organization for what you're doing.

Contracting

For the last several years, we've had the fortunate experience of being able to watch the advance of technology and its effects on organizations. Through associates and colleagues, as well as through our own experience, we've seen the ideas and concepts that we've talked about thus far work with varying degrees of success. Though it's obvious that many find success by applying these ideas, there are equally as many, if not more, who don't.

This has been a great source of frustration because the best and the brightest ideas have demonstrated that they will work if companies will only use them. As we've delved more carefully into the reason or reasons that success doesn't happen, two issues have come to the forefront. The first is the understood, written, or implied "contract" between the parties involved in the project, and the second is the commitment on the part of all those involved to make it happen.

We'll talk about commitment just a bit later, but first lets talk about the concept of "contracting."Change does happen top down, at least as far as the sponsorship is concerned. We are not counted among those who believe that there's no such thing as bottom-up change, because there is. However, from the standpoint of giving the change credence and committing the resources, it's usually a top-down process.

It's therefore important that whoever is the sponsor has a clear idea and statement about what the project is, and a good way of communicating it down through the organization. One of the best ways we've found is what we call "contracting." It means that, at the sponsor level, there's clarity and agreement among the sponsor and his or her direct subordinates as to what they're about to undertake.

If the sponsor only asks if everybody understands and doesn't take it any further than that, he or she is leaving the door open for a number of problems. Does your organization have what we call "yes" people? When a question is asked by the boss, no matter what it is, their heads bob up and down like that little dog you see in the back window of some vehicles. We've seen that a lot.

The problem seems to be that if the culture doesn't allow for much challenge to those in charge, what you get is a lot of head nodding. Assuming that you don't have to deal with whether or not the decision about what you're doing was arrived at through a participative process, the sponsor needs to take the process a couple of steps further.

The sponsor needs to contract with his or her direct subordinates for two other things. One, that when they walk out of the sponsor's office, they're not going to start shaking their heads side to side, meaning "no" instead of "yes" like they said in the office. There should be a price to be paid if they do that.

That might sound harsh, but it's what you have to do if you're on a project where you can't afford to fail. If you can't afford to fail, then everybody has to understand the price for not carrying out their end of the bargain.

Next, with a clear contract between the sponsor and his or her direct subordinates, you all know what you want to do, you all support it, and that support goes beyond the sponsor's office; what has to happen next is that the direct subordinates go have the same conversation with those that report to them, and they go do the same thing with those that report to them, etc.

This has to be done all through the organization, down to and including the first-line management. By building this network of contracts down through the organization, when something happens, you know where to look. If the sponsor ever asks either of the two following questions and gets a yes to either one, they should start looking across the contract network.

The two questions are: "Is there something happening that should not be happening?" or "Is there something not happening that should be?" A yes to either one of those questions should send the sponsor looking down through the network for a break in contract.

There are several ways those breaks in the contracting take place. Sometimes, someone has just decided they don't like what's going on anymore and they simply break the contract. However, there are a couple of other ways that are generally not thought of. One is that the contract is verbal, although we've seen a few clients put it in writing. Verbal contracts have a habit of losing strength over time if they're not carefully watched, so they need to be monitored. Second, because we play musical chairs in our organizations, we sometimes make the mistake of assuming that a new person has agreed to the contract of the person who has just left a position. Too many times that doesn't translate, so the original "contractor" must come to the new "contractee" and make a new contract.

If you do this, it will clean up and clear up the lines of the contract, and it will help greatly in building ownership for the project. This is not a process for getting a "gentlemen's agreement" for something you would "like" to do. This is for the situation where you need to be able to count on everyone involved for a project at which you feel that you can't afford to fail.

William Bridges, who wrote *Transitions*, suggests that change is external and transition is internal, which means that the psychological move from one thing to another is quite different from just doing something differently.

Your SE/CASE project is going to cause both a change and a transition. It's also going to result in a shift in your culture. When you look at all that you're going to have to do, you can see why it's so important that you have the necessary commitment, especially at the top, if you're going to make an SE/CASE project happen.

Often, we see people presume that just because someone works in the department or for the company, the commitment is there to get the job done. Commitment must be built; it can't be presumed. Commitment is an internal event. It happens in the head, but only if the head has enough information to make that decision. What's often seen as resistance is many times not resistance, but a lack of information, which is ignorance, not resistance. Commitment can only take place after a person sufficiently understands enough information about the project. The reason we say "can" take place is because "real" commitment comes from being able to take ownership of the project.

The process of change is ongoing, and you have to be careful not to try to sell your CASE project as "the" answer. At best it's "an" answer, and probably a temporary one at that. There will surely be something else not too many months or years in the future that will take us another step on the technological path. We believe it's those organizations that teach their people the principle of "*kaizen*," continuous improvement, that are going to be the industry leaders of the future.

Chapter

6

Critical Success Factors

Throughout this book we've offered tidbits of advice on how to deal with the cultural changes that lie ahead with the implementation of SE/CASE. In this chapter we put it all together by first focusing on specific critical success factors (CSFs) of an SE/CASE implementation and the potential roadblocks that can and will get in the way of achieving these factors. Then, we offer tactics to help overcome each of these roadblocks in order to fulfill the CSFs. In the next chapter, we'll present a work plan template that you can use to structure these recommendations into the proper sequence of events. This work plan template will contain the phases, activities, and tasks needed for a complete SE/CASE selection and implementation.

We separated the tactics from the work plan so you could focus on your selection and implementation strategies before creating the plan to make them happen. If these tactics were presented simultaneously with the work plan, then the tendency would be to build the plan as you go. The problem is that the tactics presented span multiple tasks, activities, and even phases of the work plan template. Thus, you'll need to fully comprehend your overall strategy before customizing the work plan.

As you review the roadblocks and tactics presented in this chapter, take extensive notes. Ideas will come to you as a natural course of events. Write these ideas down or underline any ideas or suggestions that apply to you. Remember, not everything in this book will apply to your unique situation. You'll have other, additional roadblocks and tactics not mentioned in this book. We have not provided an exhaustive list from which to pick and choose. We have provided a list of the most common roadblocks and tactics to help stimulate your thinking and start the ball rolling. Like any methodology or approach, the work plan presented is no substitute for thinking. It's a starting point, not the end point. This chapter will serve as a guide to help you customize the work plan template in the next chapter.

Another reason we separated the CSFs, roadblocks, and tactics from the work plan template is so that this chapter could be given to management to read. Since it doesn't contain the procedural, how-to information, it flows a bit quicker and at a higher level. This structure will allow more people to get involved with the development of the strategies used within the work plan. It's really not necessary to drag all of these individuals through the detailed planning process.

As we mentioned, this chapter contains the CFSs, roadblocks, and tactics for implementing SE/CASE. Critical success factors are those issues or concerns that must be addressed in order for an SE/CASE initiative to be successful. They include items within and outside the control of the IS department. Items within the control of IS include CSFs such as a stable and motivated staff and a genuine need for change. These types of items need to be proactively planned for and managed. CSFs outside the direct control of IS include stable CASE technology and strong user support. These items need to be analyzed and taken into account during the planning for the initiative.

The CSFs presented here don't represent a complete set of factors for your environment. Every organization is different. These CSFs are presented here as a starting point for you to identify your own set of factors. Add your unique set to this set and change it. The focus is on identifying the CSFs, not on validating our set of CSFs.

Roadblocks are those challenges that you'll face in trying to achieve your CSFs. Roadblocks will definitely vary between organizations. Everybody will have a different set of roadblocks. Again, we'll provide a set of roadblocks, but don't rely on this set entirely.

The tactics represent advice on how to overcome specific roadblocks. Many of the tactics will address multiple roadblocks. Tactics are the building blocks for a complete SE/CASE strategy.

The best way to understand the interactions of CSFs, roadblocks, and tactics is through an analogy. For this discussion we'll use a relatively simple example of introducing a new pet to a family.

Over the past few years, we've witnessed and read about the struggle that many organizations encounter while implementing SE/CASE. Surprisingly, for organizations both big and small, the challenges were very similar. The roadblocks and tactics might vary, but the challenges remain. We've captured the essence of these challenges within the following set of critical success factors for the implementation of SE/CASE:

Clear and genuine need for SE/CASE. Identification of the real problems that need to be solved and future opportunities that exist. These needs provide the business rationale for SE/CASE.

Vision and plan for SE/CASE. The existence of an integrated software engineering and CASE vision (i.e., where you're headed) and the associated long-term (three- to five-year) plan for achieving this vision.

Fit with the existing culture. An intent to minimize the impact of the new technology on the current IS and business cultures. A commitment to provide the best fit possible.

Shared understanding of and appreciation for SE. A common definition and understanding of what SE/CASE is all about and an appreciation for the concepts, principles, and philosophies of this new approach. The entire IS department needs to be on the same playbook with regard to SE/CASE.

Effective management sponsorship. IS and top management's unified understanding of, commitment to, and active leadership for SE/CASE.

Patience. A longer-term focus. The persistence to stay the course, to see the SE/CASE vision through without significant shifts in direction.

IS staff buy-in and acceptance. The staff's willingness to accept the new SE/CASE technology and to give it a try.

Stable and motivated staff. An IS staff that stays intact and is motivated to get the job done.

Skills to get the job done. The ability to effectively function within the new SE/CASE environment.

Support infrastructure. Support for training, mentoring/coaching, policies/procedures, reward mechanisms, and other organizational entities that support the ongoing move towards SE/CASE.

Perception of IS as a team player. The user community needs to view IS as a part of the company team—as an integral part of the organization. IS can no longer be viewed as a prima donna or a special-case department.

Strong user community support. Ultimately, the user community funds the IS department. Without continued support for SE/CASE from the user community, the effort can't go very far.

As you can see, there's a lot to implementing SE/CASE. Is it any wonder that companies today are having problems trying to "hodgepodge" in CASE technologies? Without analyzing all of these factors, a company will tend to focus on just one or two aspects of implementation. It's like going out and purchasing a house based on only a few buying criteria (e.g., location and square feet). You tend to suboptimize those two or three criteria. Perhaps you find a house that meets these criteria the best, you buy it, and then find out the neighborhood is full of snobs, the kids have no one to play with, and the taxes are astronomical. It's no wonder that purchasing a home is a very stressful period.

The normal reaction for most companies starting out with SE/CASE implementation is similar. Many companies tend to focus on two CSFs—effective management sponsorship (or commitment) and staff buy-in and commitment. The thought is that if everyone is committed to SE/CASE, then everything will just fall into place. Many people think that SE/CASE implementation is like purchasing real estate—location, location, and location. Or, in our case, commitment, commitment, and commitment. We wish it were that simple! Unlike location, the half-life of commitment is very short. We've seen commitment dissipate in just one meeting. If commitment is not backed up with real needs that are clearly understood and tangible, then most SE/CASE initiatives are dead in the water.

The following sections of this book define the CSFs previously listed. Within each section, we'll describe the CSF and its importance, identify the potential roadblocks to achieving the CSF, and recommend tactics to proactively manage the potential threats. As you read through these sections, underline or mark those roadblocks and tactics that apply to your organization. Don't allow this section to become just interesting reading. We've written this book to make a difference in organizations like yours. It's up to you to make that difference. As we unfold the suggestions, identify them and later expand them for your specific situation.

Don't allow the volume of suggestions in this book to overwhelm you. There's a lot of information presented here. Learn from our trials and tribulations and be proactive with SE/CASE. Don't get caught up in the perception that it's all too confusing and you can deal with the problems as they arise. The reality is that your successor might have to deal with the problems; you might not be around long enough! SE/CASE implementation is very complicated and much needs to be said about its implementation. However, simply ignoring the complexity of IS culture will only make matters worse. It truly is a "pay me now or pay me later" scenario.

Clear and Genuine Need for SE/CASE

In most organizations, nothing major ever happens without a reason for doing it. There's an inertia that exists within companies that forces everything to stay the same—an inertia that resists significant change, especially a change that involves spending money.

Talk, however, is cheap. It's easy to talk about doing things. Take your own life for instance. How often do we all talk about buying a new sports car or a boat? How often do folks in the north talk about pulling up stakes and moving to where it's warm year round? How often do we talk about changing jobs or even careers? It's easy to talk. It's even fun to do a little dreaming, a little window shopping, or to review a brochure or two. We often have the sincere intention to acquire a major item or to move, but it's not until a clear and genuine need exists that we commit to the change and move forward with sincerity and drive.

The same scenario is true of SE/CASE implementation. Almost everyone is talking about SE/CASE. Many organizations have acquired the brochures. Many have been to the SE/CASE conferences. Some have even "test driven" the tools/techniques a few times. However, we've found that if the needs of these organizations are not real and visual, progress beyond this point is often difficult, if not downright dangerous!

It's difficult because SE/CASE implementation requires a sustained drive to get you though the rough times. If you get anything out of this book, you should at least get the feeling that SE/CASE implementation is not easy. It's a hard and long process. There will be many times when you or others within the company feel like it's just not worth it. At these times, a visual, real need will help sustain the momentum. This is similar to a diet and exercise regimen. If the need is simply to look better, chances are the sustaining drive will be much less intense than if you've just had a heart attack and need to reduce weight to survive! Business survival is just as sustaining.

SE/CASE implementation is dangerous without a real and visual need because you might get lucky at first and make some real headway. You might actually get the organization to expend significant resources and start to change the direction of the large freighter sometimes referred to as the USS IS Department. Then, at a moment's notice, something goes wrong or a new player is introduced into the IS leadership. This "iceberg" touches off a round of doubt, and politics begin to kick in. Without a clear and genuine need that's documented and agreed upon, the other "officers" on board might take the easy and safe way out. They might jump ship on you and leave you alone to go down with the ship!

To help counteract this situation, the need for SE/CASE has to be genuine and real. When someone asks "Why are we doing this?," it's not enough to say, "Our competition is doing it," or, "Everyone is doing it." In addition, we cannot rely on the other organization's detailed rationale for implementing SE/CASE. Their rationale might be clear, but it's not your organization's rationale. It's not genuine. It doesn't solve your problems.

You'll need to personalize your reasons for SE/CASE. Earlier in this book we discussed specific objectives for SE/CASE. From this list you should be able to start a meaningful discussion with your department's leadership concerning your reasons for SE/CASE. If you can't agree on these reasons, don't go any farther. This situation is like trying to select package software for a user without knowing why you need the package. This represents a disaster waiting to happen.

The need for SE/CASE should also be clear and visual. All too often, we dive into a SE/CASE initiative with a vague vision espoused by the IS director in a 15-minute meeting. From this foggy direction we spend hundreds of hours and hundreds of thousands of dollars. The need for SE/CASE might be real and genuine, but the foundation for SE/CASE implementation is shaky. Without a clear need, the rationale is often extracted, expanded, forgotten, misinterpreted, folded, spindled, and mutilated. Clarity of the need will help to focus the effort and achieve the desired results. It needs to be very clear to all that you have specific problems and that SE/CASE will solve those problems.

An unclear vision has a way of attracting political maneuvering. Ambiguity invites some folks to use the SE/CASE initiative for personal gain. A few might see SE/CASE as a way to further build their empires. Others might use it as a lever to "one up" their internal rivals. It's normal and healthy for individuals to base career moves around SE/CASE, but whenever the SE/CASE initiative is put into jeopardy because of politics, it's a major roadblock.

However, the biggest roadblock to achieving a clear and genuine need is when an organization gets enamored with the technology. SE/CASE can be fun and interesting. There's some very interesting software engineering CASE technology available today—some with great graphics, some with artificial intelligence, and some with object-oriented technology. For the technologist, it can be very seductive. At times we've seen organizations select the technology and then look for the problems for the technology to solve. In one of these IS organizations, a user department started to refer to IS as the "Toys-R-Us" department. We all have a tendency to go for the glitz and to forget the problems at hand.

Whenever we do push beyond the glitz of the technology and look at the problems, we often don't look far enough past the symptoms of these problems. We want to eliminate these symptoms as quickly as possible. This short-term focus has a way of obscuring the real needs of the SE/CASE initiative.

These roadblocks can be overcome. The key is to focus on the pain caused by the problems. You'll need to focus on both the current and anticipated future pain. Examples of IS pain include:

- User community outsourcing.
- Diminishing credibility with upper management.
- Large and growing maintenance burden.
- Lack of confidence in development capabilities.
- No infrastructure to take advantage of new technologies.
- Unable to consistently deliver quality systems.

- Loss of project control.
- Inability to handle large, complex systems.
- Attrition of key staff members.
- Inability to attract top recruits.

Pain has a way of moving mountains, current pain more so than future pain. We're not recommending that you start fires, but that you find and highlight the fires. Find out where the IS department is truly hurting. What are the crucial sore spots and why? If the pain is real, once the real pain is exposed and highlighted, movement towards fixing these problems will be swift and sustained.

Be careful, however, to not assume that SE/CASE will solve all of these problems. Be open to other avenues, other solutions. Forcing SE/CASE to solve problems it was not designed to tackle can also be a dangerous situation. Once the pain is identified, document it. Documenting the pain forces you to validate and solidify it. If the pain is not real or significant, it will become apparent in the documentation process. Remember the last requirements statement that you wrote for a user. Once the requirements started to get documented, the real requirements began to emerge in a new light. Also, documenting the pain will help later on whenever many have forgotten why you were implementing SE/CASE in the first place. It's very helpful to pull out this list and refresh the organization's collective memory.

Once the pain is identified and documented, create a set of objectives and goals that focus squarely on the pain. There needs to be a clean linkage to these pain items. One of the worst scenerios would be to raise the level of pain in an organization, document it, and then proceed without addressing the pain. These goals also need to be measurable. A measurable goal will allow the organization to see the progress towards addressing the identified pain.

Even though it's not necessary to reach consensus with the department's leadership on the specific pain items, it's very necessary to reach consensus on the SE/CASE objectives and goals. These objectives and goals will serve as the SE/CASE initiative's focus and "touchstone." At every decision and major milestone, these objectives and goals should be reviewed to make sure the initiative is proceeding in the proper direction. This will help to make sure that the glitz of the technology doesn't cloud the major issues.

Vision and Plan for SE/CASE

A significant portion of IS organizations do a good job identifying their most pressing needs. They document these needs clearly and in business terms. However, at times some of these organizations do too good of a job. Once their needs are identified and the associated pain is highlighted and elevated, then everyone wants the problems fixed and they want these problems fixed right away. As a result, the majority of these organizations succumb to the seemingly inevitable decision to acquire a CASE tool from the "get go." They select the tool, pilot it, implement it, and then sit back and assess what they have!

This urgency to act can prevent an organization from optimizing their total SE/CASE environment. It leaves an organization with a hodgepodge of tools and techniques—none of which interface well with one another. To counteract this quick-hit approach, you'll need to present your organization with a vision of the future SE/CASE environment and a long-range, workable plan to get you there.

The vision needs to be broad-based and imaginative. It needs to be visual and exciting. It needs to have a long-term focus. It should address the majority of the problems in a well-integrated manner. The AD/Cycle vision from IBM is an example of this type of vision. Figure 6.1 shows IBM's vision for SE/CASE.

The AD/Cycle diagram is a good starting point from which to craft your own personalized SE/CASE vision. It contains many of the essential dimensions of SE/CASE from strategic planning on through to maintenance. This diagram also addresses such areas as configuration management, project management, reusability, and methodology. As an alternative, you might want to consider using our SE/CASE Scope diagram, Figure 3.5. There are many other alternative views. You can get these visions from CASE vendors (e.g., DEC, Texas Instruments), methodology vendors (e.g., AGS, E&Y), and even industry groups (e.g., IEEE.)

Customizing an existing vision diagram allows you to jump-start your design effort. You could leave the vision diagram as is and implement it "vanilla," but customization helps to reassure everyone that your specific needs have been attended to. It helps you to establish buy-in from the staff. Even if the basic structure of the vision stays the same, the staff will feel more comfortable with the resultant environment. People don't like the "one-size-fits-all" approach, even if it's true!

Customizing an existing vision (like AD/Cycle) works to your advantage. Most of these models are solid and complete. They're visual and they can be shown on one page, thereby reducing confusion. In addition, if the "vanilla" vision gets bad press, then the customization can be used to distance yourself from this press. If they get good press, then you can stress that your environment was based on the standard vision.

Once you've established where you'd like to be with a vision, it's then time to put a plan together to get there. This is one of the biggest faults of SE/CASE implementation efforts. Many IS organizations have great ideas and foresight, but no plan beyond the immediate (and seemingly inevitable) CASE tool selection and implementation project. Without the next steps clearly laid out, many organizations languish in a seemingly endless series

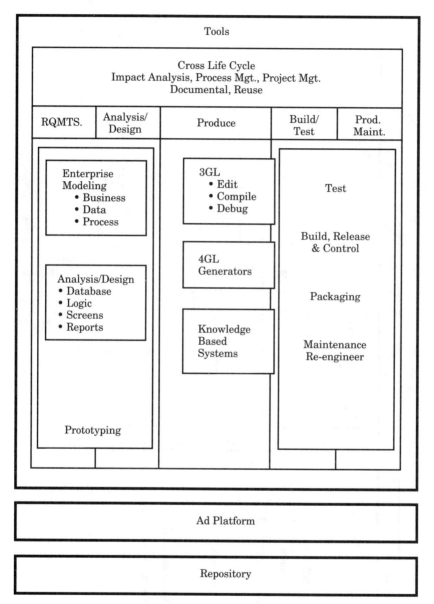

Figure 6.1 IBM's AD/CYCLE diagram.

of pilot projects trying to fine-tune the CASE tool selected. If you're not careful, you can get bogged down with one specific technology. With a clear plan, it puts pressure on the organization to continue to move forward. An example of a long-term implementation plan is shown in Figure 6.2.

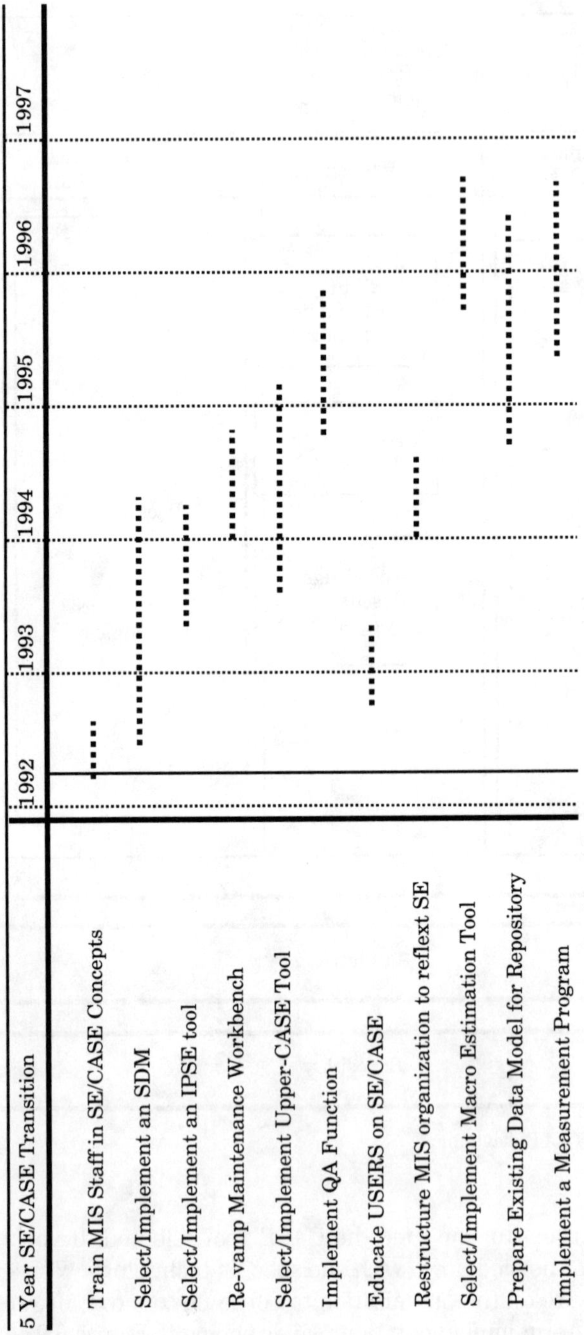

Figure 6.2 Sample five-year SE/CASE transition work plan.

This type of implementation plan needs to cover a period of from two to five years. Any less than two years and you won't be able to properly implement the core components of SE/CASE. Any more than five years, and you're just fooling yourself. There are so many potential twists and changes in the SE/CASE field that anything beyond five years is just a guess.

A long-term implementation plan lets people in the organization know the sequencing and timing of future technology implementations. This knowledge will put some people at ease. Without a plan, these people are constantly pushing for their pet technology to be next. For example, the DBA will be very interested with normalization support and schema generation technology. With a plan in place, they can be assured that their technology will be addressed in the relative time frame provided.

An implementation plan is also useful for managing the expectations of management and the staff. If your vision is complete, visual, exciting, and very compelling, then you'll have a relatively easy time selling it to the organization. This vision will help you to get momentum moving in the right direction and with a full head of steam. However, without a realistic, well-thought-out plan to make it happen, everyone will expect the full vision to be implemented overnight. To many, it's just buy a few tools and plug them in. What's the big deal?

This situation is very similar to implementing an application package into a user environment. You might have properly identified the problems, highlighted the pain, created a vision for the future, and sold the overall concept to management and the users. Now they're primed for action. However, without a clear action path, the users will forge ahead in the most direct manner. They'll want to bring in a few vendors for demos, acquire a package, and implement the package. Sounds straightforward. Who could argue with this strategy?

However, we all know that package selection is also a "pay me now or pay me later" scenario. In other words, you need to take the time to match the processes and culture embedded in the package to the processes and culture of the user department. If you don't assess these dimensions up front, you'll pay dearly during implementation.

If you have a clear, well-thought-out plan of attack ready whenever the momentum starts to gain speed towards implementation, then this energy will be properly channeled. This strategy works equally as well with package selection as with SE/CASE implementation. After all, SE/CASE can be thought of as an application package for the IS community.

There are many roadblocks that prevent an organization from establishing a well-thought-out SE/CASE vision and plan. The most common one is the short-term, tactical focus as addressed previously. This roadblock forces quick action and eventual suboptimization.

Another key roadblock is the tendency of IS organizations to focus too much on the computer aided side of CASE. It's easy to get enamored with the technology and to choose the "hot" CASE vendor at the time of selection. We all like bells and whistles. Make no mistake about it, these bells and whistles will help sell the technology to the IS staff. They like bells and whistles as well as anyone, maybe more. However, keep in mind that the technology has a job to do. Once the glamour of the tool runs its course, then the real functions and value emerge. If the purchased technology does little for the organization, then it will ultimately be abandoned. We all have a job to do. Work has to get done in the most effective and efficient way. Thus, the focus should be first on the software engineering side of CASE. In short, make sure it all fits together before the technology is selected.

IBM, with their AD/Cycle vision and Repository Manager product, made popular a very palatable selection and implementation strategy. Simply pick and choose any CASE tools with the idea that the Repository Manager will integrate them together. This strategy apparently reduces the risk of making a wrong decision, thereby speeding up the selection process. IBM's strategy perpetuates the notion of: "If you can't lose, why take your time up front? Just get moving!"

The term used by many for this strategy is component-CASE (C-CASE). To a number of organizations, this allows them to quickly select the technology without having to worry about making a bad decision. If all the tools tie together, then they're not stuck with one vendor or approach.

What this strategy doesn't yet take into consideration is the proliferation of different SE approaches and techniques and their impact on the culture of the organization. Every tool vendor puts a different twist on the use of the techniques and approaches. The tools might talk to one another, but communication is very suspect. It's like parents talking to their teenagers. There's talking going on, even yelling, but nothing of substance ever seems to get across the "great barrier."

As with most of life's truisms, if it's too easy, there must be something wrong. SE/CASE is no exception. Maybe in a few years C-CASE will be ready, but then there's always something else to worry about!

Too narrow a view of SE/CASE can also be a major roadblock to success. SE/CASE is much more than just the analyst tool that draws diagrams. I see SE/CASE encompassing strategic planning, development, maintenance, and project management. A focus on only one area will tend to suboptimize the operations of the department around the area picked.

Failure to document the SE vision happens all too often. Management is very adept at verbalizing their vision! After all, if the vision gets across to the staff, then why take the time and energy to document the words? Well, as we all know, documenting something forces you to work through the bugs and glitches. In addition, it's very easy to conveniently change the vision to suit the audience. This results in upper management hearing one scenario, the user community another, and the staff yet another. Finally, without a tangible remembrance of the vision, most people will read things into the vision that were never meant to be there.

The majority of these roadblocks can be overcome by creating an integrated vision of where you want to be. Keep this vision visual and diagrammatic. Keep it simple and straightforward. Refer to it as often and in as many different contexts and situations as possible. Keep it in front of people. Use the vision in every presentation or meeting associated with SE/CASE. Make it a part of the organization's culture. Make it an artifact of the organization.

One way in which we helped to reinforce the vision for a client organization was to etch the basic design of their customized vision into a ¾-inch thick block of glass. The glass block was held in a wooden holder and could be used as a paperweight or ornament for their desks. We produced 20 of these items and distributed them to the managers and key staff members who helped to define the vision. This was a visual sign that something important had taken place and that the vision was worth remembering. It was a constant reminder to the management team and to their staff of what the organization was striving towards. As a result, the vision didn't get put into a folder and forgotten. It was remembered and built upon daily.

Another important tactic is to build your vision from existing strengths. Every organization does something right. To throw the baby out with the bath water can kill any momentum you might have gained through all of your internal marketing efforts. If you replace something that's working reasonably well with something that might be suspect, you'll lose people very quickly.

For instance, let's say you're involved with bringing in a new project management tool to support the information engineering approach that you selected. This project management tool will be used to manage the work breakdown structure embedded within the information engineering approach. You might have overlooked or ignored the fact that within the existing environment the organization was quite good at managing change control (i.e., monitoring user change requests) on projects. Then, within the implementation of the new tool, you also change the change control process to take advantage of features within the new tool. If it's not obvious that the new change control process, supported with the tool, doesn't work better than the old process, then you're setting yourself up for a heavy round of resistance. Since the staff now has a basis of comparison from the old to the new, they'll extrapolate the unknown. Also, since their only comparison was negative, look out!

Finding the "gems" within your organization sometimes takes an objective eye. It's human nature to either downgrade or overinflate your own abilities and strengths. Some of us are optimists, some pessimists. Its hard and sometimes impossible to sit back and be truly objective. Politics plays a part. Being too close plays a part.

For these reasons, it might be necessary to bring in an outside consultant to assess your current environment. This person can identify your organization's strengths and highlight your weaknesses. Outsiders have little to fear and can sometimes be brutally honest. However, you need this knowledge in order to craft your SE/CASE vision. In addition, outsiders can also identify potential threats (e.g., user community outsourcing) and opportunities (e.g., existence of strong facilitation skills). The complete package is well worth the cost and time of putting it together.

Build your vision from high ground. Take a strategic perspective and integrate into it the corporation's goals and objectives. Integrate your vision into the other three planning architectures discussed in the Introduction. These other architectures are: data, process, and technology. The SE/CASE vision, of course, represents the SE/CASE infrastructure architecture discussed in the Introduction.

If your company has initiated a corporatewide quality focus or continuous improvement process, then make sure your vision clearly ties into it. These days, funding doesn't come easy. Tying the SE/CASE initiative to a TQM initiative can help tremendously with freeing up funds. In addition, SE/CASE fits nicely into the concepts of TQM. Both are focused on long-term improvements and on doing things right the first time. TQM can help to prepare the user community for the SE/CASE changes to come.

Fit with the Existing Culture

SE/CASE can't be easily forced into an organization. As this book points out in many ways, SE/CASE can and will affect the culture of an IS organization. The closer the fit between the technology and the culture, the better. If there's a conflict between the culture and the technology, the culture will almost always win.

The IS culture can be changed, but not without much consternation, resistance, and trouble. All of this results in a long period of inefficiency and ineffectiveness. Ironically, these are the exact problems that SE/CASE is supposed to address!

However, the cultural fit of SE/CASE is usually more a matter of perception than reality. Sure, SE/CASE does affect the processes and day-to-day activities of the IS staff. There are real and tangible changes that need to be made. However, if SE/CASE is perceived by the IS staff as an extension of what they currently do today as opposed to a completely new way of thinking and working, then the perceived change is much less. This is another important reason to build from the strengths of the department as discussed in the last section of this chapter. "Extending the current" is a very successful strategy. It might take a little longer to implement, but the results tend to be more permanent.

With some IS departments, the strategy to extend the current is too great a hurdle. They simply need to "leapfrog" into the twenty-first century with the new techniques, tools, and culture. For these organizations, the fit to the new SE/CASE culture is very crucial. With this situation, you'll need to work very hard at being practical and realistic. You'll need to acquire technology that's adaptable and flexible. You'll need to customize it. However, most importantly, you'll need to focus on two or three of the key cultural dimensions (usually quality, teamwork, and discipline). Keep it simple. Do what makes sense, not just what all of the theorists say to do. Don't overwhelm the organization. Keep an eye open to the human aspects.

In either case, make the technology look like it was fine-tuned to your environment, even if you don't need to change it much. Personalize it and name it. Give it a unique identity. Without these activities, the technology stands a greater risk of "not being invented here." The result should not appear forced or faked, but that the technology was designed for the users' unique needs.

Shooting from the hip can be a major roadblock to properly matching SE/CASE to the existing IS culture. It's easy to feel comfortable that we have a handle on the department's beliefs, behaviors, and assumptions. After all, many of us have been around the IS department and have worked side-by-side with the staff for many years.

Assuming that we're right (but being wrong) can result in the selection of the wrong set of SE approach(es), techniques, and tools. For example, if you incorrectly determine that your organization's cultural strengths include teamwork, creativity, and personal motivation, you might wrongly recommend a rapid application development (RAD) with prototyping tools. Perhaps 25 percent of the department might perform very well in the new environment, but the remaining 75 percent of the department staff are lost. They don't have a clue about how to operate in this new freedom. The results could be confusion, serious mistakes, and lots of resistance.

Another cultural-fit roadblock is not adjusting the SE/CASE environment to reflect the cultural differences as they become apparent during the implementation. A misfit in culture is hard to see up front. It's truly hard to identify beforehand. However, when you see a misfit during SE/CASE implementation, you'll know it. It's at these times that you need to truthfully ask yourself if the technology, the technique, the procedure (or whatever) is that important. Is it a crucial piece to making it all hang together? If it's that important, than stick to your guns and fight to change the culture. If it's not that important, than let it slide. It's much more important to fit the technology into the existing culture than it is to fight for purity of the technology.

I know this is a very brash statement. To some, it borders on blasphemy! SE/CASE gurus have been preaching for many years to take an "all-or-nothing" approach to SE/CASE implementation—not to tinker with the techniques or the approach but to use them in their "vanilla" form. These are very rigorous and exacting processes. However, these rigorous and exacting processes are not as rigorous and exacting as you would think.

Changing preestablished SE/CASE processes, however, can be very dangerous. It's like a person trying to move a post in their cellar in order to better finish the basement. You know, the ones holding up the first floor support beams. It looks easy enough to do. Simply crank down the stanchion, move it a few feet, and reextend it. However, if you know anything about construction, the simple rule is: don't move the posts! However, these posts can be moved if you know what you're doing. (Please don't try this yourself! You could damage your house!) If you get an experienced, knowledgeable engineer, he or she will determine the risk, devise a process, select the best new placement, and supervise the actual movement of the post.

In the same light, a knowledgeable and experienced SE/CASE consultant can work with you on modifying your SE approach, technique, or tools to fit your culture. He or she can help you make the difficult tradeoffs of bending for the current culture while still adhering in principle to the essence and rigor of software engineering. As with the construction engineer, you need be able to trust your consultant. The end results could be just as disastrous. However, if you're planning to implement SE/CASE alone, by all means stick to the book. Don't move the posts! Changing the SE/CASE foundation is not a job for amateurs.

The primary tactic to finding a cultural fit is relatively simple: analyze the existing culture, determine the cultural impact of the new technology, and proactively plan to adjust as you go.

To analyze your existing culture, you might want to consider administering a culture questionnaire. A sample culture questionnaire is included in chapter 7. You can use this diagnostic instrument as is or customize it for your unique environment, terminology, or situation.

The focus of this questionnaire is to identify the relative strengths and weaknesses of the existing culture. This is very much like the tests we all took in high school to indicate what we were best suited for in life. For instance, if you like the outdoors, like working with people, and have an interest in biology, then a job as a forest ranger might be just right for you.

In the same light, if your organization scores high on teamwork, leadership, creativity, and personal drive, then the RAD approach might be right for you. However, like the high-school test, we can't allow a simple diagnostic to make the decision for us. These types of decisions need to come from within, not from a score on a test.

Once the culture is more fully understood, then the work of predicting the impact can begin. This is another potential area for a consultant. Someone who has been through a few of these types of implementations will be better able to react to the potential problems and challenges based on your specific culture. These cultural impact items need to be documented and analyzed because from this list, the action items will be developed.

Another major tactic is to be able to float above it all, to be the facilitator of the cultural change, not the driver of the change. There's an important distinction between the two roles. As the driver of the change, you'll be playing a more active role in shaping the SE/CASE vision and modifying either the culture or the technology. As a facilitator of the change, you'll need to view change as a process, learn how to manage change, and focus on keeping up the momentum for the change. You can't allow yourself to get personally involved with the change. This detachment will give you the space to see conflict more clearly, to remain more objective, and to develop creative solutions to the challenges. Remember, the facilitator is not a technician, but a diplomat.

Shared Understanding of and Appreciation for SE

Software engineering is a very broad and complex discipline. As a result, there are almost as many different interpretations of this discipline as there are so-called experts in the field. I'm sure even this book presents a slightly unique interpretation of SE/CASE. The key to a successful SE/CASE implementation is not so much getting your understanding of the discipline absolutely right, but gaining a common understanding within your own organization of what you think it is.

Even if you tried, it's almost impossible to pin down an accurate definition of SE/CASE. The approaches, techniques, and tools are constantly evolving. It's like hitting a moving target with twenty or thirty people telling you where the target is. Every expert has a slightly different view as to where you should aim. Just read three or four articles about SE/CASE and see if your head doesn't spin from the different views!

It's possible, however, to at least gain a common understanding of SE/CASE within your own IS organization. This understanding needs to be shared among the key departmental leaders. It takes a little time and energy to reach this common understanding, but the struggle is well worth it. As your SE/CASE implementation unfolds, at least members within your own organization will be singing out of the same hymn book.

By itself, a common understanding is not enough. You also need an appreciation for the principles that are at the heart of SE/CASE. This appreciation must be well established and genuine. All members of the IS organization need to be committed to the principles of SE/CASE, not just to the results of applying these principles.

The principles of SE/CASE were discussed in detail in chapter 4. This discussion centered around the culture diagram in Figure 4.2. An appreciation of the SE/CASE principles starts by addressing the middle layer of this diagram. Within this layer, you'll need to weave together the concepts of discipline, leadership, teamwork, total quality, and ownership into one, cohesive view. This view should make sense for your specific organization. These principles can't just be words, they need to be ingrained within the organization and believed by everyone. They must become part of the department's everyday beliefs, behaviors, and assumptions.

The primary reason to gain this shared understanding and appreciation for the concepts of SE/CASE is to support the selection and assimilation of your SE approach(es). As we mentioned in chapter 2, the SE approach becomes the IS department's ideology. People can get very emotional and potentially very defensive when discussing development and maintenance ideology because once they realize the importance of the SE approach, they will lobby hard for their own points of view. Sharing many of these points of view up front will make the implementation go much smoother.

Often, we've seen IS organizations argue over the concepts, techniques, and approaches of SE/CASE. Many times these organizations were arguing for the same side, but they didn't know it! Taking the time up front to educate and discuss SE/CASE will eliminate many of these potentially damaging arguments.

The other major reason for gaining an understanding and appreciation is to support the sponsorship process. As we'll discuss in the next section of this chapter, sponsorship entails understanding, commitment, and leadership. Each of these aspects is supported by this CSF.

Gaining a shared understanding and appreciation of SE/CASE seems like a difficult task, but it really isn't. It just takes patience and a desire to want to learn and accept the concepts. The problem is, most people don't care how SE/CASE works; they just want it to solve their problems.

Well, the implementation of SE/CASE is not simple. It's not the same as acquiring an automobile. Many people, including myself, have no understanding or appreciation for the interworkings of an internal combustion engine or other related components of a car. We buy them, learn how to drive them, and off we go. We don't need to know much more about a car except to change the oil every 5,000 miles or so and to schedule other routine maintenance.

However, for SE/CASE to work properly, you need to know a lot more about what you're doing and why you're doing it. We're still in the early days of SE/CASE. Today's SE/CASE products can be thought of as "Model-T" vintage technology. With the Model-T you had to know much more about your car. You never knew when or where you would break down. The roads were horrendous. Mud was everywhere. Gas stations were scarce. There were few repair shops along the way to where you were headed. At times, it seemed a lot easier to go by horse than by car. (Sound familiar? Sometimes its easier to code by hand than by code generator!) Without a thorough understanding of the workings of this complex machine, you were in trouble.

Unfortunately, today's SE/CASE is not much different. You really need to thoroughly understand and appreciate it in order to achieve the desired results. On the other hand, perhaps this complexity works to our advantage. If SE/CASE were as easy as today's cars to operate, the user community would only need a few mechanics to keep the technology up and running. Thus, there would be many fewer analysts and programmers in the world today. That's a scary thought!

A major roadblock to achieving an understanding and appreciation for SE/CASE is our profession's obsession with technical details. We like to go right to the glitz of a new technology. "Show me how it works" is a lot different than, "Explain to me the principles of how it works."

We also tend to be serialistic learners. That is, many IS people need (or at least desire) the detailed, step-by-step procedures laid out in front of them in order to create their own map of how the pieces fit together. With SE/CASE, this is very difficult. SE/CASE is just too broad a subject. Most people would lose interest or comprehension before reaching the end of the procedures. Thus, SE/CASE needs to be taught in a holistic manner. With this approach, the technology is explained at a high level, then expanded into the details. This teaching approach relies on expanding layers of abstraction. For those who don't learn well in this manner, these layers could cause confusion and resistance.

In addition, many IS managers tend to quickly dismiss the importance of the principles of SE/CASE. These individuals are impatient and want to get right to the heart of SE/CASE. They want to get their hands dirty, not clutter their minds with theory. This strategy can still accomplish the goal of gaining an understanding and appreciation of SE/CASE if approached properly. Two useful approaches are:

1. Using SE/CASE-experienced consultants to do a system or two while you watch and help.

2. Trying a few smaller prototypes by yourself.

If these situations are used as learning exercises, then the IS department can benefit greatly, and an understanding and appreciation can be built.

The key to avoiding many of these roadblocks is to manage the concepts of SE/CASE. Managing a concept is different from managing a process (i.e., a project). You manage a process-oriented activity by keeping track of time expended and the deliverables produced. However, a concept doesn't have specific tasks or deliverables. For example, what tasks or deliverables can you attach directly to the management of teamwork or leadership? Thus, without tangible things to look at and react to, the concepts of SE/CASE are only espoused, but never managed.

Early in my career I had the opportunity to work for a large chemical company who learned how to manage a concept. The concept they successfully managed was "safety." They were very big on keeping safety in front of every employee—plant worker or office worker. As a producer of potentially lethal chemicals, it was critical for the company to manage safety for each and every employee.

In the early days of my tenure with the company, I felt that they overdid it. After all, I was an office worker, I didn't touch, smell, or see any chemicals. I only had to worry with bits and bytes. Also, to my knowledge, no one have ever been injured directly by a bit or byte. Can a byte bite? (Sorry!)

The focus of the company's safety management program was a monthly, two-hour safety meeting. These meetings generally focused on office safety (e.g., making sure all radios and other electrical devices were safe from electrical shock) and home safety (e.g., the proper storage of poisons). The company passed out safety pamphlets to reinforce the concepts discussed in these meetings. The company also had safety specialists. One of these specialists was even a part-time "chair inspector" who made sure that all of the chairs in the office were safe. They had routine individual office inspections to make sure that all electrical appliances had the official inspection sticker attached. They even watched as employees left the office parking lot and counted the number of employees wearing their seat belts. Seems a bit like "big brother!" Believe it or not, this was back in 1984!

The most visual and effective aspect of their safety program was the way top management treated the concept. They were very serious about safety. They didn't treat it with mockery and sarcasm, as I did at times. Safety was the first thing discussed at every staff meeting, from my project team on up to the board of directors of the company. On-the-job and off-the-job injuries statistics were kept and used for promotions and raises. Yes, it's true. They would actually slow up or even refuse the promotion of a manager if that manager's department had a bad safety record. Again, I'm not just talking about in the chemical plants where it makes perfect sense, but in the offices as well!

Now you can see why I felt that it went a bit too far. Here I am, an office worker, and part of my promotion is based on my safety record. Well, I held my concerns to myself and went along with it. After all, everyone else seemed to go along with it. There must be something to it.

Then one hot summer afternoon I was visiting a Louisiana chemical plant to get a better insight on a system I was developing. As we entered a chlorine gas production facility, an alarm went off. Schooled in the practice of mock evacuation drills, we all evacuated as soon as possible. This time, however, it wasn't for practice; it was the real thing. Luckily, I got out okay.

Later that same year I was working on another system dealing with inventory control. While documenting the requirements for that system, I suggested an added system feature that would allow the organization to better manage the shelf life of the inventory. Not that the product would go bad, but that the container used to hold lethal chemicals might deteriorate and release its chemicals. For this suggestion, I was personally praised by a vice-president of the division.

After these incidents, I began to realize how the management of the safety concept potentially saved my life as well as countless others. It might have seemed overdone, but it got the job done. Even to this day, I'm still affected by this safety program. I will not drive or ride in a car without my seat belt on. When staying at a hotel, I request the bottom few floors in case on an emergency evacuation. I even go around closing file cabinet draws so that someone will not run into them accidentally. Like it or not, safety is now a part of me.

In the same vein, SE/CASE concepts like total quality and teamwork need to be managed. You could go back to my safety example and substitute the words quality or teamwork for safety, and you'd get the idea. These SE/CASE concepts need to become a part of every individual. They can't just be words. We can't give them idle lip service. We need to live the concepts. We need to measure and reward the concepts. They need to be the focus of our status meetings. We need to provide time and resources to educate the staff on the mechanics and importance of the concepts. In short, these concepts need to be managed as well.

Another important strategy to build a shared understanding and appreciation for SE/CASE is to provide broad, high-level education on the SE approach and concepts before providing the detailed training on the tools and techniques. Then, as the techniques and tools are being used for the first few times, you should provide SE/CASE coaches to the staff to assist with the detailed use of the techniques and tools. These coaches should also reinforce the concepts of SE/CASE learned in the education step. This allows the education to be tightly integrated with the beliefs, behaviors, and assumptions of the department.

Effective Management Sponsorship

Almost every article and book on SE/CASE implementation talks about the absolute need for management commitment before implementing this new technology. These publications are absolutely correct. You can't get off first base with an SE/CASE implementation without strong management commitment. Management commitment is a true given for success. However, some CASE authorities have even gone so far as to compare SE/CASE implementation to purchasing real estate. In real estate the three most important preparation activities are "location, location, and location."

With SE/CASE, some have declared the three most important preparation activities to be "commitment, commitment, and commitment." I'll have to admit, a few years ago I was saying the same thing. However, as I helped company after company through this difficult transition, I realized that commitment wasn't nearly enough; management needed to sponsor the SE/CASE initiative.

Sponsorship goes much deeper than just commitment. You can be committed to buying American; you can even be committed to the Cleveland Indians. However, you can be committed to these causes without really knowing the whys and hows of what you're committed to. Both of these causes sound appropriate to focus on (assuming, of course, you're from Cleveland). However, with a better understanding of the cause, your commitment could waver. Once you realize that some American products are assembled with a significant portion of foreign parts and some foreign products are assembled with a significant portion of American parts, then your commitment might waiver. Also, once you realize that the Cleveland Indian's front office might not be willing to pay the big bucks for major talent, then your commitment might also waiver.

To us, sponsorship means commitment, understanding, and leadership. Commitment for software engineering and CASE, an understanding of the concepts and technology, and the leadership to carry through with the implied commitment. Many times we've seen IS management committed to a specific CASE tool without having any idea of the concepts, approach, or techniques associated with the tool. This is similar to a marketing manager being committed to the use of LOTUS 1-2-3 spreadsheets, but having no understanding of the accounting principles behind the spreadsheet.

This type of commitment is only skin deep. Whenever the implementation gets a little rough, this type of commitment dissipates with the first good alternative idea. For example, at one organization we visited, a CASE pilot team was having a difficult time internalizing data modeling concepts, specifically the entity relationship diagramming (ERD) technique. This put the pilot project behind by two weeks.

At first, management stood staunchly behind the CASE tool and insisted that the project team not proceed any further without this logical data model in place. Then a team member suggested bypassing the logical data models and going right into the physical database design model, a technique the team was comfortable with. Since both the logical ERD and the physical database design were produced by and documented in the new CASE tool, management accepted this change in approach. They were committed to using the CASE tool and, to them, the project team was still using it. Politically, they were covered. They were committed to CASE, but not really sure of what they were committed to. To them, it was simply the use of a software product, not the compliance to a development approach.

For a while, all appeared fine. However, as the project proceeded, the physical database had to be modified countless times because of the skipped step. This put the project further and further behind. The end result was a pilot project that was two-and-a-half months late (on a six-month project) and lots of questions and doubts about the relative merits of the new SE/CASE approach. Luckily, a later project didn't encounter the same problem, and the tool and accompanying techniques are firmly in place at this company.

The key, however, is to make sure management understands what they're committing to. Committing to SE/CASE is similar to getting married. At the wedding, each party takes the vow "to have and to hold, for richer and poorer, through sickness and in health, . . ." Hopefully, you don't enter into this lifelong type of a commitment based on words alone. Each party needs to fully understand the implications of their words before they get married. Once the real implications are fully understood and agreed to, then the couple has a better chance of a long and happy marriage. Then, if times get rough with the marriage, each party can rely on this important commitment to see them through.

The same type of full understanding and strong commitment needs to be addressed with SE/CASE technology. Sure, SE/CASE is not a lifelong commitment like a marriage, but it should be thought of and implemented as though it were permanent. The IS department is in effect wedding the SE/CASE approach and ideology.

Active leadership is also an important dimension of effective sponsorship. The old adage, "People watch management's legs, not their lips," is never more true than with SE/CASE implementation. Often, executives' actions don't match their words. IS management needs to take a front-and-center stance with SE/CASE. They need to take the flag and make the first move forward. This move needs to be visible, genuine, and significant. Simply making a presentation and espousing their commitment towards SE/CASE is not enough. Many within the IS organization have seen the "idea of the month" dissipate as soon as the next new concept of technology came along. As we said, "Talk is cheap."

Staff members respond well whenever they see management putting their "skin into the game." This can be accomplished by IS management taking courses in the specific techniques to be used. Not a four-hour overview, but the full three- to five-day workshops. Sure, this takes a lot of time, and IS management will probably never actually have to use these skills. However, if IS management is truly committed to making this long-term initiative happen, a week is a small investment. This training will provide the management team with the understanding and the insight to make the tough tradeoffs as projects experience implementation problems. Another visual activity for IS management team involvement is to join a CASE user group or consortium in order to learn from others going through the same type of an initiative. This is a great opportunity for management to effectively get involved, but, unfortunately, this is often delegated to the staff.

Getting people excited about SE/CASE is important. Management still needs to be the cheerleaders of the initiative. However, staying on the sidelines and cheering for the home team is not enough. Management needs to put down the pom-poms and get into the game. They need to directly support the staff to pull through this difficult transition. Unless IS management is comfortable with being around and even in the trenches of IS, the SE/CASE initiative is put into an unnecessary risk. SE/CASE is just too different for management to operate as normal business.

One visible activity that's not recommended for IS management is attending the annual user's group meeting for the new technology. These meetings are usually held in warm, interesting spots like Palm Springs, San Diego, or Orlando. It seems like the only time management shows any interest with the new technology is when a vacation is on the line. The staff looks at this scenario with skepticism. It definitely works against building an effective sponsorship for the new technology.

Another major roadblock towards building an effective sponsorship is a lack of a high-level champion(s). You'll need to go as high in the organization as possible for this sponsor. From the IS side, you need to at least have the IS vice-president or director as the sponsor. Even if this individual really doesn't care and is very comfortable delegating responsibility to the development manager or project managers, it doesn't send the right message to the staff. This person needs to be seen spearheading and driving the initiative. Remember, you're not just selecting a software tool, you're potentially changing the IS culture and infrastructure with this initiative. It needs the visible support of the department's leader. All eyes will be looking for this support.

This champion needs to be able to make and hold to crucial SE/CASE decisions. One of the biggest roadblocks for an SE/CASE initiative is a sponsor who cannot or will not make the tough decisions. Many times, SE/CASE decisions (e.g., which approach, methodology, tool) are made by default or made by middle management. As a result, they're forever revisited by the staff and the management team. It's easy to second-guess someone else's choice, but it's difficult to make the decision up front. However, if the top guy is seen making an informed decision based upon sound corporate strategies, then the decision is much less likely to be scrutinized. People will just accept the decision and move on.

Gaining a high-level sponsor from within IS is also very crucial to implementation success. Obtaining the support and backing of corporate management outside of IS is equally, if not more, important. Upper management support brings energy, funds, focus, and visibility to the implementation. Getting the top guy or gal of the company to spend time and attention on the SE/CASE implementation will do much more than any internal marketing program. The sheer fact that this individual is interested puts a very positive spin on the initiative. The IS staff will feel like this initiative might in fact make a difference to the corporate bottom line. As a result, they will be less likely to resist the change. The change will be deemed good for the company, not just for the IS leadership.

You need to get serious and focused with the selection process. You need to make your SE/CASE decisions as early as possible—no poking around. Selecting SE/CASE technology is not a hobby or a perk, but a real part of your job. You need to do it. You need to get it done. I know this sounds a bit condescending, but many initiatives have failed because nothing was ever selected! People are just too afraid to make decisions.

In addition, the longer a choice goes unmade, the more time there is for individuals within the organization to join the different ideological camps. Once into these camps, it will be difficult or almost impossible to pull them back to a common ideology. Delaying the SE/CASE decisions gives the staff the extra time and energy that they'll use to learn the candidate technology. Once this investment is made, many will not want to lose the value it provides. The delay also provides more opportunities for political sides to form and for battles to be waged. With political infighting, no one wins. It's truly a lose-lose situation. Quick decisions will limit the opportunity for these sides to form.

Now, we're not saying to pick the first tool that comes along. You still need to make a fair and complete assessment of your situation and of the technology. As you'll see in the next chapter, there's an awful lot that needs to be done before selections are made. However, when it's time to make these decisions, you need the guts to make the decisions and to finalize them. Don't permit yourself to fall for the next-release syndrome. Each CASE vendor offers a product, but each vendor also offers a vision. We all like the products, but we fall in love with the vision. Since the fulfillment is always right around the corner, then there's a tendency to want to wait until the new technology arrives. The problem is that:

1. The vendors never quite deliver the visions the way you imagined.

2. There's always another vendor with another, more enticing vision.

This syndrome is similar to waiting for the perfect notebook PC. Every few months, notebook PCs are smaller, faster, cheaper, lighter, hold more data, and have better screens. They were okay last year, they're great today, but they'll be even better next year. Four years ago I bought the best laptop PC on the market. This laptop was equipped with a 286 chip, 40Mb of memory, 4Mb RAM, and a two-hour battery.

This PC weighed about 11 pounds and cost around $5,000. Looking at today's price/performance ratio, I might have wanted to wait to acquire a PC. However, I also need to look at the value it has provided me over the years. The portability of the PC has allowed me to get more than 300 more billable hours while on airplanes, to have quick access to many of my files wherever I am, to occasionally work at home, and to even write this book. I think I got my money's worth and more.

SE/CASE is not much different. The current crop of tools do provide value. In addition, these tools can be upgraded as the technology evolves, so you're not really stuck with one generation of technology as with the PC example. There might be a six- to twelve-month lag, but most of the popular CASE tools follow each other almost feature for feature. It's almost getting to the point of where word processors or spreadsheets were a few years ago. You just need to pick one and go with it. Stop worrying about what the other companies are doing.

Also, don't let your current projects make your approach and tool decisions for you. Many organizations select their SE approach and CASE tool based on a specific project at hand. These organizations soon realize that their selection became the *de facto* approach and tool for the department. This is a very easy trap to fall into. It's much easier to compare technology with a solution in mind than to gaze into a "crystal ball." However, we need to be visionary leaders, look past the present, and determine how we'll use the technology two to five years from now.

As we mentioned earlier, understanding SE/CASE is key to building an effective sponsorship for the technology. Insufficient understanding of SE/CASE, therefore, can be a major roadblock. SE/CASE is a relatively complex technology and thus difficult to comprehend, both the hard side (i.e., technology) and the soft side (i.e., cultural). In addition, management has other pressing issues to attend to and might not have the time it takes to fully comprehend the interworkings of the technology. However, spending the time up front with management to get them to fully understand what SE/CASE is all about is very worthwhile. Be forewarned—this understanding might kill your initiative once they realize the tangible benefits and the true costs of SE/CASE, but at least the initiative is killed before any harm occurs to your career.

Backsliding is another roadblock to building the sponsorship. Backsliding is a natural human response. With SE/CASE, it means going back to the old ways of defining and producing systems. The IS profession has a certain inertia that likes things the way they were. Whenever things start to go wrong with the new technology and approaches, there's a strong urge to resort to the tried-and-true ways of old. As we mentioned earlier, IS runs on the principle of "WISCY"—why isn't Sam coding yet. Backsliding into this old routine is very natural and almost expected behavior. Regardless of all of the fantastic productivity claims, SE/CASE will take longer in the front end of a project. As a result, backsliding needs to be monitored and managed throughout the duration of the implementation.

Over the last few years, SE/CASE has been wildly oversold in many organizations. Sure, the technology vendors have a habit of overselling the benefits and are responsible for part of this unwarranted hype. However, for the most part, many of them have recently been much better at selling their products on real, measured benefits. The overhype problem is coming from the internal team implementing the technology. This team wants the initiative to be accepted with open arms and is willing and ready to promise the moon. It's this group that sets unrealistic expectations with management, not the vendors.

As a result, SE/CASE is often introduced to the management team as a savior. This "savior" label just sets the technology up for failure. SE/CASE technology is good, but it doesn't do it by itself. The staff and management need to work together to make it work. If the focus is on the "saving technology" and not on the people, then it will never work.

Not only are the benefits of SE/CASE oversold, but the cost of implementing the technology is vastly underestimated—often by orders of magnitude. SE/CASE implementation takes lots of money, time, and energy. In addition to the price for acquiring the technology, you also need to consider maintenance costs, selection time, time in classes and seminars, learning curve, coaching time, and many, many other support costs. The problem is not justifying this high cost. These true costs can be justified for most organizations. No, the problem is the effect these "in-stream revelations" have on the implementation momentum. As unexpected costs emerge during the SE/CASE implementation, management might tend to draw back support for the effort, even if the benefits are being achieved. These revelations tend to put doubts in their minds. This reduced sponsorship position could weaken the organization's resolve to get it done. Also, with SE/CASE, it's an all-or-nothing proposition. You really can't afford anyone having doubts halfway through an implementation.

Whenever large sums of money, significant change, and the management of staff are concerned, then internal politics will undoubtedly play a part. SE/CASE is hardly the exception. In one rare case, we've actually seen the implementation of SE/CASE technology fail because a certain individual was supporting the technology. This individual was not well liked within the department, and the project manager core was more concerned with getting this individual out than in making SE/CASE work. In other cases, where certain leaders were against the new technology, it also didn't gain the type of early momentum that was possible and needed for a successful SE/CASE implementation. Your implementation plan needs to address these types of political issues. Ignoring them will not make them go away; it will only allow them to grow bigger.

All of these roadblocks are important, but the number one roadblock to effective sponsorship for SE/CASE is still the failure of a pilot project. All eyes are on the pilot. Many of the best people are often used for the project. In many cases, the tool vendor has been holding the hands of the project team. The thought is that if this perfect scenario doesn't produce fruits, then what will happen whenever the technology is implemented in less-than-perfect conditions?

Pilot failures, however, do not occur only because the wrong technology was selected. This is rarely the case. Most all CASE technology can be made to work for most organizations. In many cases, the pilot team was selected based on their technical capabilities and not on their project management skills. Project management skills are very crucial to the success of a pilot or, for that matter, any project. However, for a pilot, someone needs to determine when "fiddling around" with a particular SE/CASE technique or tool feature needs to end and the project needs to keep moving forward. If the project is staffed with only technical wizards, then the project will not move off the dime until the particular technical problem at hand is resolved to perfection.

Pilots also fail because of a lack of team synergy. Often, the pilot project team is made up of the best "hotshots" that the department has to offer. These individuals are used to shinning and blazing trails. Well, whenever you get too many "hotshots" together, you run the risk of conflict. It's like the National Basketball Association's yearly all-star game. Everyone is special and used to the limelight, but whenever you get them together on the same team, they don't work well together. The same is true of a pilot team. This effect is also compounded by the relatively short duration of most pilots. These projects usually last for only three to six months, hardly time for a team of "prima donnas" to properly gel.

A pilot failure doesn't have to occur within your company to put a damper on your SE/CASE implementation. A failure that appears on the cover of *Computerworld* or *Datamation* or that occurred recently down the street from you can be equally as devastating as one in your own company. You need to stay ahead of these types of situations and move quickly to squelch any fallout. If there's a failure down the street, call the company. Find out why and objectively compare these reasons against your own environment. If the same could happen in your own environment, then reconsider your choices. If the environments are truly different, then document and publish the differences. Be honest, open, and especially quick. Fallout from others' failures can move very quickly, and sometimes the damage can be irreversible.

Whatever you do, don't use SE/CASE technology to rescue a failing project. This roadblock only fuels the fire of the failed pilot scenario just discussed. If you develop the system yourself, SE/CASE will not save you much if any time on your first project. In fact, in most cases, it will take you 20 percent to 40 percent longer than doing it the old way. These are hardly the statistics a project manager of a failing project needs to hear. Sure, the spotlight of the technology takes people's eyes off the real problems of the project for a while and puts a glint of hope into these eyes, but reality will set in and the technology will most likely fail. One possible alternative is to use a consulting organization experienced with SE/CASE to help the proj-ect. However, if the project is already well into analysis and design, even this attempt at using SE/CASE will not help. There will be too much retrofitting to deal with.

So, how can you overcome these roadblocks? How can you get management to understand SE/CASE and become its disciples? How can you avoid internal politics, backsliding, pilot failure, and the lack of a high-level sponsor. The key is to get management to own the initiative—to make it their's.

Getting management to own the initiative is accomplished by first and foremost tying the initiative to the SE/CASE objectives identified at the outset of the SE/CASE initiative. These objectives were management's objectives in the first place. If the SE/CASE technology directly and clearly supports these management objectives, then management will naturally want to own the SE/CASE initiative. If the tie is not clear, then management will tend to distance themselves from SE/CASE. Under this scenario,

SE/CASE will be just another toy for IS, not something useful for the good of the department. The key is to make it a win/win situation. You need to consider what's in it for management.

Personalizing the benefits of SE/CASE is another important dimension of gaining management ownership for SE/CASE. However, this is a little harder than it appears. For some IS executives, writing articles and speaking at conferences about their experiences with SE/CASE is seen as a career booster. It puts them in the limelight outside of their own companies and positions them for future career moves. This scares the hell out of other managers. Thus, you really need to know your audience.

Connecting SE/CASE to your company's total quality movement (TQM) is another way of personalizing the benefits of SE/CASE. Within many organizations, upper management is now rated and rewarded on their individual contributions to improving quality and the process that produces quality. SE/CASE represents a very tangible and solid improvement in the development process and the resultant quality. By highlighting these TQM-like benefits, management will see SE/CASE implementation as a career-enhancing mechanism. Once this connection with SE/CASE is made, you'll have gained a strong and long-lasting sponsorship for SE/CASE.

Education and involvement of the management team is, of course, a necessary ingredient to gaining management ownership. The key, however, is to do it in unison. You'll need to treat the management team as a team. If you train them and involve them as individuals, then you might end up with as many different SE/CASE interpretations as there are people on the team. The whole team needs a common understanding, not individual interpretations. This common understanding breeds team ownership. If individuals are seen as owning the initiative, then there's much more potential for political maneuvering.

Once the management team has formed a consensus of what needs to happen and jointly owns the initiative, it's then time to cascade the sponsorship. Cascading the sponsorship implies taking the vision, ideas, and concepts of SE/CASE and getting the next layer in the organization to buy into the initiative. Once this layer is committed, then you move to the next layer. Cascading continues until the entire organization is converted.

Two problems that people run into cascading the sponsorship for SE/CASE are:

1. The understanding and ownership was not cemented in the management team before the sponsorship was cascaded down.
2. Management skips the middle layer(s) of the organization and goes right to the staff.

If the understanding and ownership for SE/CASE is not well established before passing the implementation baton, then the inevitable direction changes will kill any implementation momentum. The management team will be seen as weak, ineffective, political, bumbling, and indecisive. Remember, when implementing SE/CASE you'll be asking the staff to change the way they earn their livelihood. Any wavering in direction will be seen as a threat to their ability to earn a living. This will undoubtedly affect the implementation by increasing resistance, thereby slowing momentum.

If management skips the middle layers (i.e., the project managers and leaders), then you better have selected the perfect technology. Remember, in many organizations, the project managers are the ones who really control what happens within projects. They're the ones who are ultimately responsible for quality delivered and the schedule. If they have not bought into the new concepts and technology, they will find every excuse not to use it—especially if they perceive that management is trying to pull a fast one on them. Trying to force something on them that they don't fully understand while still holding them responsible for quality and schedule is very dangerous. If the technology is just perfect, most project managers will see the value and come around. However, most technology is not perfect. In short, don't forget the project managers.

Ownership is difficult to obtain and sometimes even more difficult to maintain. All too often an organization is able to achieve consensus on the whys and the whats of SE/CASE but unable to maintain this consensus and resultant ownership as the vision starts to unfold. This is because the vision needs to be flexible as new concepts and technology become available and the technology is better understood by the company. Any change in course can potentially affect sponsorship and ownership. Also, other pressing issues and time itself can cause sponsorship and ownership to be affected. Thus, it's important to manage this sponsorship.

Sponsorship is managed by obtaining visible support for the initiative from the management team and reinforcing this support periodically. It's very important for them to show personal interest and active involvement in the day-to-day incremental steps necessary to make SE/CASE happen. Never assume that sponsorship is perpetual. The half-life of sponsorship can be as short as one meeting!

It's also very useful to get the sponsorship and commitment in writing. Getting it in writing forces the management team to really think through what they're committing to. No one signs a piece of paper without reading and understanding the contents. Getting it in writing is a good checkpoint to make sure that management understands the initiative and is on board with it. Getting it in writing also helps to keep the initiative going whenever there are management changes. It's also useful for large organizations where the management team is far removed from the staff.

Understanding SE/CASE is much more than just learning the techniques and tools. It involves understanding why the approach and tools works so that trade-offs can be properly made later on projects. It involves getting your hands dirty and experiencing the technology firsthand. It also involves understanding the limitations and shortcomings of the approach and tools selected. With today's technology, no approach and tool combination is perfect for every situation. Management needs to be aware of the specific strengths and weaknesses of the approach and tools selected for your organization. This prepares them for the eventual resistance as the use of the technology unfolds. By being prepared, they can expect resistance and proactively manage towards success.

For sponsorship to be effective, management needs to lead the organization with SE/CASE by example. Leadership is a missing commodity in many IS organizations today. Oh, they have management all right—management by threat, demand, and edict. However, they seldom have leadership by example. With the implementation of SE/CASE, management needs to "walk their talk." If you talk about high-quality project deliverables, then produce high-quality plans, reports, and presentations. If you talk of efficient projects, then run your status meetings efficiently. If you talk about building partnerships with users on projects, then form strong alliances with upper management. These items can't just be bottom-up initiatives. They also need to start from the top. The staff is watching with a critical eye.

The final tactic towards building an effective sponsorship is keeping expectations realistic and obtainable. If you shoot for the moon and only get halfway there, you've failed. If you shoot for Toledo and get way past Detroit, then you're a hero and the momentum continues (assuming of course you're on your way to Canada from Columbus). The key is calculating the benefits and being honest to yourself and your company. If the benefits are soft, say so. If they're long-term, say so. Also, calculate all of the costs up front. Include all costs, not just the visible outlay of dollars. Include learning-curve time, training and orientation time, resistance time, and all of the other causes of expended resources. It's better to figure out that SE/CASE is not worth the effort up front than halfway through an initiative.

Patience

Patience is a virtue—with SE/CASE implementation or with any other major cultural change. You can't rush or force your culture. You have to plant the seeds, nurture them, and watch them grow. You can't expect an instant SE/CASE culture to spring up from a few inspirational speeches. If you could, there wouldn't be a need for this book or for others like it (or, for that matter consultants who specialize in changing the culture).

We've seen a few IS organizations force SE/CASE into their culture. Or should we say forced their culture to accept the principles of SE/CASE? At one organization, IS management simply declared that SE/CASE would be used from that day forward. At first, the staff appeared to accept the declaration, but resistance started to build. Then management came in, fired a few people, declared the party line, then left the staff to sit and brew for a while. This action got the staff's attention very quickly. They were clear on the changes that needed to occur, but the focus was now on management and not on the SE/CASE implementation. SE/CASE now became a weapon with which to fight back. Giving in meant being submissive. Remember, IS staff members are proud; we don't acquiesce easily. Needless to say, a political cat-and-mouse game ensued for years.

As a result, the SE/CASE initiative was never truly successful, and resentment carried forward long after the reasons were forgotten. Had management simply been patient and softly coaxed SE/CASE into the organization rather than forcing it in, they would have been much more successful. As we've said many times in this book, "Pay me now or pay me later."

The major roadblock for patience is simple human nature. We all want things fast. We're all impatient. It's ingrained in the American culture. The other day my five-year-old daughter, Melissa, asked me why it took so long to get our hamburger order at McDonald's. It took almost a full two minutes to get served! Her mind-set is one of instant gratification. After all, she said, "people get served on commercials much faster!"

Many of the CASE vendors have been guilty of this type of advertising. McDonald's can usually produce. CASE vendors, however, are a different story. They're getting better at managing the realities of implementation, but the hopes and aspirations of a quick strike still remain. It's very hard for a sales managers with half a million dollars of revenue staring them in the face to say the words, "Twelve- to eighteen-month learning curve."

As mentioned before, a lack of understanding of the concepts and principles of SE/CASE can also lead to impatience. There's a constant tendency to underestimate the unknown. We're all eternal optimists.

Another major roadblock to building patience is the "hurry up and wait scenario" that's played out in many SE/CASE implementations. The primary focus of the implementation is on key events like orientation classes, demonstrations, and pilot tests. This is much like running to catch flights at an airport. Everyone needs to "be on" these events. However, each of these events disrupts the normal operation of the department, pulling the resources from productive activities. These events always seem to be rushed for one reason or another. Then there are long delays of inactivity between events. How many times have you heard people talk about redoing their entire schedule to take a class, then waiting 12 months to use what they learned (and most likely forgot). This scenario doesn't help to build the paced momentum so desperately needed.

Paced momentum doesn't come naturally; it needs to be planned. It needs to be built on a series of minisuccesses. These successes provide visible proof of movement and improvement. This proof helps to build steady support for the SE/CASE initiative. Too much or too quick an improvement, and the momentum will undoubtedly hit a plateau and peter out. Too little or no incremental improvement, and the staff will lose heart. The ultimate goal will seem unobtainable. The key, then, is to balance the long-term focus and goals of the SE/CASE initiative with a series of short-term successes.

Building a plan to optimize these two dimensions will be difficult, but not impossible. It will be different for every organization, but the key elements are similar. Your implementation strategy should focus on keeping the implementation simple, understandable, modular, and measurable. Remember, it can be done.

IS Staff Buy-In and Acceptance

Next to management sponsorship, staff buy-in and acceptance is the most obvious critical success factor to the implementation of SE/CASE. Interestingly enough, however, the staff doesn't need to be as committed to SE/CASE as the management team. This is just the opposite of what many people would think. Many would feel that since the staff is in the trenches and using the technology daily that they need to fully understand and internalize the new concepts and techniques.

However, the staff just needs to accept the technology, not love it. Sure, it helps if everyone is fully on board with the new techniques and tools and they have all internalized the concepts as their own. However, this just isn't possible or necessary. They just need to accept the fact that management has the staff's and the department's best interest at heart and that management can make the right decision on technology. The staff needs to feel confident that management knows what they're doing. The staff needs to know and understand enough to be effective, but a complete understanding is not necessary.

Even at this more limited level of buy-in, there are still many roadblocks to successful implementation of SE/CASE. If the staff is unclear as to why the organization is pursuing SE/CASE or sees a tentative management position towards SE/CASE, then the initiative is in jeopardy. Many within the department might look at SE/CASE as the "initiative of the month"—only to disappear whenever the next initiative emerges. Or if the initiative is moving too slowly, the staff could get restless. The worst scenario often played out by many organizations is the situation of "trying out" multiple SE/CASE alternatives at the same time. This causes confusion over real direction, uncertainty over management commitment, and lots of lost time. In addition, it sets up some of the staff to be losers if their technology was not selected. This puts them on the defensive immediately.

If the staff mistrusts the department's leadership, then buy-in and acceptance is much more difficult. Remember, the staff usually doesn't need to fully understand the technology before they can accept it and use it. However, if mutual trust is not there, many will insist on a full understanding of SE/CASE before they buy into it. This is a very time-consuming process.

Mistrust is created whenever management doesn't share the results of self-assessment studies and other analyses, or whenever management asks for suggestions but never uses any of them. This gives the impression that management doesn't listen, that management doesn't have the best interests of the staff at heart. Mistrust is also created whenever decisions and promises of the past are not honored, or, worst of all, whenever resistance is beaten down. As we discussed in the last chapter, resistance needs to be anticipated and turned into positive action like in judo—not beaten back and squelched like in boxing.

Implementation of immature approaches and tools is another major roadblock to success. In most IS organizations, the staff using the new SE/CASE technology is technically oriented. These individuals will eventually learn the techniques and tools and then be in a position to understand if it works in your environment. This is where the rubber meets the road. If it works, then it's all fine. If it doesn't work, this group will be very vocal.

At times the technology might not be right, and the red flag raised by the staff will be useful and necessary. However, usually, the situation is not this black and white. If the technology is right, but just premature, then this situation needs to be managed properly. With premature technology:

- The approach and tool will not be well integrated.
- It might be easier to do some things manually.
- There will be a lack of full integration/standards.
- You could lose a few project deliverables.
- Not all of the desirable features will exist.
- Something better is anticipated in the future.

Each of those situations will need to be dealt with carefully. Don't make excuses for the tool or approach. Just explain the full vision to the staff and get them to buy into the big picture and to overlook the smaller, short-term inconveniences.

A worse scenario is if the staff rejects the basic principles of software engineering. This could come through a misunderstanding of the concepts of rigor, quality, engineering, automation, and effectiveness. Or it could be that the staff fully understands these principles, but they just don't fit with their individual styles. If it's a misunderstanding, then a class, a book, or an article or two could do the trick. However, these individuals might need to experience SE a while before those materials are of any use.

If they do understand these principles and they still reject them, then, and only then, is it time for drastic action. If the management team is truly committed towards SE/CASE for the long-term, it might be time to outplace these individuals. We're all for converting as many people over from the old to the new, and for giving them all the opportunities possible. However, whenever you run into the occasional brick wall, you just need to move the wall to the side. This initiative is bigger than just a few people.

If not removed, these individuals will be a major source of resistance for years to come—not just their own resistance, but with others whom they will consciously or unconsciously influence. After a few of these outplacements, others will get the message that management is serious about making SE/CASE happen. If done properly, this will turn into a very positive event, not a fearful negative event.

The worst and most feared roadblock to staff buy-in and acceptance is the relentless time pressures to get the job done. SE/CASE or no SE/CASE, the pressure is always there. Management might give the pilot team a few extra weeks to learn the new techniques and tools, but everyone knows that this time is never enough. There will always be unforeseen events that occur on every project, and these will put pressure on the staff to revert back to the old tried-and-true approaches and techniques. "We'll do it right next time" is a constant battle cry for most organizations. Of course, we always seem to have time to do it over. However, that never seems to be said at the right time.

Of course, the general resistance to any new technology or change is a major roadblock to buy-in and acceptance by the staff. In the last chapter, we addressed the major reasons for IS resistance and many of the signs of this resistance.

The most important tactic for helping to build buy-in and acceptance is staff involvement. It would be great if everyone in the IS department could be directly involved with the evaluation, selection, and implementation planning for the SE/CASE technology. For the majority of the IS department, this is, of course, impossible. With each person added to the core team, which needs to understand the decisions and reach a consensus, you add an exponential amount of time. It isn't just that person's time, but the added time for the larger group to be able to reach consensus. Thus, the team size needs to be balanced between the amount of time it will take and the extent of staff representation on the selection and implementation team. As discussed earlier, this representation needs to be fair and well proportioned.

Another way of achieving broad-range staff involvement in the selection and implementation process is through surveys and interviews. This way, each individual at least has an opportunity to affect their own future. This helps later on with implementation because the staff will tend to give the new technology more time and patience than if they had not been involved.

However, if the implementation lags too long behind the surveys (two to three years), then the effect of the survey is minimal. If this is your situation, you might want to resurvey the staff for implementation issues. They might not feel like they affected the selection of the technology, but at least they had input into its use.

A fun and very effective way to get broad-based input is to run a contest to name the new environment. Giving the approach and tool environment an internal name like "Concept 2000" or "Rapid Rosy" will help to build excitement and ownership for the new environment.

As mentioned a few times throughout this book, the project manager is a very, very important individual to win over. If management is convinced of the new approach, and the analysts and programmers are also convinced, the job is still not done. Without the project manager's buy-in and acceptance, the project team will not use the new tools and techniques. You might find visual compliance. However, project managers know how to do just enough to get by politically. The project will still be done the old way. The key to winning the project managers over is taking the time to transfer sponsorship of the initiative and understanding of SE/CASE over to them. Of course, give them extra time on the project to make sure the new approaches and tools are properly used.

An often overlooked tactic in building staff buy-in and acceptance is through the development and execution of an internal marketing plan—a plan that follows the classic product marketing strategy of defining the product, place, price, and promotion.

The product is the full SE/CASE environment, not just the visual CASE tool(s). The product is also: the change in the organizational structure to support SE/CASE; the methodology and techniques behind the CASE tool(s); the cultural changes that need to be made; and the skills that need to be acquired.

The place is the physical environment in which the new environment needs to run. In their interesting book, *Peopleware*, Tom Demarco and Tim Lister talk about the physical environment of the IS department. Staff members are very interested in this discussion.

The price to the organization is obvious. It includes the out-of-pocket expenses as well as all of the added time to learn, apply, and support the new environment. The price to the staff is not as obvious. This price includes:

- Disruption of their normal work lives.
- The risk of changing career direction.
- The risk of acquiring new skills. (What if they can't do it?)
- Potential overtime due to training and learning-curve time.
- Increased stress due to the constant pressures of the job.

The other side of the price equation is the benefits to the staff. For maximum effect, you'll need to personalize these benefits like you did with the management team. Make the staff aware of such benefits as the increased market value of their new skills, the reduced confusion and fingerprinting on projects, and the satisfaction of doing things right for a change. As with the management team, keep the expectation for achieving these benefits both realistic and obtainable. Also, personalize the potential threats to the individual. If they truly will not be around long if they don't convert, let it be known. It sounds like a mean thing to do, but it's truly worse not to tell them early!

The important aspects of the marketing strategy are the message and its method of delivery. The message needs to be crisp, forthright, visionary, and dynamic—not an easy set of attributes to fulfill. You'll need to develop this message in a set of overlapping presentations—one for the users, one for management, and one for the staff. Each will vary in detail and differ in emphasis, but the central themes should stay the same. Don't get into the trap of saying conflicting things to these different groups. This will come back to haunt you if you do.

Start the development of this marketing plan by identifying and stratifying your targets. Identify who will most likely support your initiative and who will not. Try to determine why these groups would support or reject the initiative. Form your marketing plans around these issues.

To help carry the message forward, use the active leaders in the department who are most receptive to the new approach and tools. Don't try to go it alone. Also, consider using guest speakers to support the message. This delivery technique was used very successfully at one of our past clients' company, where industry experts were brought in at just the right time to reinforce the momentum of the SE/CASE movement. However, be careful not to bring these speakers in too soon. This will breed impatience. It's like telling your children that you have candy, but they can only have it that evening. (If your child is like my Michael, you know what I mean.) Also, be careful to inform the speaker of your marketing message and of your vision. This preparation will allow the speaker to properly reinforce your message and not introduce anything contrary to your proposed vision.

Encourage full use of the SE/CASE technologies. Set up internal user groups to discuss common experiences and problems. Run lunch or evening minitraining sessions to reinforce specific elements of the new environment. Publish a newsletter to reinforce any successes. Never acquiesce without a good reason to back off of the new technologies.

A very hard tactic for many organizations to practice is to manage the staff's resistance to SE/CASE. Most organizations have an instinctive tendency to squelch resistance whenever and as soon as it occurs. The natural belief is that if the symptoms go away, then the problem is solved. The only result of squelching resistance is that the resistance goes underground or, worse yet, it's repressed for another day when there's more pressure and a better (potentially more damaging) political stage for releasing it again.

The best approach to managing resistance is to expect it, respond to it, and monitor it. Learn from the mistakes of the past. Assess similar initiatives (e.g., putting in a new DBMS). Where did you go wrong? Where was the resistance? How was it effectively overcome?

Schedule regular debriefing sessions up front before implementation starts. Don't wait until there are numerous problems and the emotions are running high. At these stressful times, a debriefing session only helps to fuel the fires, not to put out the fires. If the sessions are scheduled up front before the problems arise, it tells the staff that resistance is natural and expected. The message is that it's okay to have concerns and to be open about them. If properly vented, these concerns will truly help to fine-tune the environment. Everyone is a winner. Sure, it takes a little extra time, but its "pay me now or pay me later." You make the choice.

Monitor the resistance as the implementation unfolds. Ask the staff how things are going and truly listen. Ask the tough questions; don't just make the rounds. It will probably take a few rounds of posing the same questions to the same individuals before they'll be able to express their true feelings about the situation.

Don't only ask the questions in a full room with all of the staff or at formal staff meetings. This platform is more for politicking by both sides than getting to the truth. You need to get one-on-one with the staff to get a real read of the situation. Also, be aware of the subtle comments and jokes. Many times the real feelings are very quiet whispers from an unlikely corner of the department.

A formal way to monitor resistance is through the old-fashioned suggestion box and through surveys. Again it takes time, but knowing about the resistance is very important.

Stable and Motivated Staff

No SE/CASE implementation, no matter how good it is, will work without staff. Don't fool yourself; good staff make it all happen. SE/CASE is not magical. SE/CASE doesn't produce the software by itself. No one has yet invented a "Vulcan mind meld" device that can fit over the user's head and simply suck in the requirements. Interestingly enough, there's a trend in some of the vendor research departments to produce "client CASE"—tools and techniques that are used solely by the user to produce the products they need. This is the topic of a future book.

However, for the foreseeable future, the production and maintenance of software will still be a people business. Thus, keeping the IS staff somewhat intact and motivated is very crucial to the success of the SE/CASE implementation. Given all that goes on with an SE/CASE implementation, this is no small task.

A very obvious roadblock to this CSF is the loss of good people. Not so obvious, however, is how these individuals are lost to the organization. The first loss is straightforward. Once the talented staff members learn a new and highly marketable skill, they jump ship for more money and challenge. This loss needs to be proactively managed. Don't wait until you lose two or three good people. They're probably among your best, and you can ill afford to lose them. Don't expect or assume any loyalty for giving them the opportunity to learn the new skills. Plan for salary boosts as the skills are acquired. As we've said many times, SE/CASE is not cheap!

Those who don't initially get the chance to acquire and exercise these new skills will begin to realize a devaluation of their talents. They might look across town to an organization who is not planning to implement SE/CASE for some time and feel that those opportunities and salary will be greater for them. They might jump ship on you as well. Some of these individuals you might want to go—especially the higher-priced technicians who will have a very hard time making the adjustment to SE/CASE. They've been the kingpins for so long that whenever the game changes, they might not be able to make the necessary adjustments in technology and ego. For those that you want to stay, make sure you counsel these individuals early on and assure them of their financial stability and future technical challenges.

As the implementation unfolds, there might be a few staff members who feel that they will not be able to make it in the new environment. These individuals will lack the self-confidence described in chapter 4. These individuals might stay around, but their motivation and corresponding productivity will drop as their fears intensify. These individuals need special counseling. One of our clients used an industrial psychologist to aid in this type of counseling. In addition, you might want to implement a special SE/CASE mentoring program for these types of individuals. Within this type of program, each newly converted staff member will be assigned a relatively experienced mentor who will help them through the trials and tribulations of learning a new skill.

Impatience can also result in the loss of staff and motivation. It's almost impossible and surely unwise to convert everyone in the department at the same time. Those individuals not initially involved might get excited about the new technology and jump ship to another organization that can provide these new challenges sooner.

The biggest loss is seldom noticed, but often experienced in many of the larger IS organizations. This is the loss of hidden talents. In the past, the successful staff members were those who could deal with ambiguity, play the politics, scramble like mad, and still pull the thing together at the last minute. Hopefully, these characteristics will not be necessary in new SE/CASE environment. Thus, individuals who didn't flourish in the old environment have a new opportunity in the new. A different set of personal characteristics are now needed. The ability to follow a disciplined approach, the ability to work as a team player, and the focus on quality are all now very essential in each person. Look at your so-called "poor performers." Are there a few in this group because they always strived towards doing the right thing but never got a fair chance to do it? Be honest and open. You might just find a few gems!

Motivation can be affected by the constant changes in direction and organizational structure. Many staff members are just starting to get used to one another, and then the next wave of reorganization hits. As a result, the staff members are constantly changing responsibilities, roles, and priorities. This type of instability prompts a certain degree of complacency. Why put energy and effort forward if someone keeps changing the game on you. This results in individuals who simply show up, go through the motions, and pick up their paychecks.

The primary tactic employed to deal with the challenges of keeping the staff stable and motivated is to review and restructure the:

- Job descriptions.
- Career path within the department.
- Training curriculum.
- Salary structure.
- Reward mechanisms.

These areas are tightly connected and integrated. Together, they all play an important role in keeping the department intact and driven. This area is also very sensitive in many IS organizations. This is definitely an area to get human resources involved with early on.

You should first start by reviewing and updating the job descriptions for the department, focusing on the new roles and responsibilities for each position. Try to write the descriptions with the new environment in mind. Be creative and break the old mold. Remember, you're attempting to incorporate teamwork, quality, and engineering concepts into the job, not just the techniques and tools of SE/CASE. You'll need to weave these concepts into the descriptions.

Once these job descriptions are reestablished, then the current and future departmental skills should be assessed. Note—you'll need to assess the current skills that will be used in the new environment. It does little good to assess skills such as Assembler programming if you're headed towards COBOL code generation. By assessing future skills, you're looking for skills that might be lying dormant in the current environment, and you might be able to tap into them. For example, you might have a few staff members who have attended or run JAD sessions for a prior employer. Knowing this type of information at this point is very useful.

There are three ways to assess the current skill set. First, ask the individual, through survey or directly. Next, ask the person's manager who is relying on and using these skills. This individual will have a very objective opinion of the specific skills used. Finally, consider testing for the skills. There are a few testing companies that will come in and administer tests on specific skills.

The information gathered in the skills assessment should then be mapped to the specific job descriptions reviewed earlier. Analysis of this mapping will highlight the IS department's education and training challenges. From this analysis, the department's training and education curriculum should be established.

On the individual level, this type of information will be useful for career development planning. This is where a revised career path is needed. The department's official career path should reflect the concepts and technologies of SE/CASE. The old progression of programmer to analyst to project manager to IS management might not properly support SE/CASE. This progression needs to be tempered with the concepts of teamwork and leadership. The focus should be on the team entity, not the individual position. Perhaps the path should focus on a blending of team skills that progress outward as the individual progresses from novice to associate to master.

Once you modify the job descriptions, career paths, and training curriculum, nothing will change until the reward system is altered to reflect these new changes. Quite simply, what you reward is what you get. Modifying this mechanism is not an easy thing to do. Not surprisingly, politics play a major role in keeping things as they were.

The key to a successful reward system is to reward those aspects of the environment that make SE/CASE successful. Those aspects include a diverse skill set, personal motivation, and teamwork. Simply rewarding personal results (e.g., the number of programs written for the year) will tend to suboptimize the environment. Rewarding the triad of skills, personal results, and team results forces the individual to spread his or her energies and talents across a broader spectrum.

A diverse skill set refers to the number and depth of different skills that an individual possesses. In the past, many individuals were rewarded for knowing one skill and knowing it very, very well. In the new environment of SE/CASE, these types of masters will still be very important. We'll still need database experts, artificial intelligence gurus, and communication wizards. The major differences are that:

1. We won't need as many.

2. A broad understanding of the other areas of IS will makes these experts even better at what they do.

The teamwork concept of SE/CASE also puts a heavy demand on the diverse skill set requirement. Within an effective team, each member should have a solid working understanding of the jobs of others on the team.

Specialists who don't understand other team members' areas of specialization will rely on a formal structure and approach that will not be very dynamic as the realities of business occur.

I know this concept is a bit contrary to the popular notion of software engineering being a very structured process that supports specialization. With a very rigorous process, a team member shouldn't have to know what happened previously or what will happen down the line. However, we're just trying to be practical. We've yet to see a textbook system. Each one has nuances that challenge the formal approach. A diverse skill set will better position the team to make the necessary project trade-offs earlier and with better results. Even if you do subscribe to the "software factory" mentality approach, then a diverse skill set will at least position individuals to better support those down the line from them. They will be able to know the implications of their actions.

A diverse set of skills also allows for better cross-checking of work within the team structure. All too often, people tend to bow to the expert without challenging him or her. They just don't know if the expert is right, so they assume the expert is right. Cross-checking of work is especially useful if the expert happens to be an outside resource. A diverse skill set also provides some backup for a project team if someone happens to leave unexpectedly.

A diverse set of skills will also position the department for future changes. Since the staff members would not have all of their talents in one technical basket, they would be much more willing to move on and to change to new and future SE approaches and tools.

Finally, the diverse skill set approach will make it more fun for the individual. Sure, it's nice to be an expert at something, but you reach a point of incremental learning and experiencing, a point where the major challenges of the area of concern become commonplace, a point where little is new. Some people enjoy the comfort of this position. They don't have to stretch any longer. They can put it on autopilot and coast through the day. As managers, we need to guard against this complacency. We need to challenge these experts to become masters in other areas. If they can do it in one area, they can do it in another.

The only way to get many people from this comfortable perch is through reward mechanisms. You can talk and preach all you want about self-improvement and new skills, but until you take action, nothing will happen. You'll only get good intentions and plans. You need to reward for people for skills acquired, not just skills used. You'll need to make part of the annual promotion/raise performance review dependent on the acquisition of new skills. Make it very clear that you're rewarding for the future as well as for the present. This will get people away from focusing solely on suboptimizing the present.

Of course, you don't want to forget about rewarding skills used. The staff still needs to produce. The present projects and requests still need to get completed on time, within budget, and to quality standards. This production needs to be visible and measurable. The challenge here is to objectively measure the quality and productivity of the work and to fold this into the performance review system.

Anyone involved with establishing measurement programs will instantly tell you that tying the measurements directly to the reward system will result in unreliable data. The staff will see to it that the data reported will make each individual look great. This will happen if there's a direct link between the two. Your challenge is to be able to use the aggregate measurement data for the performance review while still keeping a subjective distance. This is not easy. Good luck.

You'll also need to blend in the team's performance with the individual's performance review. By rewarding the team's performance, it will force the individual to better support the other members of the team. This support will result in the proper leveraging of the key members of the group and the proper level of team optimization. The measurement systems can be tied a little closer to the team's performance than to the individual. Another tactic to keep the staff stable and motivated is to identify who you want to keep and who is to be let go as early in the process as possible. Again, we recommend keeping as much of the old department together as possible. There's a lot of knowledge of the current systems in their heads, and a mass exodus might be political suicide. However, if you feel that you must clean house a bit, do it early and all at once.

By doing it early and quickly, you'll avoid the unnecessary worry about who is next. Sure, this quick-strike scenario will impact momentum significantly, but it will be a one-time event, not a series of events.

Motivation can also be improved by concentrating on many of the nontechnical aspects of work. The amount of usable work space, the level of noise and interruption, and the effectiveness of team synergies can all play a part in improving motivation. Be open to new ideas and use resources from outside of the IS discipline. Without motivation driving the SE/CASE environment, it's all just a collection of approaches and tools that can and will sit on the shelf.

Skills to Get the Job Done

Having the right skills is a very obvious CSF of SE/CASE implementation, or for that matter, any major change. Put simply, to be successful you need to know what it is you're doing. For this reason, education and training has been addressed in almost every article and book dealing with SE/CASE implementation. Yet, few organizations have gotten it right. These publications have raised the interest and attention of management towards education and training, and more money and time is being spent, but the results have been very dismal.

We're constantly educating and training our staff too soon, too late, and sometimes even the wrong people. Just because an organization has a full education and training curriculum, that doesn't mean that they will successfully and effectively train their staff.

Many of these curriculums focus on the mechanics of getting the job done. Again, it's the WISCY mentality coming forward. The thought is, if we train the staff on how to produce visible results, that's what we'll get. As a result, there will be a quick return on investment for our training dollar. What we do, then, is to focus on building the following skills:

1. General skills.
    - Project management.
       a. Critical path scheduling.
       b. PERT charting.
       c. GANTT charting.
    - Programming and construction.
       a. DBMS.
       b. JCL.
       c. Languages.
    - Testing.
    - PC.
    - Mainframe.
2. SE skills
    - Data flow diagraming.
    - Decomposition diagramming.
    - Entity relationship modeling.
    - Data normalization.
    - Consensus building (JAD).
    - Prototyping.
    - Structure charting.
    - Structured walk-throughs.
    - Structured programming.
    - Structured testing.

All of these skills are very important to the success of an SE/CASE implementation. They form the basic building blocks of getting the job done. However, to be truly successful, the following soft skills also need to be developed within the organization:

1. Facilitation.
2. Presentation.
3. Meeting skills.
4. Listening.

5. Interviewing.
6. Problem solving.
7. Verbal communication.
8. Written communication.
9. Interpersonal skills.
10. Leadership.
11. Administration.

The main objective of a complete education and training curriculum should be more than just imparting these skills. It should also aspire towards a loftier goal. This goal should be to develop professional software engineers. Professional software engineers should know more than just the technology and tools of SE/CASE. If this is all you need, then the legions of off-shore programmers would have a field day. What's needed for success is a professional attitude to support the basic skill sets. Elements of this attitude include:

1. Open-mindedness, willing to try new ways.
2. Versatile, demonstrates the ability to play new or different roles.
3. A team player, does whatever it takes.
4. Hands-on, not afraid to get hands dirty.
5. Self-confident, self-starter.
6. Business oriented.
7. User-friendly, able to effectively communicate.
8. Politically astute.
9. High energy level.

The biggest roadblock to developing professional software engineers is the constant focus on the training aspects of learning and little focus on the educational aspects. People need to know how SE/CASE all ties together. They need to be educated in these concepts, not just trained to push the buttons. They need a broad base from which to work.

The practical use of SE/CASE involves many trade-offs. The staff needs to be prepared to make the right decisions as they occur. The methodologies of SE/CASE are meant to be a starting point and a guide. The methodologies were not meant to be the final word on how systems are developed. In addition, the techniques of SE/CASE can be applied in many different ways. Even the tools of SE/CASE can be adjusted for different results. SE/CASE is not as mature a discipline as many people would like to think. As a result, there's still plenty of responsibility that a project team must assume. Simply being prepared to operate the environment is not enough. You can't simply go through the motions. SE/CASE is not a substitute for thinking, it's an elevated platform for thinking. Thus, you need to be properly prepared to manage this complex and interrelated environment.

In the process of using and managing the SE/CASE environment, the project team must be prepared for making numerous trade-offs. For this, they need the knowledge to make these decisions and the authority to carry through with them. The following are a few of these trade-offs.

Flexibility versus rigor. Doing things by the book is admirable, but when it takes three to five times longer, then you need to look seriously at the activities and tasks of a project work plan. You need to make the tough decisions of what really needs to be done. These decisions can only be made with a thorough understanding of what you're doing.

Perfection versus excellence. Crossing all of the "Ts" and dotting all of the "Is" is not what SE/CASE is all about. Sure, we all want to do a solid, professional job, but sometimes people focus too much on the surface and not enough on where it counts—on the architectures of the systems. Filling out the forms and drawing pretty diagrams will definitely make management feel that the team is adhering to the rigors of the SE/CASE approach, but this doesn't guarantee success. We need to make sure we focus on doing the right things the right way, not on simply following detailed directions. We need to focus on excellence, not perfection. However, this is not an excuse to do a sloppy job; thus, there's a trade-off that needs to be made.

Process orientation versus end results. The philosophies of TQM emphasize a focus on the process as opposed to the deliverables. The theory is that if the process is right, then the results will be of high quality. However, the realities of a specific project often dictate a focus on the deliverables. The project team needs to be able to dynamically shift their focus, depending on the situation.

MIS driven versus end-user driven. Users are starting to get very involved with the development and maintenance process, even to the point of being active team members and getting their hands dirty with IS technology. You should make every effort to encourage this type of behavior, but you need to manage it. There will be some areas that users are not prepared to handle. The project team needs to know these areas up front.

Another major roadblock to acquiring the needed skills is the constant pressure to produce. If projects are late and the users are demanding systems, then it's politically difficult to free your best people for training. The result is that the available staff members get trained. You know, the ones who never seem to be right for the important assignments and are constantly in training classes. As a result, you're training the wrong people first. To be effective, you need to get your departmental leaders educated and trained first. Through their leadership, the rest of the staff members will learn better.

One recommendation to address this challenge is to offer education and training classes at night after business hours, or even on weekends. I know, this doesn't go over well with the staff. We don't like it; no one likes it. We all have families and lives outside of work, but times are changing. International competition is changing the American workplace. We all need to be more productive. However, look at it this way. What's worse—a few lost weekends or the unemployment line? Consulting organizations have trained their staffs using this technique for years. It's not popular, but the strategy works. You're not being cruel to the staff, but fair. At least you're providing the opportunity for them to learn.

A temptation many companies face is getting their initial orientation to SE/CASE from a technology vendor. Many CASE vendors will offer free seminars to potential clients to explain all about SE and CASE. The problem with this tempting offer is that this type of education tends to be shallow and primarily focused on the tools. After all, the vendor is ultimately trying to sell a CASE product, not to objectively inform you about SE/CASE. This type of education could get your SE/CASE implementation effort off on the wrong foot. There are plenty of independent sources of education and training. Sure, it costs a little, but remember, nothing is really free. By accepting the vendors' offers, you might be doing more harm than the class was worth.

Training budgets are usually one of the first items that get slashed in rough economic times. It's always politically easier to cut training costs than to cut the people who are actually producing the systems. At times, this is an appropriate strategy, but not always. Remember the often-spoken adage, "If you thought training was expensive, try ignorance." Yes, you need to be responsible and cut back in tough times, but you should also look in other areas, not just training. If you cut too deeply into training, you'll lose any ability to bounce back quickly once the recession is over. By the way, a good rule of thumb is to allocate about five percent of the IS budget for training and education. Like we said, training is not cheap!

The advent of newer technologies provides us with an interesting training strategy. There are interactive video instruction (IVI) classes available today for such subjects as data flow diagramming, entity relationship diagramming, and structure charting. In addition, the familiar training tapes have gotten much better in recent years. Companies are finally learning how to inform people without putting them to sleep. These types of training devices are self-paced and, if purchased, don't go away during tough economic times. This strategy provides a stable source of education and training.

These training mechanisms also provide a just-in-time training capability not available with stand-up classes. As a team member needs the understanding, they can take the class, acquire the skill, and quickly apply it in a real situation. JIT training has proven very effective in optimizing the training dollar.

The worst roadblock to acquiring the skills needed to get the job done is to use training as a reward. Many organizations reward successful work with a class in a warm, sunny spot. There are other ways to reward staff. Don't mix rewards with training. Training needs to be serious and purposeful. If you mix the two together, then people will start to take courses they don't need because the class is offered in a spot that they would like to go to! It just gets too political.

The primary tactics for addressing these roadblocks are to instill a self-improvement mentality and to focus on developing your resources. We talked about self-improvement back in chapter 4. This cultural dimension focuses on the individual taking personal responsibility for their own career. It represents the personal and active drive to improve their own knowledge and skills.

For the organization to take advantage of this self-improvement mentality, you need to give each individual a focus. You can't inspire staff members to improve without giving them a plan to follow. If there's no plan, this could result in anarchy—everyone running around learning new tools and techniques, but no one working in unison.

The IS organization will need to help each individual with a personal development plan based on their current skills and experiences and their long-term hopes and aspirations. Employees need opportunities to apply what they've learned. They also need coaches and mentors to help them whenever the going gets tough. These monitors will be able to make sure the individuals are using the technology and using it right. In essence, the IS department needs to be ready to support the individual development plans. Self-improvement doesn't only involve the individual; it also involves the organization enabling the individual to self-improve.

The basis of your training strategy should be to improve the masses over time, not to just make a few people more effective and productive. You need to be able to leverage your best people—to use them as coaches on multiple projects, not just buried on one key project. This is very difficult. To take a key person from a hot project is very political. However, it needs to be done. To optimize the whole department, you need to spread the wealth around.

Measuring skill levels is very controversial but often very effective. There are a number of companies springing up who can certify your staff members in many different areas of SE/CASE. Measuring a skill level can put added pressure on the staff to truly learn the skill, not just attend the class. If you know that you'll need to take a test at the end of a class or after using the skill for a while, you tend to take training much more seriously. No one likes to fail, and few like to take tests. To some, it's demeaning. However, look at who tends to be most vocal. Not those who will have no trouble certifying, but those on the borderline.

Certification also provides a mechanism to better manage your departmental skill base. You'll find out who has what skills and who doesn't. This can provide information for building new training curriculums. With this knowledge, you can also start to pay for skills. Like many auto assembly lines, workers get extra pay if they can perform more than one job. If your staff members are more versatile, it provides the IS organization with more staffing options, reduces the impact of losing a key individual on a project, and makes the job more fun.

A key message for every education and training class is for the staff to park their egos at the door. SE/CASE training is new and different. The stars of yesterday will not necessarily be the stars of tomorrow. Again, times are changing and everyone needs to wake up and smell the coffee. It takes a different makeup and attitude to be successful with SE/CASE. With some, it also takes complete retraining. That's why it's always easier to train a relatively junior staff member in SE/CASE than to train a 20-year COBOL, CICS programmer. However, don't discount these seasoned individuals. They still have a storehouse of knowledge in their heads. We just need to be able to tap into their capabilities and convert it over to the new approach. This takes time and patience, but it can be done. Don't give up on these individuals too soon. However, be honest and forthright with them. They have to be able to see the writing on the wall if they don't convert.

IS Viewed as a Team Player

For many years, IS has been looked at as a stepchild of the corporation. A department that needs to be around, but a department that no one knows what to do with. We're sort of looked at as a "necessary evil." However, for SE/CASE to truly achieve the grandiose benefits touted by the vendors and industry experts, this image has to change.

Over the years, this image has actually worked to our selfish advantage. By leaving IS alone, we've enjoyed a free reign in the acquisition of technical toys and other related material. As long as the payroll checks were done on time and the general ledger balanced, we were left to do the voodoo that we do so well. We bought bigger and faster computers, layer upon layer of software platforms (e.g., operating systems, security systems), and development tools of every type.

However, today this stepchild image hurts IS. With the advent of SE/CASE concepts and technology, we're moving to form true partnerships with the user community. Many of the more significant benefits of SE/CASE are only applicable if the corporation intends to use IS for strategic advantage. As a support group, we can only enable IS to be used for competitive advantage. It's up to the users themselves to employ this weapon. If we're part of the corporate team, then this transition will occur naturally. If we appear as outsiders, then the transition is unlikely. We'll simply be the same outcast organization looking for a cause with updated tools and techniques.

The obvious roadblock for this CSF is our "prima donna" style. We tend to dress differently, act differently, and use different language than the rest of the organization. As a result, we're constantly shooting ourselves in the foot. We're saying to the company that we're not team players, that we like to go it alone.

Many IS organizations mean well, but it's very hard for them to realize that we're a service organization. For years we've acted as if the business revolved around us. How many time have you heard, "That can't be done because of this problem or that situation." We're forever limiting the company due to technical difficulties. However, be realistic. How many times were these excuses just jumble-ese? Nice technical jargon that really means that IS is too busy, not interested, or doesn't want to be bothered. We're being self-serving, not corporate team players.

The tactics are simple. Get involved in business-planning activities. Keep an internal customer focus (i.e., the user community is the customer base). Also, act like a business department. Team playing is a series of individual activities that forms a new image of the IS department. Everyone needs to pitch in.

Strong User-Community Support

Without the strong support of the user community, an SE/CASE implementation is dead in the water because the user community ultimately pays the bills for an SE/CASE implementation. Few pay directly, but most are ultimately funding the operations of IS in one way or another. It's from this funding that SE/CASE technologies are acquired.

If the user community is against a major initiative like SE/CASE, then there are many ways in which they can apply pressure to IS to change their strategies. The most effective way is to go outside the IS organization for development and maintenance services. In many organizations, outsourcing is beginning to be an acceptable and even preferred method of getting the job done.

In addition, the implementation of SE/CASE will probably change the way you interact with the user community. A few of the techniques and SE approaches (e.g., RAD) even require the user community to play a more active and involved role in the development process. Without user support from the beginning, you're simply wasting your time.

Most organizations wait far too long before they get the user community involved. Some organizations are intimidated by the users. Others are afraid that the complexities of SE/CASE will overwhelm the users or that the users will not care which approaches or techniques we select and use. A few are even afraid that, if given an early chance, the users might actually influence the SE/CASE technology selections.

Within a TQM program, the key to success is to focus on the customer. An SE/CASE implementation is no different. IS needs to start looking at the user community as our own internal customer. We need to involve them with the selection and implementation of SE approaches and techniques. We can't assume that we know all about our internal customers. We simply need to partner with them. SE/CASE is not an IS-only technology. It's a shared technology that's used by and benefits both IS and the user community.

An interesting trend with CASE technology is a concept called "client CASE." Client CASE is CASE technology designed for direct use by the user community. It's technology that integrates artificial intelligence with predefined system templates. This combination takes much of the technical nuances out of systems development. If you ever intend to evolve into aspects of "client CASE," then the user community must be involved from day one.

The most common roadblock to user support is that the benefits of SE/CASE are not readily apparent to the user community. From their perspective, they see the benefits of SE/CASE only advancing the IS department. In fact, some organizations even see SE/CASE as having a negative impact on their own time and effort. In essence, they perceive SE/CASE as a way of off-loading IS grunt work onto their laps. In addition, the user community has a tough time accepting their own benefits. Many of these benefits are long-term (e.g., better support) and are realized beyond a manager's individual tenure within a user department.

Business pressures will also affect an SE/CASE implementation. Because of the learning curve and potential for unexpected problems, many users will not accept their projects as "guinea pigs" for SE/CASE. Since many organizations run lean to begin with, every project developed is a crucial project. The result is a constant stream of "next-time" decisions.

Once a project is started with SE/CASE, business emergencies and political pressures can force a project to abort the SE/CASE approach and tools. This is a very common situation. User support is really tested in these types of situations.

The most important tactic in overcoming these roadblocks is to know your customers. You'll need to know what they expect from IS, how much they're willing to change, how much they're willing to get involved, and how much risk they're willing to take.

Surveys and interviews are very useful techniques for getting to know customers. Making the surveys and interviews formal will help to surface the crucial information you need. With informal, one-on-one chats, you tend to get an "all's okay" message from the users. They're people too; they really don't want to upset the apple cart. However, when the assessment gets more formal, they feel more free and compelled to open up and let it out. You want and need to get to this core understanding.

You'll also need to educate your user community on the fundamentals of SE/CASE. They need to understand the basic process, concepts, and principles of SE/CASE. These concepts are not as foreign to them as you would think. After all, many of the engineering principles found within SE are borrowed from the engineering field. Engineering is something many business users are already comfortable with. To the user community, SE is not a new or novel idea, it's just the way that IS should have been developing systems all along! They can get quite comfortable with the concepts, often more quickly than the IS community!

Educating the users is not enough. You also need to create and execute a user marketing plan. You should sell SE/CASE on quality, but justify it with productivity improvements. For unless your organization has a well-established Corporate Quality Initiative, quality benefits will not be enough. You'll need to personalize the benefits of SE/CASE to each user group. You'll need to inform them of their changing roles. Most of all, you must maintain a business-centered focus. You can't let the technology run rampant and obscure the real message. This message must be that SE/CASE ultimately benefits the users—that IS is not just having fun with new technology again, but is doing something real to help the users.

Chapter

7

Stages of SE/CASE
Implementation

Our initial intention with this final chapter was to provide a step-by-step method for bridging the gap between the SE/CASE technology selected and the surrounding IS culture. However, we encountered two problems. First, we were not able to effectively separate the activities and tasks used to select and implement the SE/CASE technology from the tasks that deal solely with realigning the culture. The activities just too interrelated. Thus, what we'll be providing is a set of activities and tasks that do both.

Secondly, we couldn't craft a rigid approach that every reader could use. The problem we foresaw is that each of you is in a different situation with regard to SE/CASE. Some of you are at the beginning, some have tried a few things and are looking to expand, and a few are even fully implemented and are looking to fine-tune the culture around the technical environment. For this reason, we've provided the step-by-step advice by implementation stages.

The advice we provide is like a systems development methodology in that it should be used as a guide or boilerplate for your planning effort. Like an SDM, don't follow this template verbatim. Add, subtract, and modify the activities and tasks. Be creative, but be honest with yourself. Take a realistic look at the challenges that lie ahead of you. Look at chapter 5 again if you need to review the complexities involved with SE/CASE implementation. Our template is based on the CSFs, roadblocks, and tactics outlined in that chapter. Don't shortchange yourself in responding to this challenge.

You'll need to make adjustments to this template in order to respond to the following type of organizational variables:

- Size of the organization (the larger the organization, the more tasks you'll need).
- Need for formality/documentation (i.e., an audit trail of your decisions).
- Size of the transition team.
- Including the users in the selection/implementation process.
- Past successes and failures with similar activities.
- Current stage of SE/CASE implementation.

Realize that there's no truly right or wrong way to proceed. This is a one-time event for you and many others like yourself. Go with your gut feeling, but think through the implications of any task deletions from the template. The key is to use common sense.

Be ready to change directions in midstream. The project plan you craft from our template will be a good start, but it needs to be dynamic. Whenever you're dealing with the culture of an organization, anything is possible. People don't behave in predictable ways like data. You need to stay loose on your feet and expect almost anything.

As mentioned earlier, our template is partitioned into the different stages of SE/CASE implementation. You'll need to assess where your company is and apply those sections that are appropriate. This partitioning is meant to help you focus on the key activities and tasks that are right for you, but also consider the earlier stages for activities and tasks that might still apply.

The stages identified in the template are as follows:

Stage one—Considering SE/CASE. The activities and tasks in this section of the template are for organizations who are just starting out and have very little idea what SE/CASE is all about. It's also for organizations that want to know if SE/CASE is for them.

Stage two—Creating the SE/CASE vision. Once a company is serious and committed to bringing in SE/CASE technology, then these activities and tasks will help focus on creating the future vision for SE/CASE. From this vision, the culture of the organization is assessed and its realignment is planned for. For those organizations interested primarily in cultural re-alignment, this should be your primary focus.

Stage three—Selecting the technology.

Stage four—Planning for the transition.

Stage five—Deploying SE/CASE.

We'll now describe all of the tasks within each of these stages. These tasks are presented in a somewhat sequential order, but they don't necessarily need to be executed in this order. Again, the tasks presented are ideas for your individual work plan.

For each of the tasks, we'll present a description, a rationale for performing the task, and the implications of not performing the task. We'll also provide tips, guidance, questionnaires, checklists, sample deliverables and other aids for the execution of the task, and, if appropriate, we include a set of work steps to complete the tasks.

Stage One—Considering SE/CASE

1-A. Gain a common understanding of SE/CASE

Description. Create a common understanding within the IS department of what software engineering and CASE technology represents. Make sure everyone views this new technology in the same light, from the same perspective.

Rationale. SE/CASE is a very broad and diverse discipline. As a result, there are many opportunities during its implementation for an organization to form differences of opinion of what its SE/CASE is. From these differences might stem many discussions, arguments, and disagreements. Most of these conflicts can be avoided if everyone is on the same page of the "hymn book" from the very start.

Work steps.
1. Review SE/CASE technology.
   - Read books and articles. Get smart before you begin. A solid understanding will allow everything else to fall into place. There are a number of good books out today. Use your local SE/CASE vendor or consultant to point you in the right direction. Don't rely on a vendor's or consultant's understanding. Form your own. Keep the vendor and consultant honest.
   - Attend SE/CASE conferences. Attend conferences based on the topics discussed, not the tools displayed. Try to select a conference that matches your stage of implementation. There are now conferences for those organizations who have already been into SE/CASE for years. These conferences can add value to an organization just starting out, but a more general and basic conference will serve the novice better.
   - Attend vendor tool demonstrations. Be careful not to get lulled into selecting the technology too quickly. Remember, the objective is to learn about SE/CASE, not to select it. That comes later in this process.
   - Map SE/CASE terminology to your organization's vernacular.

2. Experience the technology.
   - Visit similar-size sites that are using SE/CASE technology. Simply telephoning an organization or talking to a person at a conference is

not enough to really understand what SE/CASE is all about. By visiting a site, you'll be able to react to the technology, not just discuss it. Visit a few different organizations. Not everyone attacks SE/CASE in the same way. Make sure you address these organizations from a win-win position. Make sure there's something in it for them. For example, share something that your organization does well (e.g., metrics, database design, user surveys).

— Engage a SE/CASE-experienced consultant to perform a smaller project using the technology. This is a great way to see firsthand the effectiveness and challenges of the technology within your environment. The consultant should bring in the technology. Thus, you won't need to acquire the technology and go through the ordeal of getting management's approval. However, the technology used should not be allowed to become the *de facto* technology for the IS department. This is a very natural temptation, especially if it worked well. However, remember that almost all of the SE/CASE technology can be made to work. Your job in this process will be to find the most effective technology for your organization, considering your unique set of skills, experiences, and cultural dimensions.

3. Reach Consensus on Understanding SE/CASE
   — Document what SE/CASE means to your organization. Make it visible, common, and shared. If at all possible, write it down.
   — Involve staff and management. Don't just keep this understanding of SE/CASE within the management ranks. Remember, the staff members are the primary ones who will use this technology. Without staff representation early in this process, you might find it much harder to get commitment later on.
   — Strive towards consensus. You'll never be able to get everybody to agree. It's almost impossible. However, you do want management and staff to at least speak the same language.

1-B. Assess organizational readiness for SE/CASE

Description.   Assess the degree to which the IS organization is ready for SE/CASE technology and ready for the implementation process. This task helps ensure that you have a real need, a potential fit with the culture, the skills to pull off the implementation, the money to do it, and most of all, the right timing.

Rationale.   SE/CASE can and will cost significant amounts of money, energy, and political goodwill to implement. Before you invest these valuable resources by investigating and evaluating SE/CASE technology, you'll need to make sure that the technology is right for you. To be honest, SE/CASE implementation is not for everybody, and its implementation is definitely very difficult. There are times when it's best to delay or even abort an SE/CASE implementation. This tasks helps you determine if the time is right.

Work steps.
1. Administer the Readiness Survey (appendix A).
   - Review the survey for applicability. If you're past this step or it's a dictate that SE/CASE will be implemented, bypass this task.
   - Determine who should have input into the survey. It might only be necessary for the driver of the initiative to fill out the questionnaire, or for the transition team or management team.
   - Complete survey. A group review is a good way to review the survey. This survey is provided more to provide fuel for a discussion than to collect actual responses.
2. Assess your readiness for SE/CASE.
   - Document the pros and cons of SE/CASE for your environment. This survey doesn't produce a simple numerical rating that can be used to decide if SE/CASE is right or wrong for you. In fact, many of the questions are positive factors for some organizations and negative factors for others. It all depends on your particular situation. This task is an exercise for you to think through these questions and arrive at the right decision for your unique needs.
   - Make a decision to abort, postpone, or move ahead with SE/CASE. If you're indecisive, move ahead. The abort or postpone options are really for those organizations for whom SE/CASE is clearly not appropriate.

Task tips. A consultant can truly help you with this decision, if you can find an objective consultant. The problem is that some consultants will tell you that you need SE/CASE right now, with the expectation that they'll be able to help you during the implementation. This presents a conflict of interest. One way to get objective advice from the consultant is to declare up front that whoever provides the readiness assessment can't help with the selection/implementation process.

This entire task should take no more than a day or two, no more than a week for a close call. Remember, you're not selecting the technology, just looking for a potential fit. Use the JAD process to gain concurrence. The survey was designed for just such a process.

Be honest with yourself. If SE/CASE doesn't fit, don't force it. You can always wait for a better time.

1-C. Prepare for the transition

Description. Perform related activities to get ready for the transition process.

Rationale. The better prepared you are, the quicker you'll get through the process.

Work steps.
1. Identify existing pockets of SE/CASE within the organization. Many times, organizations go through a long process of evaluating SE/CASE technology only to find out that their parent or sister organization has already implemented the technology. If they have SE/CASE, take advantage of their pricing arrangements, training, customization, etc. Don't assume that the same technology is right for you, but it should at least be a major candidate.

2. Dust off/update IS strategic plans. SE/CASE represents one of the four IS planning architectures (i.e., data, process, technology, and infrastructure). SE/CASE is in the infrastructure architecture. The other three planning architectures are very interrelated with SE/CASE. Reviewing and updating your strategic plan will be very useful for this effort.

3. Review corporate plans and strategic initiatives. Review ongoing corporate initiatives like TQM, downsizing, decentralization, etc. Determine how these initiatives are related to SE/CASE.

4. Review past IS technology selection reports, CASE reports, or related ones.

5. Align with consultants/consortiums/internal groups. There are many consortiums forming to help member organizations understand and implement SE technology. There's often a price to be paid, but it's usually well worth it.

6. Identify IS leaders and influencers.

Stage Two—Getting Ready to Act

2-A. Make the case for SE/CASE

Description. Document the reason, rationale, and pain for moving to SE/CASE.

Rationale. SE/CASE is a major investment in terms of money, time, and energy. If there aren't good, solid reasons for this expenditure, then sooner or later the initiative will be suspended. Knowing and documenting these reasons up front will reduce the risk of delays or unwarranted cancellation of an SE/CASE initiative.

Work steps.

1. Interview user-community management. The user community ultimately pays for the IS department. In some organizations this payment is direct, in others indirect. Either way, if the users are not on board with the benefits of SE/CASE, then they'll fight it as another one of IS's toys. SE/CASE can't be seen as an "IS-only" technology. There has to be something significant and tangible in it for the user community. Identify and document these benefits.

2. Interview key IS leaders. These individuals are not only the formal IS managers, but they're also the project manager core and the quiet influencers.

3. Identify and document current IS pain. Potential sources of pain include:
   – Outsourcing pressure.
   – Diminishing credibility with users.
   – Missed estimates.
   – Unable to prove value to the user community.
   – Quality inconsistencies.
   – Maintenance burden.
   – Loss of control over development.
   – Attrition of key staff members.
   – Pressure to do more with less.

4. Identify and document future IS pain.

5. Map pain/needs to SE/CASE technology. For the identified pain to be effective in securing management sponsorship, the SE/CASE technology has to be clearly seen as an effective way to alleviate the pain at hand. If the pain/SE/CASE connection is not clear, then the pain identification might get management to act, but they might completely overlook SE/CASE as a potential solution.

6. Identify potential non-SE/CASE solutions. SE/CASE will not solve all of the problems raised in the prior steps. Identify alternative solutions where appropriate.

Task tips. Even if management is not asking for a rationale to proceed with SE/CASE, you should still do this task. Sooner or later they'll ask, and usually at an inappropriate time. To avoid this situation, just provide a rationale early. This is another task where a consultant could add a valuable objective, outside viewpoint.

2-B. Encapsulate IS management's perceptions

Description. Clearly define where management wants to take the IS organization.

Rationale. Most IS managers usually know early on where they would like to take the SE/CASE initiative. It's from this early, somewhat premature perspective that they'll view the progress, success, and viability of the SE/CASE initiative. Rather than fighting these early visions, it's best to document their vision and evolve the final vision from the vision of the IS managers.

Work steps.

1. Identify IS management's aspirations and hopes. What are they expecting in terms of technology, benefits, and results?

2. Define and document the objectives of SE/CASE. Clarify management's goals from SE/CASE technology. Example objectives include:
   - Consistently produce quality systems.
   - Effectively use MIS resources.
   - Ensure cost effectiveness of MIS resources.
   - Improve productivity.
   - Control the development/maintenance process.
   - Improve predictability of the processes.
   - Improve the maintainability/adaptability of software.
   - Accelerate software development.
   - Meet user requirements.
   - Satisfy user expectations.

3. Map SE/CASE objectives to corporate objectives and goals. Make sure that the stated objectives ultimately benefit the organization, not just make life in IS easier.

4. Map SE/CASE objectives to pain. Identify which objectives address which problems and challenges. It's this mapping that will provide the staying power later whenever the implementation hits a rough spot or two.

5. Scope the SE/CASE initiative. Will the full SE/CASE environment include or exclude areas such as strategic planning, development, maintenance, or project management?

6. Identify budget issues/limitations.

7. Set measurable goals. These need to be based on the objectives stated previously.

Task tips. A JAD-like meeting with IS management and key influencers is the best way to capture management's vision of what SE/CASE should be.

2-C. Assess the sponsorship for SE/CASE

Description. Determine the strength and staying power of management's commitment for SE/CASE.

Rationale. SE/CASE needs strong management sponsorship in order to take hold in an organization. Measuring and assessing potential sponsorship before the technology is selected allows you to reduce the SE/CASE vision if sponsorship is weaker or add to the vision if sponsorship is stronger than anticipated.

Work steps.

1. Determine the degree of sponsorship needed. Determine the amount of support needed to implement management's SE/CASE vision. The amount of sponsorship needed is in direct proportion to the amount the culture needs to change, the amount of money spent, and the time needed to make it all happen. Look at past initiatives of similar magnitude (e.g., DBMS implementation). Extrapolate for SE/CASE.

2. Document the internal influence structure. Review the organizational reporting structure. Identify influencers and decision makers. Identify and address political issues.

3. Identify and assess potential sponsorship sources. Consider IS, corporate, and user-community management members. Look outside the traditional structure. Be creative.

4. Define mechanisms to acquire and maintain sponsorship. Consider getting sponsor commitment in writing. Create a steering body.

5. Adjust management's SE/CASE vision accordingly.

2-C. Establish a justification mechanism

Description. Establish a way to track the progress of the SE/CASE implementation in order to prove its worth.

Rationale. Even if management is not asking for a formal justification of the SE/CASE technology, you should still consider this task. Sooner or later, someone will ask you for the "proof," and usually at the worst time. Sure, benefits can be achieved with SE/CASE without measurement, but no benefit can be realized without measurement. A "gut feeling" estimate will not be appropriate when there's a significant amount of money waiting to be approved.

In most organizations, SE/CASE might be impossible to justify financially up front. The costs are just too high, and the benefits are just too soft and long-term. However, if upper management sees a concerted effort to measure as you go, then they might relax stringent guidelines that force you to justify the investment up front. With a measurement approach, at least it's not a pure trust-me scenario. There's a mechanism in place to confirm the expectations. This also keeps you from having to take a short-term or chopped-up implementation strategy.

Work steps.

1. Define the justification approach/method. Think through all possible justification scenarios that management might at some point ask for. Define an approach that's inclusive of the majority of needs while still remaining relatively simple. Note: Don't go overboard with justification. You need enough information to be objective, but not so much information that you lose sight of the goal.

2. Identify measurements for ongoing justification. Define specific quality and productivity measurements needed to justify SE/CASE now and in the future. Assess the degree of formality and precision that's needed. Keep all measurement at the same level of precision. Determine how the measurements will be collected, analyzed, stored, and reported. Measurements can scare a lot of people, so be very specific as to their handling. If there's even the slightest hint that the measurements will be used to measure performance, look out. Keep in mind the stated objective of this task—to justify SE/CASE. Keep focused on this objective. Some potential measurements include:

   – User satisfaction rating (from a simple survey).
   – Function points produced per person-month.
   – Percentage of development time spent fixing bugs.
   – Percentage of code/design reused.
   – Number of change requests per one thousand function points.

3. Develop a baseline metric set of the current processes. In order to prove that SE/CASE has the expected results, it will be necessary to take a snapshot of the IS department before SE/CASE is implemented. Since it will probably take at least a year or perhaps two before full deployment of SE/CASE is possible, you do have enough time to take a before snapshot. Of course, you'll want to use the same measures that you'll be capturing with SE/CASE.

Task tips.   There are a few good consulting organizations in the U.S. who specialize in measurements. To help you establish a plan of attack, consider bringing in an experienced measurement consultant for a few days. However, this is another area that you need to be careful not to go too far with. Consultants have a way of expanding even the simplest of tasks. The objective of this task is solely to establish a justification approach, not to set up a full-blown measurement program to fine-tune the process. That comes later, after you've selected and implemented a process.

2-E. Create a transition work plan

Description.   Create a work plan to successfully evaluate, select, and implement SE/CASE.

Rationale. With SE/CASE, you're trying to formalize and structure the development and maintenance processes. With this task, you're trying to formalize and structure the evaluation, selection, and implementation process. This is a major critical success factor. You need to treat this process like any other project—with a work plan, project manager, team members, objectives, strategies, and all of the other aspects of an application project.

Work steps.
1. Set the transition scope/objectives. Define the bounds of this project. What's within the scope of study and outside the scope? How will management know when this process is complete and successful?

2. Identify transition constraints. Define uncontrollable, negotiable, and controllable constraints for the initiative. *Uncontrollable constraints* are those considered and/or declared unchangeable by management. Examples include organizational structure, physical locations, or a total budget of $xxx,xxx. These are limits that the transition team should just consider fixed. *Negotiable constraints* are those that are currently fixed but still might be capable of being changed if the right justification can be made. Examples might include job descriptions and change control mechanisms. *Controllable constraints* are those that the transition team has at their discretion to balance within the course of the transition project. Examples include implementation duration and training curriculum.

3. Assess risks. Identify the technical, business, and political risks of the transition project. Use any application project risk questionnaire to help identify these risks. A transition project is not much different in terms of risks. Sample questions include:
   – Technical:
     a. Does technology currently exist for identified scope items?
     b. Can identified CASE technology run on existing hardware?
     c. Do you have anyone in-house with SE/CASE experience?
   – Business:
     a. How well is the company doing financially?
     b. Do the users want/need IS to get better?
     c. How solid is the user/IS relationship?
   – Political:
     a. Have similar initiatives failed in the past?
     b. How many different locations need to be coordinated?
     c. Have you identified a sponsor(s) for SE/CASE?
     d. Have you used higher-level consultants before?
     e. Are there other cultural change initiatives underway?

4. Define transition strategies. Think through each of the following areas. Your resultant strategy will be used in the next work step to create the transition project work plan.
   - Planning horizon. How far out will the transition plan go? This usually extends three to five years.
   - Speed of implementation. How quickly does the technology need to be implemented?
   - Top down (management oriented) versus bottom up (staff oriented). Is this transition effort directed from the top or built from grass-roots efforts? You can achieve the vision both ways, but your approach will change, depending on your strategy.
   - Technology versus peopleware solution. SE/CASE means more than just technology residing within a PC. You can have a very successful initiative without purchasing one single CASE tool.
   - Determine the depth of analysis needed. How deep do you need to go before you feel comfortable making a decision?
   - Determine the degree of deliverable detail needed. Decisions will be made as the transition project unfolds. Determine how detailed the documentation needs to be for these decisions.
   - Develop a detailed transition work plan. Using this chapter, create a detailed work plan for the transition. Decide which stages, tasks, and work steps are needed. Document these activities with a project management tool.
   - Define the transition milestones. Within the work plan, identify milestones that can be used to gauge progress.
   - Obtain approval to proceed.

Task tips.   This is an area where it's okay to overdo it a little, and it's a step that's often overlooked by many transition efforts. People feel that they can implement SE/CASE "in their spare time," and thus they don't need the formality of a work plan. In fact, the transition effort is a real part of a person's job and needs to be planned in as much detail, if not more, as any other part of the job.

Don't follow verbatim the approach prescribed in this chapter. Our approach is generic and is meant to apply to a very wide range of organizations. As such, we were not able to add in many of the organization-specific activities.

2-F. Staff the transition team

Description.   Assign staff to the transition work plan.

Rationale.   Nothing ever gets done unless staff members are assigned. This project needs to be part of their job, not a side issue to do during lunch or in the evenings. Without assigned staff, the SE/CASE transition effort will wander aimlessly in hit-or-miss fashion.

Work steps.

1. Define needed skills and representation. Identify the type of individual(s) to assign to the transition team. List the characteristics for these individual(s). Note: There's a tendency to assign technologically proficient transition team members, those who will be able to quickly pick up the complexities of SE/CASE. While this is an important attribute, it's not the primary attribute. The following is a list of other important attributes of the individuals:
   - Technologically competent.
     a. An understanding of SE/CASE.
     b. Ability to learn quickly.
   - Respected by peers.
   - Strong communicator.
     a. Listen emphatically.
     b. Talk clearly.
     c. Write plainly.
     d. Able to teach and sell concepts.
   - Change agents.
     a. Able to constructively deal with resistance.
     b. Able to weave in team involvement.
     c. Able to manage the pain/sponsorship.
     d. Visionary leadership.
   - Politically astute.
   - A broad representation of the target audience.
     a. Functional areas.
     b. Age. (It's good to get both the new kids and the older veterans rep resented).
     c. User representative.

2. Identify transition team members and define roles. Identify who will be on the transition team. Consider management, staff members, users, and even outsiders. Sometimes a consultant can play an important role in keeping the transition initiative objective.

3. Define the reporting and administrative structure of the team. Define who reports to whom, who is managing the transition team, and how time will be reported. Again, this is a real project and it needs all of the tight controls of a regular application project.

4. Schedule the transition project. Using a project management tool, insert the team members and their individual availabilities. Schedule the project. Review milestone date with management for their approval. Commit to this schedule. Make it happen.

5. Kick off the transition process. Orient the team on the transition approach. Perhaps give them a copy of this book to read and refer to.

Stage Three—Forming the SE/CASE Vision

3-A. Prepare for current environmental assessments

Description. Get ready to assess the current development and maintenance environments.

Rationale. Doing an effective assessment takes planning. You can't just "wing it." If you do, the assessment might not be objective, it might not cover the needed areas of concern, or it might not be detailed enough to be useful.

Work steps.
1. Determine method(s) of assessment. Identify the mechanism(s) used to collect information about the current environment. Potential mechanisms include:
   - Survey/questionnaires—The objectives for using surveys include:
     a. To quickly understand your current situation.
     b. To provide the needed information to make decisions.
     c. To prepare the staff for the interview process.
     d. To obtain facts/opinions in a safe, nonthreatening manner.
   - Interviews. This mechanism allows the interviewee to open up in an unstructured forum. The results of interviews are much harder to tabulate, but are sometimes much more useful. Unexpected gems come from interviews. Interviews can be conducted one-on-one or in group settings. One-on-one interviews are useful for management or for sensitive issues. Group interviews are useful for getting programmers and analysts-type staff members to open up. Many times these individuals need a group around them to get them started. Once started, some very interesting things can come out.
   - Phone interviews. These are not recommended except in cases of different locations.
   - E-mail. This is a creative way to get information. It shouldn't be used as the primary mechanism, but as a supplemental mechanism. The key is hitting the staff in many different ways. This will help to get people to open up.
2. Determine the appropriate degree of accuracy. You don't need to know everything about everybody. The focus on this assessment needs to be on accurately identifying the department's strengths, weaknesses, opportunities, and threats. From this basis, determine who you'll survey/interview, the percentage of coverage, and the depth needed to achieve the needed results.

3. Prepare assessment instruments/diagnostics. Customize the question-naires found in appendix A for your transition initiative. These surveys include:

   — MIS Environment/Technology Profile. This diagnostic only needs to be filled out by the transition team. It shouldn't be disseminated to the general audience. Most of the information asked for in this diagnostic is used later for reference. This diagnostic is simply a convenient device to capture and store this type of information.

   — MIS Organization, Policies, and Strategies. This survey is used to assess the general operations of the MIS department. Of all of the surveys provided in this book, you'll most likely change this survey the most. No organization is the same, and some of the questions asked in this area are politically sensitive. Review this survey carefully. It will at least provide a starting point for the development of your survey.

   — MIS Culture Assessment. This key questionnaire captures the staff members' beliefs about the culture of MIS and the staff members' skills and experiences. It asks questions from both the overall perspective and the individual's perspective. This is another survey that needs to be looked over very carefully. There are some very sensitive questions asked within this survey diagnostic.

   — Skills and Abilities. This diagnostic collects data on the current skill and experience base.

   — Work Practices. This diagnostic is provided in three parts: 6a) Development Work Practices, 6b) Project Management Work practices, and 6c) Maintenance Work Practices. Together, these three parts assess the effectiveness of the current MIS processes. This information will be used in the SE approach and methodology selection activities.

   — MIS/User Relationship. This diagnostic is to be administered to members of the user community. You might want to reverse the questions and use this diagnostic with the MIS staff as well. This way, you'll have both sides of the relationship captured.

     These questionnaires should be considered template material, not the final diagnostic instruments. You'll need to tailor the questionnaires for differences within your organization, such as:

   a. Regional/company nomenclature.
   b. Elimination of sensitive questions.
   c. Elimination of obvious questions.
   d. Addition of questions.

4. Package and copy the customized assessment instruments/diagnostics. Organize the selected sections of the survey into a cohesive package. Add a cover page (a sample in provided in appendix A) to classify the person filling out the questionnaire. Provide a confidentiality statement to the staff and stick to it. Let the staff know exactly how the data will be

used. Remember, any breach of confidence could potentially kill the entire SE/CASE initiative.

5. Identify follow-up interview questions. Create a checklist of questions that you need to personally ask members in the organization.

6. Configure the mechanics to collect and analyze the assessment data. Identify the technique to be used and the tool to capture the data. You might want to consider Lotus or one of the available survey analysis tools on the market today. Please note: The tool you use to collect the data might influence the surveys themselves. Your numbering scheme might need to be changed.

7. Identify/categorize the target audience. Identify specifically who will receive a questionnaire and who will be interviewed.

Task tips.   This is a great task for hiring a consultant to help you. The consultant will be perceived by the staff as neutral and objective. In addition, the consultant will have the distance from your organization to be able to probe into the seemingly obvious, only to find interesting twists.

Make sure that you review all of the surveys carefully, question by question. We've included questions from many different perspectives, at times probing into sensitive areas. Also, make sure that these surveys have been reviewed by the proper authorities before they're sent out. Don't assume that because the questions are in a book that they're so generic that there's nothing to worry about. To be honest, we like to put a little spice into our questions. Our wording might be a bit too much for your particular organization.

3-B. Assess the current development/maintenance environment

Description.   Administer the surveys and assess the results. Provide a statement of the organization's strengths, weaknesses, opportunities and threats.

Rationale.   You can't implement an SE/CASE environment from ground zero, for very few organizations are at ground zero. Every MIS organization has done something in the past. This task attempts to document the relative successes and failures of those past attempts. This knowledge is useful so that the new environment can be tailored to better fit into the existing culture, tools, and work practices.

Work steps.
1. Administer the diagnostics. Disseminate the surveys. One technique that's very useful is to pass out the surveys in a large room. Have the staff fill them out right there. This will provide them an opportunity to

ask questions and will ensure a 100 percent return. Tabulate the responses within the collection tool. Verify that the diagnostic statistical validity is appropriate.

2. Identify key assessment issues and points that need to be verified.

3. Interview users, staff, management.

4. Review related sources such as the MIS policy manual, measurement statistics, turnover, and tenure statistics.

5. Assess/document current work practices. Using the results of Surveys 2, 6a, 6b, and 6c and your interview notes, document the current set of MIS work practices. Assess your coverage of the full development and maintenance life cycle. Compare these results against industry norms. For this task, use a consultant or use the Software Engineering Institute Software Maturity model. This is a one through five rating on how advanced your development and maintenance processes are.

6. Document the current IS culture. Map the questions in the Culture Survey against the cultural dimensions identified in chapter 4. Use the matrix shown in appendix E to identify the appropriate question for each cultural dimension. Provide a summary chart like the one in Figure 7.1. Make a statement about the staff's attitude, morale, and value system.

7. Inventory the current technical capabilities/skills/experiences. Review the results of the survey. Summarize the data into the strengths and weaknesses of the department.

8. Assess the MIS/user-community relationship. Review the survey results and interview notes. Produce a statement about the strength of the relationship and major issues.

9. Summarize and document SWOT items. That's the focus point of this task. The surveys and interview notes will provide the data. In this task, you take this data and turn it into information that will be useful throughout the entire implementation process.

10. Identify implications of SWOT items. Assess and react to the SWOT items. How will these points affect the upcoming implementation?

11. Review/validate findings with IS leadership. Review each of the SWOT items with the leaders and/or management groups. Make sure that everyone is in general agreement with the findings.

12. Present to management/staff.

Task tips. Again, an outside perspective is useful. However, don't be conned by the consultants, this is a task that you can do successfully yourself. It's just that a consultant can do it faster and a bit more objectively.

3-C. Assess the current/future application portfolio

Description. Assess and categorize your current and future applications for technical and functional quality.

Rationale. SE/CASE environments are built for different types of systems. For example, a RAD approach with a CASE front end and a 4GL code engine is best for online applications that are not tightly coupled. On the other hand, for applications that are huge, interconnected, and complex, an information engineering environment complete with an I-CASE tool might be appropriate.

Don't allow yourself to select the SE/CASE environment based on one or two upcoming applications. These might be an abnormality and not the normal operations of the department. By reviewing the existing applications, you'll be able to determine which ones are ready to be redeveloped, reengineered, or restructured. Each of these actions requires a different type of SE/CASE environment. A redeveloped action requires the traditional I-CASE or C-CASE tool and methodology approach. Reengineering requires a code reengineering with an accompanying forward engineering (i.e., I-CASE) tool. The restructured action might only require a few maintenance assistance tools. Reviewing future applications will also provide you with information for future SE/CASE strategy. As someone once said, "There are no new applications these days, only reborn applications."

Work steps.
1. List all current applications. Include in this list the age, language, and business (e.g., financial) importance of each of the applications.

2. Rate the functional and technical quality of each application.
   Functional quality is the fit of the system to the business needs. Does the system do what the users need it to do? *Technical quality* deals with the maintainability and language/platform architectures. How solid is the architecture? Rate the two dimensions on a scale from one to ten; one is low and ten is high.

3. Map the technical quality against the functional quality. Draw a grid with the rating of functional quality being the X-axis and technical quality being the Y-axis. Figure 7.1 shows a sample mapping.

4. Review future IS and user application plans. Estimate the future percentage of development, enhancement, and maintenance activities. Estimate the percent of custom-built, package-selection, transaction-processing, executive-information, decision-support, client-server, and imaging-multimedia applications.

5. Define your SE/CASE strategy. Should the environment be tuned for replacing, restructuring, or reengineering systems?

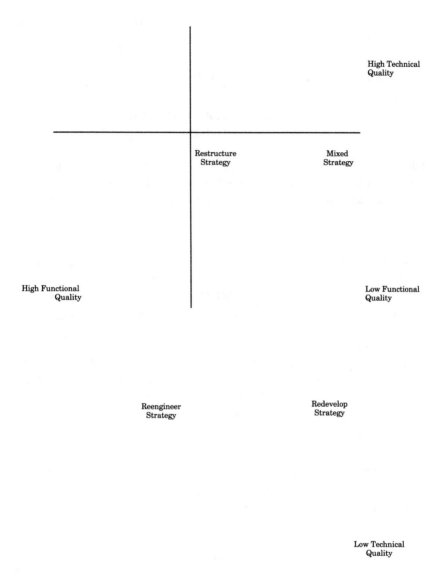

Figure 7.1   Application portfolio view.

Task tips.   Don't shortchange this task. Many people initially feel that they have a good handle on their current application portfolio until it's mapped out on the grid. This picture usually changes their perception of their application reality. I know we're all drawn to the flash and glimmer of the I-CASE solutions to completely redevelop systems from the ground up. However, remember, the "shoe has to fit." Nothing will hurt your implementation success more than an obvious mismatch. Do what's right for the organization, not what's best for your career.

3-D. Review/integrate other planning architectures

Description. Review the corporation's strategic plans for data, processes, and related technology (e.g., DBMS, LAN, platforms). Define how the SE Infrastructure relates to these other planning architectures.

Rationale. You can't define SE/CASE in a vacuum. There are many other factors that go into pulling it all together. This task focuses on integrating the SE/CASE strategy into the other previously discussed strategies for one cohesive strategy and vision.

Work steps.
1. Review the existing planning architectures. Review all planning and budgeting documents. Look at reports and deliverables that focus on data, process, and technology strategies and plans.
2. Surface and resolve interrelated architectural issues. Document any issues or items that could or should relate to SE/CASE. For example, if the company is moving from an IBM platform to a DEC/VAX platform, this will definitely affect the choice of a code generator. Also, if the organization is looking to outsource more development or maintenance, this will affect the methodology and degree of structure needed. Define any architectural solution to the problems.
3. Identify/review other corporate initiatives (e.g., TQM).

3-E. Select the SE approach(es)

Description. Select the appropriate software engineering approach or approaches for your organization. Document your reasons for selecting the SE approach(es).

Rationale. The most important decision in this whole initiative is the selection of the SE approach. This decision provides the ideology that the MIS department will work within for the next three to five years, if not longer. This is the basic approach that will be used to get systems developed and maintained. Thus, this decision needs to be made consciously, and the reasons need to be clearly documented. The staff needs to clearly see the rationale for the selection. All too often, this decision is made by default or by a few managers behind closed doors. In either case, staff support for the decision will be weak or even nonexistent.

Work steps.

1. Review past findings:
   - SWOT items and issues.
   - Percentage of time in maintenance versus development.
   - Types of systems to be developed in the future.
   - Assessment of current culture.

2. Define selection-of-SE-approach criteria. Define the points that will really make a difference in the decision. Map these to the SE objectives identified earlier in this IC/VISION process. Example criteria include:
   - Minimum cultural disruption.
   - Maximum use of user community personnel.
   - Ability to hire staff experienced in the approach.
   - Ability to migrate approach to an object-oriented approach.
   - Technique-based.
   - Modifiable/flexible.
   - Data oriented.
   - Quickest delivery of new systems.

   Please note: These are sample criteria. You'll need to define your own criteria for your specific needs.

3. Review alternative approaches. Review approaches such as information engineering, structured analysis and design, rapid application development, reverse engineering, package software selection, reusable templates, and object-oriented development. Consider combining a few into a hybrid approach.

4. Select the approach. This is a perfect time for a JAD-style session. There are many issues that need to be put on the table and understood by all. A JAD-style session is a great vehicle for achieving the needed consensus for this type of a decision.

5. Document the selection rationale.

3-F. Establish and document the SE/CASE vision

Description. Document the SE/CASE vision in as much detail as needed. The resulting vision statement is in essence the requirements for your SE/CASE environment.

Rationale. Documenting the SE/CASE vision is a crucial factor for the success of the SE/CASE implementation process. Without this deliverable, the SE/CASE initiative will tend to wander around following every new technology that hits the street. A documented vision will help keep the organization focused on your primary goals while still allowing the focus to be dynamic. A documented vision is really a mechanism for change, not a barrier to change.

A documented vision also helps the organization to visualize the final goal. Visualizing a common goal will help the organization to pull together as a team to get the job done. Without this common, visual picture, there will be many different versions of the vision, each an individual interpretation of what was meant. These different interpretations can and have resulted in political infighting.

Work steps.

1. Review management's pain, objectives, and goals.

2. Review the industry vision diagrams/architectures. Talk to industry experts. Get copies of IBM's AD/Cycle diagram and DEC Cohesion diagram. Talk to the I-CASE vendors. They have a slightly narrow viewpoint, but one that at least keeps an organization focused. Read articles and books from standards committees. Join SE/CASE consortiums. Don't reinvent the wheel with the SE/CASE vision. Your focus should be on customizing someone else's vision.

3. Scope your vision. Many of the industry visions listed above cover a wide range of SE/CASE technology, from strategic planning to development to maintenance to project management. Determine where your vision starts and ends. Remember, you're planning this vision for three to five years. Don't be too restrictive. The purpose for this scope statement is be able to confine the number of issues and concerns whenever it gets down to selecting technology. For example, if strategic planning is within the scope of your vision, then whenever you select a data modeling tool, you'll need to look at future strategic planning considerations along with development issues. If strategic planning was not within your scope, then the data modeling decision would be much easier, much less constrained. As the scope widens, the issues "baggage" widens.

4. Set the simplicity/complexity nature of the vision diagram. The vision diagram should be very visual. There should be a diagram that ties all aspects of the full scope together. This overall diagram is a must; it's really not optional. What's optional is how deep and complex the vision needs to get. If it's simple and direct, then this task will be very quick, and communication will be straightforward. The problem with a simple SE/CASE diagram is that it overlooks many important issues that need to be highlighted. It also gives the organization a bit too much rope to interpret the meaning of the high-level vision. You'll need to determine up front how detailed this vision needs to get. A key to determining the level of detail is to first define the objectives and uses of the vision diagram.

5. Customize/create your vision diagram. Using an industry diagram (e.g., AD/Cycle), customize the diagram to fit your organization's view of SE/CASE. Even if you adopt someone else's vision diagram, you should still personalize it. Brand it yours. Name it. Give people an opportunity to react to it.

6. Specify the vision requirements. This task produces the vision statement. A sample of this statement is provided in appendix C. Within this statement are the following types of requirements:

   — Functional requirements. These requirements define specific functions that will be covered by the new SE/CASE environment. At times, a decomposition diagram is used to graphically define these requirements.

   — Operational requirements. These requirements specify the details of the SE/CASE technology. They include:

      a. Recommended development approach(es).
      b. Recommended techniques.
      c. Methodology requirements.
      d. Required tool categories.
      e. Vendor requirements.

   — Technical requirements. These requirements deal with the target and development platforms of the organization. They're often overlooked by many organizations because people assume that everyone knows all of the issues surrounding the different platforms. These requirements never get written down, and wrong assumptions are made.

   — Organizational requirements. SE/CASE will influence the organizational structure. Roles, responsibilities, policies, procedures, and support mechanisms might all need to be changed to some degree. This section of the vision statement lays out these organizational changes.

   — Cultural requirements. These requirements identify the specific cultural dimensions and skills that need to be changed/enhanced in order to support the new paradigm of SE/CASE. In this section, you'll be defining your ideal culture.

Task tips. Treat this task as if the SE/CASE environment were a system and the vision statement the requirements statement. You need to be detailed enough to be able to go out and select the appropriate technology, but not so detailed that everything is written down. Use the sample vision statement in appendix C as a guide to how detailed to make the requirements. Again, this sample report is meant to initiate and spur on requirements. It's not a checklist of all of the possible requirements. The actual size of the vision statement should be around 2 to 25 pages.

3-G. Assess cultural changes introduced by SE/CASE vision

Description. Assess the impact of changes introduced by the new SE/CASE vision on the MIS and user-community culture.

Rationale. As previously pointed out, the impact of SE/CASE on the culture is probably the most crucial challenge that the transition team will face. This task attempts to analyze and quantify this impact.

Work steps.
1. Compare the current culture to the ideal culture. Compare the results of the cultural assessment to the cultural requirements listed in the vision statement. Identify specific issues that are worth noting. Document the significance impact on your organization.

2. Calculate the cultural impact (CIPs) of specific technologies. Using the worksheet found in appendix D, calculate the impact for each of the operational requirements (e.g., tool types) listed in the vision statement. List the results in numerical sequence, with the highest CIP ratings at the top. These results are used for deciding how to implement the technology and later for sequencing the technology implementation.

3. Identify potential pockets of resistance/acceptance. Who in the organization will most likely embrace and who will most likely resist the new changes? You shouldn't identify specific names, but specify the general groups of staff members. If possible, also document the reasons why these groups would support or resist the changes. For example the supporters might include:
   - The Engineering Department. They've been pushing for SE/CASE for the last four years.
   - Newer staff members with less than four years of experience. Many have had the basic concepts in college, and they're eager to get back to this approach.
   - User community management. Being primarily engineering oriented, the new approaches will fit right into management's idea of how to run projects.

   Resisters might include:
   - CICS-seasoned individuals. The new code generator will decrease their relative value. It automatically does most of the screen mapping and related activities.
   - The technical writing staff. There's a perception that SE/CASE will eliminate the need to manually create user and programming documentation. While this is a goal of the SE/CASE vendors, this will probably not happen for five years, but yet this group is still concerned.
   - The DBA group. This group has the most to gain from the new environment, yet they feel threatened. They currently have a data model-

ing tool, and it looks like they might have to give it up in favor of a companywide tool.

4. If appropriate, modify the vision.

3-H. Assess the organization's ability to assimilate change

Description. Determine if the MIS organization can take on this large change effort.

Rationale. Change is not restricted to one department. We're all getting bombarded by change daily. Your organization might be in the midst of remodeling or moving, your pay/performance structure might be changing, you might be currently going through a "right sizing" effort, or your user community might be changing its business direction. Each of these changes could affect an MIS staff member. If all of this change happens at once, you can imagine the potential for disruption. Each of these distractions will negatively affect your SE/CASE change plan. You need to be aware of these other activities and try your best to mitigate and plan around these distractions.

Work steps.
1. Identify other changes that are occurring or are soon to occur. Look for changes within and outside of MIS. These changes could also be outside the organization. For instance, if a major bridge will be closed for a year and the majority of the staff members will need to spend more time on the road each day getting to work, this will have an impact that needs to be assessed.

2. Assess similar past initiatives. Research past initiatives that are similar in scope and nature to SE/CASE implementation. A good example is the implementation of a new DBMS like DB/2. Objectively look at this past initiative and try to identify the barriers that were met. Ask yourself or others the following questions:
   − Did MIS provide appropriate training?
   − Was enough time provided for MIS to assimilate the change?
   − Did management own the initiative?
   − Did management visually support the change?
   − Were the staff members involved enough early on?
   − Was there a lot of politicking going on?
   − Was the implementation plan followed?
   − Were the changes clear to the staff members?
   − Did management do a good job handling resistance?
   − Were people rewarded for moving to the new culture?

   From your responses, identify the areas that were weak. Experience has shown that if an area is weak for one change, chances are that

the same weakness will shine through with a SE/CASE implementation. These areas will be very important whenever you plan for the cultural change.

3. Assess the organization's change management skills. Do you have people who are astute enough to direct a change of this magnitude? This takes a certain type of individual. They need to be able to manage a project, but they also need to be able to handle people. They need to be able to listen, communicate, negotiate, be emphatic, be sincere, and be honest. If you're missing these types of traits within the transition team, either scale back the initiative or get training. These are very important skills.

4. Summarize the organization's ability to assimilate change.

3-I. Define vision implementation approach

Description. Document the way in which the SE/CASE vision will be implemented.

Rationale. This is a planning step to tie all of the pieces together. This step is similar to phasing an application project into subsystems and defining how each will get accomplished.

Work steps.
1. Define implementation approaches. Define the mechanics of making it all happen. Determine the appropriate speed, resources, and phases to implementation.

2. Select an anchor technology that will serve as a base from which to build other supporting technologies. Candidate choices are a systems development methodology, a project management or IPSE tool, the IBM repository, or an I-CASE tool.

3. Determine the sequence of SE/CASE technology implementation. Define which technologies will be implemented when. Document the reasons for the sequence.

4. Define the implementation team structure. Who will be responsible for what?

5. Present the package to management.

3-J. Solidify sponsorship for the vision

Description. Make sure that the SE/CASE vision and the implementation strategies surrounding it are supported by management.

Rationale. Without support, you're dead in the water.

Work steps.

1. Identify/assess the sponsor(s). Who kicked off this initiative and why? Are these same people the driving sponsors now? Are there additional sponsors who have entered the picture? Are these individuals at the right level to be effective sponsors? Do they have the political clout to get things done? In short, what kind of sponsorship do you have?

2. Solicit specific involvement from sponsor(s). Identify when, where, and how the sponsor(s) will be able to provide the needed message, energy, and support for the SE/CASE initiative. Don't just assume that the sponsors will automatically rally to the SE/CASE initiative. They also have other things to do. In addition, defining the types of involvement (e.g., present vision to departmental staff, write justification report) that the sponsors are willing to assume will tell you how committed your sponsors really are.

3. Document the cascading chain of sponsorship. From the initiating sponsors come the sustaining sponsors. Identify this chain. Most likely, the core of project managers will represent the bulk of this lower layer of sponsorship.

4. Educate sponsors—both initiating and sustaining sponsors.

5. Draft a sponsorship declaration. Put the sponsorship in writing. Identify specific commitment to the change. This task will again tell you how committed the sponsors really are.

Stage Four—Planning the Transition

4-A. Develop a strategy for changing culture

Description. Develop a strategy and plan for proactively changing the MIS culture to align with the new SE/CASE paradigm.

Rationale. A culture realignment just doesn't happen because you've defined the ideal culture. You need to put a strategy and plan together to proactively make a change in culture happen.

Work steps.

1. Review cultural assessment components. Review the initial cultural assessment, the Culture Impact Points, and the summary of the organization's ability to assimilate change.

2. Determine the speed of cultural assimilation needed/possible. In essence, how fast can you comfortably push the MIS staff?

3. Identify the critical success factors. Review the factors discussed in chapter 6. Document those that apply to your organization.

4. Identify associated roadblocks. Also review those presented in chapter 6. Document those that apply for your organization.

5. Identify tactics needed to manage the cultural transition. Also review chapter 6 again for specific tactics. Document those that apply for your organization.

6. Package the identified CSFs, roadblocks, and tactics into a cultural change strategy statement.

Task tips.   You really can't do this task without a good understanding of the concepts in chapter 6.

4-B. Develop a training strategy

Description.   Develop a strategy and plan for proactively developing the needed skills to support the new SE/CASE paradigm.

Rationale.   Training and education is a fundamental need for the initiative to be successful. Again, you need to be proactive and integrate the acquired skills with the opportunities to exercise these newly learned skills before they're forgotten.

Work steps.
1. Review/update skill requirements. Review the list from the SE/CASE vision statement.

2. Develop an integrated training curriculum. Update your current education and training curriculum with the classes needed for SE/CASE. Determine the appropriate delivery method(s). Examples include: In-house, consultant lead, CBT, Interactive Video Instruction (IVI), tapes, and/or books.

3. Define training support mechanisms. Determine the role that certification and testing will play within your organization. Determine the official role for the coach or mentor position. Decide if you'll use official or informal coaches. Identify the mechanisms to monitor to gauge the attainment and use of skills (e.g., skills inventory database).

4. Solidify the training budget.

Task tips.   Get your training department involved very early on. However, don't let them completely drive the effort. It needs to be an integrated effort.

4-C. Develop a pilot strategy

Description.   Describe how technology pilots will be run during the SE/CASE initiative.

Rationale. You'll need to prove the new concepts to the organization and to yourself. This task provides the proof you'll need.

Work steps.
1. Determine the role and objectives of the pilot(s). Document how and why technology pilots will be used.
   Potential objectives include:
   — To validate new technology/concepts.
   — To learn about new technology.
   — To learn how to best implement new technology.
   — To initiate momentum.
   — To train core staff members.

2. Identify potential technology pilots. List the characteristics that you'd like in the pilot. Suggestions include:
   — A real project—not a disposable activity.
   — Mainline activity/technology—stuff that your organization does often.
   — Visibility—something that gets people's attention.
   — Low project risk/urgency. If something goes wrong, there needs to be room to maneuver.
   — Medium to small size—but not too small.
   — A limited user involved.
   — A project staffed with MIS technology leaders.
   — A project staffed with enthusiasm.
   — An environment where you can fail and learn.
   — The ability to measure success.
   — Provides the opportunity to stage technology implementation.
   — Identify specific pilot projects that best meet those criteria.

4-D. Define each transition project

Description. Define the specifics of each of the transition projects identified earlier.

Rationale. In order to create a three- to five-year transition plan and schedule, you'll need to know how long each specific transition project will take. To get an accurate estimate, the specific activities of each project need to be defined.

Work steps.
1. Identify transition projects. Review the operational and organizational requirements identified in the SE/CASE Vision Statement. Package into transition projects. The following is a partial list of potential transition projects:
   — Select/implement an SDM.
   — Select/implement an ICASE tool.

- Define/implement a quality assurance function.
- Create/implement a measurement program.
- Review/update job descriptions to reflect SE/CASE.
- Select/implement a macro-level estimating tool/technique.
- Educate the user community on JAD techniques.
- Package/implement a programmer's workbench.
- Implement a Corporate Data Administration Function.
- Prepare for the IBM Repository.
- Investigate Expert System Shells for future use.
- Establish a development center.

2. Define each project. Include:
   - Scope.
   - Description.
   - Rationale/objectives.
   - High-level work plan (5 to 10 tasks).
   - Who to get involved.
   - Rough estimate (effort and schedule).

Task tips.   Keep the definitions at a relatively high level. Remember, the intent is to be able to estimate the transition project, not to do it.

4-E. Sequence the transition projects

Description.   Define the appropriate sequence for the transition projects.

Rationale.   There are a lot of interdependencies that need to be considered to effectively sequence the transition projects.

Work steps.
1. Group the projects/activities. Package the transition projects that seem to belong together.

2. Ientify and integrate pilot projects. Match the list of candidate pilot projects with the transition projects. Identify the appropriate timing of the pilots.

3. Discuss involvement issues. Identify any timing concerns for those who are to staff the transition projects.

4. Sequence the projects.

5. Identify short-term improvement opportunities. Document any immediate, crucial needs that can be easily solved without a full transition project. Identify and estimate these short-term actions.

4-F. Create a long-term implementation plan

Description. Create a schedule of events to complete the SE/CASE Vision.

Rationale. A long-term initiative like SE/CASE has to have a plan in order to progress and achieve the stated goals.

Work steps.
1. Determine the implementation horizon. How long will the plan be for? Typical implementation plans run for three to five years.
2. Develop a GANTT chart of activities. See Figure 6.2 for a sample GANTT chart.

4-G. Develop a marketing plan

Description. Develop a plan to sell the SE/CASE vision and implementation plan.

Rationale. Just because SE/CASE seems like the best thing since sliced bread, don't assume that everyone will instantly buy into the concept. These individuals need to be sold on the relative merits of the new technology.

Work steps.
1. Define the message of the marketing program. Define the basic message that you need to tell the staff and the user community. Set your marketing objectives. Define how you're trying to change the perceptions of these individuals.
2. Stratify the audience. Analyze and categorize your target audience. Much like a car manufacturer categorizes their marketplace, you need to know who you're selling to.
3. Personalize the message for each group. Make the benefits of SE/CASE readily apparent to these different groups. Remember, not every group will appreciate every benefit. Put yourself in their place. Which of the benefits would appeal to you and why?
4. Identify the available communication vehicles (e.g., newsletters) and tie-in events (e.g., presentations, seminars).
5. Produce presentation materials. Produce some clean, high-quality marketing materials to be used for different presentations. The more canned "stuff" you have to use, the better. Not that you'll use all of the marketing materials at every opportunity, but the materials will allow you to better tune the message for different audiences.

6. Integrate the marketing activities with the activities on the implementation project work plan.

7. Document the marketing plan/strategies.

Stage Five—Selecting SE/CASE Technology

5-A. Define selection process and committees

Description. For the specific technology at hand, define the appropriate mechanics to select and implement the products.

Rationale. Not every technology transition project will be the same. Each project might need to be run differently.

Work steps.
1. Define the selection process.

2. Define and identify specific transition team members.

5-B. Develop selection criteria

Description. For the technology at hand, define the selection criteria.

Rationale. Each technology will most likely have a different set of criteria for selection.

Work steps.
1. Review other transition project selection criteria. Don't reinvent the wheel each time. Look at and use others' criteria. Customize it for the technology at hand.

2. Define the criteria.

3. Map the criteria to the SE objectives.

4. Prioritize the criteria.

5-C. Evaluate alternatives

Description. For the technology at hand, evaluate alternative solutions.

Rationale. All options need to be fairly considered.

Work steps.
1. Identify a short list of candidates. Identify the most likely products. Use the base criteria for selection. Don't allow yourself to look at more than a handful of products. If you get beyond looking at more than four or five

products, you'll begin to go numb. This is a good area for a consultant to get involved in. Most will be able to give you the top three to five tools after reviewing your SE/CASE Vision Statement.

2. Produce Request For Quotes (RFQ). Based on the requirements in the SE/CASE vision statement, create a list of features, functions, and benefits you expect. Put this list in writing and send it to the candidate vendors. Ask them to respond to your requirements in writing. An RFQ structure based on your needs will help you to compare apples to apples. If you leave it up to the vendor, you'll be left comparing apples to oranges.

3. Schedule vendor demos/benchmarks. Do these demos on your terms. Try to schedule the major two or three in the same week. This keeps you from forgetting what the other vendor said or did. Again, if the list is beyond three or four, you'll start to get confused in this process.

4. Involve management, staff, and users. Involve as many people as possible. Make sure that evaluations and reactions from the participants are in writing. Don't lose this valuable insight.

5. Select appropriate technology. Make a decision as fast as possible. Don't allow the decision to linger on unmade for a great length of time.

6. Document the rationale for selecting the specific technology.

5-D. Pilot the selected technology

Description.   Run a pilot test of the selected technology.

Rationale.   This is based on the objectives identified in the pilot strategy task earlier.

Work steps.

1. Review and approve the pilot project(s).

2. Define the criteria for success. How will you know if you're successful? These criteria need to be broader than the traditional on-time, within budget, and according to specifications. These criteria need to reflect the objectives identified in the pilot strategy tasks defined earlier.

3. Select the pilot team members. Remember the importance of this first step. Select the best staff members that you can.

4. Train the team in new technology.

5. Arrange for coaching support. Contact a consultant who's expert in the next technology. This person will be very helpful getting you through the tough times. This consultant doesn't have to be full-time. One day a week is plenty of help for most technology pilots. By not having the coach

around all of the time, you force the pilot team to really learn the new technology.

6. Adjust the technology and/or the culture. One of the objectives of conducting pilot projects is to learn how to better implement the technology. Use this information to your best advantage.

7. Document lessons learned. A pilot is truly a learning experience. Leverage the insight gained across the whole organization by writing it all down.

5-E. Create a technology-specific implementation plan

Description.   For the technology at hand, create a specific implementation plan.

Rationale.   Each technology is different and needs to be treated differently.

Work steps.
1. Schedule technology training.

2. Arrange for vendor support.

3. Identify and plan for technology-specific implementation items.

Stage Six—Deploying SE/CASE

6-A. Implement a support infrastructure

Description.   Implement the mechanics necessary to support the transition to SE/CASE.

Rationale.   The transition to SE/CASE needs support. It will not sustain itself.

Work steps.
1. Implement an integrated reward system. Define the components to reward and how to reward.

2. Revise the organizational structure (e.g., matrix, straight line) to best support SE/CASE.

3. Review and enhance the internal communication channels. Review both the formal and the informal channels. Define needed changes.

4. Recruit and hire "culture seed." Identify and hire those individuals who possess the required skills and cultural attitude.

5. Train internal staff to be better change agents.

6-B. Maintain implementation momentum

Description. Help to focus and fortify the department's momentum towards reaching the SE vision.

Rationale. Again, momentum doesn't sustain itself. It needs to be managed.

Work steps.
1. Monitor resistance. Put together a survey to ask the staff how the specific implementation is going. Reassess the staff every couple of months. Schedule "gripe sessions" to allow the staff to express their views.

2. Proclaim the successes. As pilot projects start to show the fruits of the technology, document the results and let the organization know the benefits.

3. Execute the marketing plan.

4. Execute the culture change tactics.

5. Manage the sponsorship. Talk to the sponsors often. Keep these individuals as up-to-date as possible.

6-C. Adjust vision periodically

Description. Make modifications to the SE Vision Statement as appropriate.

Rationale. The vision was not meant to be static—just the opposite. By documenting the vision, you're now positioned to properly assess the impact of changes and to comfortably make the changes.

Work steps.
1. Establish a mechanism to update the vision. Determine who will monitor for changes and who has authority to approve changes. Determine a medium to maintain the master.

2. Periodically review the effectiveness of the selected tools, approach, and culture.

3. Make the appropriate changes to the SE/CASE Vision Statement.

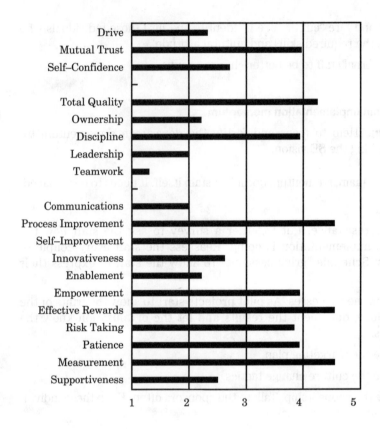

Assessment Results

(1=High, 5=Low)

Figure 7.2. MIS culture profile, XYZ Corporation.

Chapter

8

Looking Forward

We'd like to share with you some final thoughts, especially in light of all the changes we've been reading about in some of America's most recognizable names in business and industry. Clearly, many businesses are undergoing what might be called a de-layering of their corporate structures. The thinking is that this will make the organization more responsive and able to adapt to the changing needs of the marketplace and ever-changing technology. With this de-layering, the height of the vertical line in the organization will shorten, which will "flatten" most organizations, and that in turn will affect how CASE implementation projects will be handled.

This structural change in organizations will bring senior management, at least as far as proximity is concerned, much closer to where the technological changes are actually taking place. The benefit of that should be that the old "out- of- sight, out- of- mind" mentality that has prevailed in so many organizations will disappear (especially concerning "technical" things that nontechnical executives don't understand). That should help force leaders to get "educated" on things that heretofore they've "hired" done.

It will also help to bring the IS departments more into the family of the rest of the organization. In a flattened organization, the opportunities to more fully participate in the general strategic direction of the entire organization should be greatly enhanced. It should force more direct communication and team efforts between IS and other departments.

This de-layering phenomenon should serve notice on IS management to prepare their staff for:

- Much closer scrutiny than they've probably been used to.
- An increased sharing of their skills with others in the organization.

The old "if I can do it and you can't, I have power over you" routine is not going to wash in organizations of the future.

The traditional role of many IS people has been that of technical expert and not strategic partner. We believe that's about to change. There are clear indications that what the leading-edge organizations are starting to look for are people who can function across a much wider range of issues and not be significantly limited because of their "technical" bent.

This latest change in management philosophy means that as we look for people to work in the IS areas, we're going to have to be looking for those who could possibly mature into other assignments, or else we might be hiring people whose future advancement opportunities could be severely limited.

Another effect of all this is that if our hiring practices change in the way we're anticipating, you could see a positive effect come out of this because people could rotate out of IS for growth, either upward or horizontally, and then can come back to IS at some point in the future. This could mean that rather than losing people to the competition, you could temporarily lose them to other opportunities within the company, but still expect to get a nice "return" when they come back sometime in the future. This means we're going to have to be willing to "let go" of some people to be able to keep them. This could be a nice problem to have.

Another clear paradigm that's starting to develop on a wider and wider scale is that of an increased effort to make "inclusion" an ongoing and everyday part of the idea of participative management. For so many years in this country, the vertical nature of organizations has had a "top-down" effect on how decisions are made and distributed. The increasing need to get the organization to be more responsive and time sensitive has driven the issue of participation home in many organizations.

The participative management process has been resisted at all levels in many different organizations, but clearly it's resisted most where there's a perceived "threat" to the power structure of the organization. No place has this been more evident than in the ranks of middle management.

At several levels this is easy to understand. It's perceived to be more efficient simply to just tell people what to do and be done with it. In fact, some still argue that all this participation stuff takes more time than it's worth. Also, many reward systems in companies are designed is such a way that telling people what to do is the only way to get the reward. Some of this might be culture based. The higher-ups got to where they are using this system, therefore it gets reinforced by them, and those trying to climb the corporate ladder see this system as the way to get ahead.

What management is beginning to understand is that investment and ownership by most people in the organization has the effect of tapping a heretofore untapped gold mine of ideas, effort, and commitment to the success of the company. The best way to get that feeling of ownership and investment is to participate in the decision-making process.

A world-class participative management process:

- Asks for input.

- Manages the expectations of those giving ideas by making sure they realize that theirs is but one piece of input.

- Makes clear who the decision maker is.

- Reports back the decision made from the input, not by memorandum or videotape, but through the person who solicited the input in the first place. This provides an opportunity for questions and allows for again thanking those who do provide input.

- Asks for ideas again in the future.

Another barrier to this shift has been that historically we've rewarded management for giving orders and not coaching and facilitating job performance. What must happen if this paradigm is going to change is that the reward for treating the employee as a "volunteer" and getting things done through motivating and coaching will have to be higher than the reward for telling people what to do.

This shift or attempted shift will mean that there must be many people educated on how to deal with people in a much different way than they're used to. Today this shift is meeting with a lot of resistance, and it will take a determined effort on the part of senior management to make it work.

With the flattening of organizations, this shift will have the added effect of integrating the IS technical professional and manager into many other facets of running the organization, facets that they previously had not been inclined to or had not been invited to. So, the idea of inclusion will definitely have an effect on the IS professional move into the mainstream of the organization.

Another subject that's getting much attention is empowerment. The difficulty is that there's a general impression that the organization can empower its own people. This simply is not true. The choice to act or not act as an empowered person is made by the individual, not the company. The company can provide an empowering environment for people who choose to be empowered, but the company can't actually empower people.

The reality of all that means there will be some people who choose not to act as empowered persons. In some positions that might be alright. The concern has to be that if there's a major effort to get people to assume responsibility and accountability to make the organization more responsive, you might have people in the organization who will have to be replaced because they won't assume responsibility for their own empowerment. This is a hard reality in some organizations, but a reality nonetheless.

The secret to this issue is in the reward systems that are present in the organization. Whether you're talking about participation or empowerment, the reward systems, both formal and informal, must be structured to support participation and empowerment. You can't ask for risk takers in a culture that fails to reward risk takers.

Over the years there have been many things that have had either positive or negative effects on the outcome of major change projects in organizations. We'd would like to give you the latest thinking (from our experience and others) about what the factors are that you must pay particular attention to.

The first and by far still considered the most important is the support and commitment of management, especially at the top. This concerns senior management's long-term commitment and "ownership" of the project. The issue relates not only to the existence of the commitment, but also the "visibility" of that commitment. Rhetoric is not enough; it has to be backed up by actions that the organization can see and interpret as supportive of the change.

This also means that there must be accountability for the results, not only at the senior level, but also at the middle-manager level. At the senior level, there must be both a modeling of the behavior needed for success, and an assurance that others in the organization do so as well.

The leadership must be seen as coming not just from the CEO and/or staff, but from the "management team." The line managers must be seen as being in charge, and not somebody from Human Resources or from outside consultants. This last point can't be emphasized enough. We've seen many projects get only "lip service" from middle management, thereby thwarting or at least severely hampering the effort. There must be buy-in at that middle level to achieve the maximum amount of success.

Also on the list of positive impact factors is making sure that there's adequate up-front planning and preparation before the actual change is undertaken. Part of that preparation is to use a process from which a "shared vision" can be constructed. Developing "ownership" to the lowest levels of the organization still continues to be a crying need in most organizations.

As a part of the need for adequate preparation, the development of "realistic" time schedules and "next steps" is also very important. To get realistic time frames, the current and anticipated work loads have to be understood and taken into consideration, and the project has to be given high enough priority that other things can wait.

When someone's plate is already full and you come along and put something else on it, you can expect resistance. At the very least, you're going to have to prioritize the order in which things have to be done. It doesn't work anymore to tell people to "do it all" because they can't and won't.

How many times have you heard in the organization the question, "Well, what are the next steps?" People work better when they have a road map of where this is all headed, and the sponsors of the project must provide this road map.

Equally important in this area is the need to do a thorough and complete diagnosis of where the organization is before going ahead. A comprehensive implementation plan can't be completed until the organization's current position can be determined and then compared to where it needs to be.

Too many times, advocates for change, in their enthusiasm to get things accomplished, either embellish or underestimate the amount of resources necessary for the project. There's hardly anything that will kill a change faster than unexpectedly high invoices compared to what the sponsor anticipated. When "selling" a project, the rule has to be to tell it like it is, with no surprises. You must not sell the "bells and whistles" of change; you've got to sell the real cost of change.

As part of providing resources, the sponsors and management of the project must be forthcoming with any training that's necessary either to understand the change or to be able to produce the change. We've seen a number of projects where the change required new skills for the project to be a success, but the cost of the training had not been anticipated as a part of the resource requirement.

Finally, under the heading of successful preparation, the roles and responsibilities at each level must be spelled out very clearly. Once this is done, we would even go so far as to say that if something comes up that had not been specifically assigned, the attitude on the part of everyone is that it's their job until otherwise notified. Successful change in today's organization requires that the "functional silos" that have existed in organizations are going to have to disappear if the company is going to be responsive.

The third important area that can have a positive impact on the success of change is employee participation. The evidence now is incontrovertible that the more you make people a part of the decision-making and implementation process, the higher the investment and ownership they have, the more successful the change is going to be.

It's important to make sure that the involvement starts at the beginning stages of the project. If you wait too long, it gives the appearance that either employee participation was not that important or that it was an afterthought. There are more good ideas buried down in your organization than you would ever believe. It's just a matter of providing the vehicle for them to surface and be of benefit.

As projects unfold, it's just as important to get input along the way as it was at the beginning. The tendency is to get the input on the front end, then not ask again. If the reward systems in the organization are innovative, you'll continue to get a stream of innovative ideas from all levels.

Managers who feel threatened by ideas from those who work for them will not support this effort unless top management builds it into the managers' reward system. This then becomes a matter for senior executives to exercise great diligence toward.

A last point with regard to participation is that wherever possible you should make every effort to let people from all levels of the organization assume leadership responsibilities. Many times, the experience and training to assume some leadership responsibility is there, but it's never used. Use it!

The next positive impact area is the effective and continuous use of good communication during the life of the project. The need seems to be especially great from the top down, but we believe that it's equally as important bottom-up and horizontally. The top-down communication is important if for no other reason than to reassure the organization of the "top's" ongoing support.

There are several other aspects of the communication issue that bear discussion. First, the evidence is now overwhelming that the best way to communicate is not by memorandum or videotape, but in person. The flow of communication should be through the management structure and not around it through some mechanical or paper device.

Middle management who are a part of the communication system have to buy into the change. If they don't, they become a part of the problem and not the solution. Their role in communication becomes one of "messenger" rather than "owner" and participant. The effective communication systems in the organizations we've seen have managers as conduits. They're able to do this because everybody in the management structure has been a part of a participative management system as well.

Having had the chance to question and give input, management in the middle must step up or step out. No organization can long afford management team members who aren't fully invested in the messages they're asked to carry. We know that this is tough, but the consequences of this problem are so far-reaching and devastating that it can't be any other way.

We're strong proponents of the strategy of celebrating your victories. Nothing will silence the naysayers of projects faster than public celebration of progress. This presupposes that in the planning process you've provided benchmarks and milestones that can be measured. If you have, at each juncture you should be letting people know about your success.

This advice goes for letting people outside of the organization know of your successes as well. Customers, suppliers, and other significant contributors to how well your business does should have the benefit of this information. When you're celebrating progress, why wouldn't you want the whole world to know? You would!

Another factor is communication between groups who are working on different parts of the project. By keeping each other informed of what's happening and how it's going, team members provide an ongoing stream of valuable information that allows for course corrections to be made effectively and efficiently. Much time and effort can be conserved by team members just keeping each other abreast of where they are in their part of the process and of any unexpected problems that might affect other areas.

A final suggestion in this area would be to get representatives of the various elements of the project together on a predetermined schedule. Communication also means coordination, and this is the best way we've seen it done.

The most effective way to get both input and buy-in to a project is to visibly link it to current business-related issues, so that it's evident that the change is tied strongly to a business-related need. This has the effect of making the change a visible, logical activity that makes sense to people in the overall context of what's going on in the organization.

Being able to show the congruency of the program with the needs of the organization is one thing, but another key element is that as there's a greater and greater feeling of ownership on the part of the employees, the congruency should be among the employees as well because of their increased investment in all that happens inside the company.

We know that it probably seems as though we've put an awful lot of emphasis on the idea of employee participation to increase ownership and investment, but the evidence has become overwhelming that the real winners are seeing this as a key element in their future success.

The best way to see your results in this area of tying change to business-related needs is tying the program directly to behaviors that you want to see on the job, and to results. When the measure of the change can be taken through observable behaviors, it then becomes something that everyone has evidence of; it's not just someone's word that things are changing. Differences in behavior are probably the most visible measurements of change. Use them!

A lot of good change projects fail because they're seen as "change du jours." There are so many changes or directives that come and go, often without follow-through, that after a while the effect is to teach the employees to ignore many, if not all, of the directives they get. This happens because the change is seen as a program or a specific executive's pet project, rather than a part of the way you do your business.

You need to make every effort to make the strategic change projects look "seamless" with the way the organization does its business; change projects should not look like just another program. A lot of times the reaction to programs is, "If we wait long enough, this too shall pass."

One final thing that can have a crucial, positive impact on your change is building a reward system that supports the change or changes you're trying to make. Reward systems tend to get overlooked or ignored. They get overlooked because the organization often isn't aware of how important it is for the reward systems to be reviewed and aligned with the change requirements. They get ignored because companies try to hedge their bets by changing their rhetoric, but leaving the old reward system in place.

The idea behind leaving the old system in place is somewhat understandable, but it's counterproductive. Old reward systems are often seen as what got you whatever measure of success you've previously accomplished, and therefore you're reluctant to change them. The problem is that the reward systems must align with the change because if you give people the option of responding to your new rhetoric or complying with the reward system, they'll comply with the prevailing reward system every time.

A part of your reward system should include ways to recognize people for their active and positive participation. A lot of times managers think that people should do these things just because they work for the company, and employees will do a lot of things for that reason. However, when you're asking people to make significant and difficult changes, you need to establish special ways of recognizing effort towards that goal.

A part of any reward system is for the employees to understand what's in it for them. They need to understand what the change will do for their company, but even more importantly, they need to understand it at the micro level. How are they going to be better off on their job?

In looking at our research and the research done throughout the 1980s and into the early 1990s, the crucial, significant issues have been pretty consistent, with one exception. The increasing emphasis on participation by more and more people has emerged significantly. Nowhere was this more evident than in our review of the factors that have the most negative impact on the success of organizational change.

The first will surely not come as any surprise, since it's just the opposite of what was at the top of the positive list. The subject is management support. This topic, when weighted with others in the negative list, was clearly at the top. However the top three negative factors were more closely bunched together than the three at the top of the positive list.

We could only conclude that, over time, management support as a positive influence has remained clearly the leader on that side of things. However, management support and the two other issues we're going to talk about, management forcing change and management behaviors being inconsistent with their rhetoric, will become indistinguishable in their impact over time if the pattern continues.

The visible lack of commitment by the CEO heads this category as well. That position and how it's perceived is very important to the success of change projects. The appearance of or the fact of an apparent disagreement between the CEO and the senior management team got a lot of mention as well. The CEO must treat everyone, including the remainder of the senior management team, as targets of the change first. If you don't ever get past the resistance of senior management, you'll never make them advocates or agents or, better yet, supporting sponsors of a change.

This is another good reason why you should use the management structure as the communication vehicle. If there's resistance somewhere in that system, it will hopefully have a chance to surface and be dealt with when they're asked to carry the message.

There are some companies where members of the management team openly work against the desired changes. This is allowed to go on in the name of participative management. What you have to remember is that there's a point at which this behavior becomes destructive and not participative. Someone, usually the CEO, at some point has to say the decision is made, now let's get on with it. When the time for input is over and everyone has had their reasonable opportunity to have their say, it's time to either get with the program or decide to work somewhere else. As strong as that sounds, we've found that it's the only way that today's organizations are going to be able to meet the changing demands that are put upon it. This same philosophy applies to middle management also. There's no need to repeat it here, other than to say that what applies to the senior team applies all the way down the line.

The second most crucial subject on the negative impact side is that of management trying to force a change down the organizational gullet. I remember how it used to irk me when it came time for the United Way Fund drive. I had nothing against giving to the United Way, but the way the company went about it made it obvious that they were mostly interested in their community image and the percentage of participation they got. It was top down, with very little or no selling. Sound familiar?

There are probably a lot of things that could again be said here, but we don't feel like beating a dead horse. Suffice it to say that the clear message for running the company of the future is not to try to run it by force, but by inclusion.

Next on this list is a subject that ties back well with our discussion of the reward systems. Management's inconsistency between actions and words ranks right up there at the top in terms of negative impact. "Do as I say, not as I do" doesn't work anymore. The sooner you get that message throughout the management organization, the faster the progress will be. However, we find that the reason that it still goes on is that the reward system for managers either allows it or encourages it. That behavior won't change until the reward system changes.

One of the negative impact issues that didn't show up in its opposite on the positive side is having unrealistic expectations. You probably didn't get to where the company is today overnight, and you're certainly not going to change it dramatically overnight either. Pain does drive change, but if you try to push the cure too fast, the cure might be worse than the illness.

Another unrealistic expectation that we run into a lot, and we've alluded to this previously, is that of a "silver bullet." There's no such thing as a quick fix when you're talking about long-term, substantive change. No consultant, no change program can provide that for you or even tell you how to do it yourself. It's long, time-consuming, and expensive to turn most of these great organizations in a different direction, and everyone needs to understand that.

Closely allied to this is an unrealistic view of the amount of resources that it's going to take to get the job done. Advocates would generally like to get it done no matter what it costs, while the CEO would like to get it done at the least possible cost. There's probably a middle ground in there somewhere, but if the change is a must, then everyone has to be ready, willing, and able to pay the price if it's that important.

We've worked with a lot or organizations where, with its announcements, management raised the hopes of a lot of people about what needed to be done and what management was going to do about it. Managers are sometimes surprised at the level of understanding that a lot of employees already have about some of the problems that an organization has.

In this scenario, when change pronouncements are made, they come with almost a sigh of relief that finally somebody is going to do something about the problems that employees have known about for a long time. However, if what management is saying is just out of desperation to "say something," they'd be better off not saying anything.

Dashed hopes aren't a new phenomenon in many companies. Too many projects have been started and then never heard from again. As we've said before, it doesn't take long before you teach your people to ignore what they're hearing because they have no faith that any substantial follow-through will take place. Be realistic in what you say you're going to do, and let the employees help you do it.

Another in the list of the eight most crucial issues that will negatively impact organizational change is a feeling that employee participation is superficial. Sometimes this happens because it's expected that the CEO has the job of changing the company and he should do it. In this case, there's no effort made by the senior management team to involve people because they believe this is the job of management.

In other cases, senior management believe only they are in a position to formulate answers to the company problems and therefore they don't include the rest of the organization. Finally, we see situations where the facade of participation is put up when everyone already knows that the decisions have already been made and the participative process is a waste of time.

People do want to help! We've seen evidence of this over and over again. They want the executives and the company to be a success, and they want to participate in bringing that about, but not if participation is meaningless. If the decisions had to be made by upper management for whatever reason, just say it and get on with it. If there's a way to let people help formulate the answers and be meaningfully involved, then do that. Just be sure to call it what it is.

One note to those of you who work in an environment where there's a union. Get the union involved in the beginning. There are still a number of places where the we-they mentality exists between management and the union, and we understand that. What we see that we don't understand is acting as if the union doesn't exist. We're seeing more cooperation and less adversarial relationships than ever before in America's businesses. Employee representation units can be a strong ally if you'll let them.

In our review of the positive issues, we talked about the need for good communication and tying the change strongly to business-related issues. So, it should come as no surprise that poor communication and the lack of a clear purpose for a change program show up on the negative side. We don't see a need to restate all of that, which leaves just one last subject from our list, and that's placement of responsibility for getting the change accomplished.

High on the list of criticisms is when the execution of tasks is delegated too much to staff or consultants. A certain amount of that is understood, but in excess it again gives the appearance of a lack of commitment at the top because they're not willing to invest their own time in the project.

Using outside consultants when it's believed that the resources exist internally can be another sore subject. The decision to use outside people should be discussed and explained long before they show up on your doorstep. We've been put in the position of arriving as the "enemy" and not as a helpful resource. This is uncomfortable for both parties, and it's an unneeded problem.

Have you ever found yourself in the position of trying to get to the bottom of something by trying to get to the decision maker and not being able to get there or even identify who that person is? Clear lines of responsibility and accountability need to be drawn so that all concerned know where the resources are.

There's one last thing we should mention in this area, and that's putting someone in charge of a project who lacks credibility in the organization. You need to choose your champions carefully because in all likelihood you're going to be asking people to follow this person through some rough times. It's important that people will follow this person and that the leader can lead.

So there you have them, the six positive and eight negative issues that have the most impact on the success of your change. If you give these 14 things the required attention, you'll already be a long way towards success in your organization's transformation.

Over the years the approach to making change happen has taken many forms. In our work with CASE projects, we've found that a systematic approach to implementation is as important as the CASE tools and methodology. With that in mind, we'd like to share with you a system for implementing change.

In the years that Jim has worked with organizations all over the world, he has done consulting and research to put together a system for implementation that could be customized to the needs of each organization. What he developed is called Organizational Change Implementation Design Systems (ORCHIDS).

ORCHIDS is designed to provide a framework within which the universal principles of change management can be applied while developing an implementation plan in a seven-step process that's tailored to the specific needs of a particular organization. ORCHIDS is not a lock-step approach to the planned implementation of change. Experience has proven that each organization is unique in the way it does its business. This program was designed to accommodate differences in companies and to encourage incorporating that uniqueness into the plan. The system was designed from successful experiences in many companies.

The ONE-DAY PROGRAM is designed to educate the participants. It will give participants an extensive overview of the principles of planned implementation of change. Participants are interviewed by telephone in advance of the program to get a list of their needs and objectives. These are incorporated by the presenting consultant into the discussion during the day. Every effort is made to tailor the session to the needs of the audience.

The TWO-DAY PROGRAM is designed as a working session. It's particularly well designed for teams working on a change project. Teams should be from three to five people and should include the change sponsor whenever possible. The two-day session can also be designed for up to 35 individuals working on separate change issues.

Participants have the opportunity to do a diagnosis of five crucial areas related to their particular change. They can work to the point of being able to prepare a preliminary implementation plan. The presenting consultant will work with each team during the session to provide individual help where it's needed.

The EXECUTIVE SESSION is designed for transformational leaders or sponsors of change. These are usually two- to four-hour sessions for senior-level executives. They give an overview of the entire ORCHIDS approach, and discussions are centered around the leaders' key roles in the change process.

All of the programs have a segment in them we call "68." That's the discussion of the six positive and eight negative impact issues that we've already presented in this book.

The "Seven Steps to Successful Change" process is used to construct the strategy for change implementation. The seven steps include:

1. Definition. Defining clearly what needs to change means at all levels affected by the change. The definition must take into account the "ripple" effect across functional lines. Any proposed change must be accounted for in its effect on the other parts of the organization.

2. Options. The best possible options must be developed with the broadest participation among those who will be asked to make changes in

how or what they do. Options must be considered in light of their ability to be implemented.

3. Diagnosis and benchmarking. It's important to know the current state of the organization. The diagnosis includes implementation history, sponsorship, resistance, change agents, and culture. The organization is "benchmarked" on these and other issues deemed crucial by the organization.

4. Gap analysis. Once the change needs are defined and the benchmarking is completed, the gap between where you are and where you want to be becomes clearer. This process helps everyone understand the magnitude of the job ahead.

5. Plan development.This step uses all of the information in steps one through four to prioritize tasks and assign responsibility. Time frames for the successful completion of the change must also be established. A preliminary implementation plan is designed. This step will decide how to close the gaps.

6. Plan progress reviews. With the crucial areas benchmarked, it's important to monitor and track the progress of the project. The crucial piece in this step is to be able to measure the progress of various elements of the change. This can be done because measurable result indicators will have been built into the process. This step also allows for needed adjustments to be made to the implementation plan.

7. Final analysis. This is a lessons-learned and final evaluation step. Every change project has with it lessons that will make the next project more successful. It pays high dividends to look back and see what worked, what didn't, and why. The analysis results should be made an ongoing part of the leadership development program in the organization.

Three lessons stand out from our years of experience. Lesson one is that pain/cost drives change. Lesson two is that there's no such thing as a "quick fix." Finally, lesson three reminds us that it will take tremendous commitment, especially at the top, for change strategies to be successful.

The challenge of change never stops. Today's organizations are always going to be in a constant state of transition. It will be the "adaptive" organization that will survive. We look forward to working with those companies who have the vision to see a future, and the commitment to make it happen.

SE/CASE Assessment

SE/CASE ASSESSMENT

Number: _____   Date: ___ / ___ / ___

Company Name: _____

Location: _____

Position: ____   MIS Management
              ____   Project Manager/Leader
              ____   Analyst
              ____   Programmer

              ____   _____

Amount of MIS Experience: ____ years

Length of Company Service: ____ years

INSTRUCTIONS

This questionnaire is part of the assessment phase of the SE/CASE Transition Project. It is used to gather facts and opinions about the current MIS development and maintenance environments in our organization. Follow-up interviews may be scheduled with you for more in-depth information concerning relevant areas highlighted by this questionnaire.

Please answer each question as honestly and accurately as possible. For a "range-type" (e.g. 1 - 5) answer, simply circle the appropriate number. On "selection-type" answers, check the appropriate choice(s). If you do not understand or know the answer to a question, check "Unknown". Do not leave any questions blank.

All individual responses will remain confidential. Only summarized information will be provided to management.

RETURN TO: _____ BY __/__/__

1 - SE/CASE READINESS DISCUSSION GUIDE

A - MOTIVATION

1.1   What are the primary reasons for considering SE/CASE?

1.2   How effective is MIS with the following:

        a) Establishing priorities
        b) Planning projects
        c) Delivering on schedule
        d) Delivering within cost estimate
        e) Training MIS staff
        f) Training users
        g) Understanding the business needs
        h) Designing solutions/systems to meet user needs
        i) Building the right systems
        j) Communicating progress against plans
        k) Maintaining existing systems
        l) Converting systems to new platforms

1.3   Is there sufficient rationale to put the organization through a difficult and costly selection and
        implementation process?

1.4   What are your goals? Does management share these goals?

1.5   Will upper management have the sustaining reasons to carry through with the implementation
        whenever times get tough during implementation? Do they feel the pain?

1.6   Will it play in Peoria? Are the reasons for SE/CASE just smoke and mirror justifications for new
        "toys" or are they real?

1.7   How large is the development/enhancement backlog, including both documented and unreported
        projects?

1.8   How satisfied is corporate management with the current development/maintenance process?

1.9   How is the software development process viewed by upper management?

        a) As a Necessary evil or as a Strategic Weapon
        b) As a cost or as an asset

1 - SE/CASE READINESS DISCUSSION GUIDE

B - TIMING

1.10   Which of the following major organizational activities either recently happened, is in process, or will soon happen?

GOOD TIMES FOR SE/CASE

a) MIS leadership change - This is usually a great time to launch SE/CASE. New leaders will almost always be looking to make their mark and they have a relatively long time frame in which to do it. They are still in the "honeymoon period" with upper management and they probably have a bit more clout to get things moving.

b) Large, complex project upcoming - These projects provide a convenient mechanism to help force decisions and justify the funds.

c) Major project failure - Depends on why project was a failure, could be a good time or a bad time. If SE/CASE will solve the apparent problems, it could be just what you need.

d) Major project success - Normally a good time, but look out for the opinion "If we can do it without SE/CASE, then why force the new technology?"

e) Quality initiatives underway - Another great time for SE/CASE. Quality will be a convenient mechanism to justify SE/CASE.

f) Periods of low IS morale - Good time to provide a "shot in the arm".

1 - SE/CASE READINESS DISCUSSION GUIDE

BAD TIME FOR SE/CASE

a) Re-organization of Business Depts - Not a good time. Too much political maneuvering.

b) Re-organization of MIS Depts - Also not a good time, to much confusion at once. Give it at least 3 months for the dust to settle.

c) When everyone is happy and results are plentiful - If it ain't broke don't fix it. (at least this is management's attitude, there is always room for improvement)

d) During critical survival times

e) During periods of other major change (e.g., downsizing, moving physical location, other major technology implementation)

.11   Estimate MIS involvement in the following activities. Consider both current and future.

New Development (primary reason for SE/CASE)
Package selection (SE/CASE still useful, but less so)
Outsourcing (SE/CASE has a place, but a small one)
Major Enhancement (SE/CASE can be very useful in this are)
Maintenance/Support
    Corrective/bug fix
    Adaptive/Minor enhancement
    Preventative
    Performance improvement

1 - SE/CASE READINESS DISCUSSION GUIDE

C - INVESTMENT

1.12   How much do your expect to spend on SE/CASE over the next 3 to 5 years?

1.13   How much do you spend today on IS? What percentage is the estimated cost of SE/CASE?

1.14   How soon do you expect to break even on the investment? Does this investment horizon fit within the organization's investment "comfort zone"?

1.15   How much can the organization afford "per seat"?

1.16   How tangible (e.g., specific cost savings) do the benefits have to be?

1.17   Identify a few of the largest, most costly improvement initiatives undertaken by the company (in any department) in the last 3 years (e.g. quality improvement, 4GL). Do these compare to your estimate for the cost of SE/CASE?

1.18   Do you have a productivity and/or quality measurement program in place? (this will help to justify the benefits)

1 - SE/CASE READINESS DISCUSSION GUIDE

D - APPLICABILITY

1.19   What was your last major organizational change? How long ago was it?

1.20   How well did it go? What problems occurred? Were there any casualties?

1.21   Is your organization bleeding-edge, leading-edge, mainstream, lagers, or in the dark?

1.22   How willing is the IS staff to learn new concepts?

1.23   How quickly are new concepts assimilated within IS?

1.24   How strong are the forces who may have to change? In numbers? In political strength?

1.25   How closely does the IS and corporate management culture align with the staff culture?

1.26   Is it possible to change these people? Are you fighting an impossible battle?

1.27   Define the characteristics of the IS organization. (better to be on the right hand side with these characteristics)

        a) Risk takers   -   Conservative
        b) Formal   -   Informal
        c) Many Layers   -   Flat Organization
        d) Controlling   -   Hands Off
        e) Static Env   -   Dynamic Env
        f) Complacent   -   Energetic
        g) Myopic   -   Open Minded
        h) Political   -   Apolitical
        i) Just a job   -   A Fun Place

1.28   Why do people want to work at your IS organization?

        Competitive salaries
        Secure work place
        Exciting challenges
        Upward career mobility
        Good team spirit

2 - MIS ENVIRONMENT/TECHNOLOGY PROFILE

2.1   Please indicate the total number of each of the following positions within your organization, along with the average length of service in years for each.

POSITION	TOTAL NUMBER	AVERAGE YRS OF SERVICE
Project Manager/Leader	_____	_____
Systems Analyst	_____	_____
Programmer/Analyst	_____	_____
Application Programmer	_____	_____
Systems Support Programmer	_____	_____
DA/DBA	_____	_____
Information Center Specialist	_____	_____
Development Center Specialist	_____	_____
Quality Assurance/Support Spec.	_____	_____
Trainers	_____	_____
Contractors	_____	
_____	_____	____
_____	_____	____
_____	_____	____

2.2   If readily available, attach a job description for each job title (position) associated with software development and maintenance.

2.3   Attach an organization chart for MIS. Indicate the number of people at the various levels and locations.

2.4   List business unit(s) supported by MIS (e.g. XYZ division).

_____

_____

_____

_____

2.5   Indicate the number of user locations supported by MIS.   ____ locations

2.6   Estimate the size of the application backlog?   ____ years

2.7   Identify the causes of the development backlog? (check all that apply)

____ Too many unneeded user requests   ____ Infrequent use of productivity tools
____ MIS staff productivity problems   ____ Spending too much time on user support
____ Not enough MIS staff members   ____ Lack of user involvement

____ _____

2.8   What is the MIS organization's mission?

_____

_____

2 - MIS ENVIRONMENT/TECHNOLOGY PROFILE

_____

_____

_____

_____

2.9   Specify recent turnover trends.

	Last Year	This Year
Company-wide	___%	___%
MIS Organization	___%	___%

2.10   Specify the percentage of MIS staff with the following degrees.

High school diploma	___%
2 year degree	___%
4 year degree	___%
Advanced degree	___%
	===
	100 %

2 - MIS ENVIRONMENT/TECHNOLOGY PROFILE

2.11   Does the MIS organization have a systems development methodology (SDM)?

_____ Yes   _____ No   _____ Unknown

2.12   Does the MIS organization have a standards manual?

_____ Yes   _____ No   _____ Unknown

2.13   Indicate existence of the following procedures.

Quality assurance	___ Formal	___ Informal	___ None
Measurement/Metrics	___ Formal	___ Informal	___ None
Risk assessment	___ Formal	___ Informal	___ None
Change control	___ Formal	___ Informal	___ None
Configuration Mgt	___ Formal	___ Informal	___ None
Project funding	___ Formal	___ Informal	___ None
Project sponsorship	___ Formal	___ Informal	___ None
Project monitoring	___ Formal	___ Informal	___ None
Production turnover	___ Formal	___ Informal	___ None

_____   ___ Formal   ___ Informal

3 - MIS ORGANIZATION, POLICIES & STRATEGIES

3.1   Please indicate the YOUR estimated involvement in the following MIS application activities
        in the appropriate spaces below:

Trend

	Percent of Effort		Future		
New Development	___%	__ Up	__ Even	__ Down
Major Enhancement (>1 man month)	___%	__ Up	__ Even	__ Down
Maintenance/Support				
Corrective (bug fix)	___%	__ Up	__ Even	__ Down
Adaptive, (minor enh <1 man month)	___%	__ Up	__ Even	__ Down
Preventative	___%	__ Up	__ Even	__ Down
Performance improvement	___%	__ Up	__ Even	__ Down
Other _____	___%			
Other _____	___%			
	===			
	100 %			

3.2   Estimate the percent of existing types of software that MIS supports:

On-line	___%	Custom Built	___%	Tran Processing	___%
Batch	___%	Package	___%	Decision Support	___%
		3rd Party	___%	Imaging	___%
		Development			
	===		===		
	100 %		100 %	_____	___%
				_____	___%
					===
					100%

3.3   Estimate the percent of future types of software to be developed:

On-line	___%	Custom Built	___%	Tran Processing	___%
Batch	___%	Package	___%	Decision Support	___%
		3rd Party	___%	Imaging	___%
		Development			
	===		===		
	100 %		100 %	_____	___%
				_____	___%
					===
					100%

2 - MIS ENVIRONMENT/TECHNOLOGY PROFILE

2.16   Describe telecommunications and distributed processing strategy.

_____

_____

_____

_____

2.17   How are PCs or microcomputers used within the development/maintenance/support environment?

_____

_____

_____

_____

2.18   Describe overall system and data security strategy.

_____

_____

_____

_____

3 - MIS ORGANIZATION, POLICIES & STRATEGIES

3.1   Please indicate the YOUR estimated involvement in the following MIS application activities in the appropriate spaces below:

Trend

	Percent of Effort		Future	
New Development	___%	__ Up	__ Even	__ Down
Major Enhancement (>1 man month)	___%	__ Up	__ Even	__ Down
Maintenance/Support				
Corrective (bug fix)	___%	__ Up	__ Even	__ Down
Adaptive, (minor enh <1 man month)	___%	__ Up	__ Even	__ Down
Preventative	___%	__ Up	__ Even	__ Down
Performance improvement	___%	__ Up	__ Even	__ Down
Other _____	___%			
Other _____	___%			
	===			
	100 %			

3.2   Estimate the percent of existing types of software that MIS supports:

On-line	___%	Custom Built	___%	Tran Processing	___%
Batch	___%	Package	___%	Decision Support	___%
		3rd Party Development	___%	Imaging	___%
	===		===		
	100 %		100 %	_____	___%
				_____	___%
					===
					100%

3.3   Estimate the percent of future types of software to be developed:

On-line	___%	Custom Built	___%	Tran Processing	___%
Batch	___%	Package	___%	Decision Support	___%
		3rd Party Development	___%	Imaging	___%
	===		===		
	100 %		100 %	_____	___%
				_____	___%
					===
					100%

3 - MIS ORGANIZATION, POLICIES & STRATEGIES

3.4   Indicate the typical team size(s) for a development project. (check all that are relevant)

_____ 1 team member
_____ 2-3 team members
_____ 4-6 team members
_____ 6-10 team members
_____ 11-20 team members
_____ 21 or more team members

3.5   As a general rule, MIS is effective at:

	Never				Always
Establishing priorities	1	2	3	4	5
Planning projects	1	2	3	4	5
Attaining schedules	1	2	3	4	5
Delivering within cost estimate	1	2	3	4	5
Training MIS staff	1	2	3	4	5
Training users	1	2	3	4	5
Designing solutions/systems to meet user needs	1	2	3	4	5
Understanding the users business needs	1	2	3	4	5
Building the right systems	1	2	3	4	5
Communicating progress against plans	1	2	3	4	5
Maintaining existing systems	1	2	3	4	5

3 - MIS ORGANIZATION, POLICIES & STRATEGIES

3.6   Indicate the importance YOU place on the following goals and objectives.

GOAL/OBJECTIVE:	Nice to Have				Critical to Survive
Reliable Software	1	2	3	4	5
Maintainable Software	1	2	3	4	5
Increase Productivity	1	2	3	4	5
Meet/Reduce Cost	1	2	3	4	5
Meet Deadlines	1	2	3	4	5
Meet Requirements	1	2	3	4	5
Satisfy Expectations	1	2	3	4	5
Effective User Support	1	2	3	4	5
Using MIS for competitive advantage	1	2	3	4	5

3.7   Indicate the importance you feel that MIS MANAGEMENT places on the following goals and objectives.

GOAL/OBJECTIVE:	Nice to Have				Critical to Survive
Reliable Software	1	2	3	4	5
Maintainable Software	1	2	3	4	5
Increase Productivity	1	2	3	4	5
Meet/Reduce Cost	1	2	3	4	5
Meet Deadlines	1	2	3	4	5
Meet Requirements	1	2	3	4	5
Satisfy Expectations	1	2	3	4	5
Effective User Support	1	2	3	4	5
Using MIS for competitive advantage	1	2	3	4	5

3 - MIS ORGANIZATION, POLICIES & STRATEGIES

3.8   In your opinion, is the current career path:

    ____ Formal and well defined   ____ Non-existent
    ____ Informal   ____ Unknown

3.9   If a career path exists, how effective is it with helping you in your career planning?

Not Helpful   Very Helpful   Unknown
1   2   3   4   5   X

3.10   How well do you know the existing set of MIS policies?

Not at All   Very Well   Unknown
1   2   3   4   5   X

3.11   How well are the existing set of MIS policies followed by the MIS staff?

Not at All   Very Well   Unknown
1   2   3   4   5   X

3.12   Identify any MIS policies or procedures which need to be reworked and/or removed.

_____

_____

_____

_____

_____

_____

3.13   Indicate the current MIS employee turnover rate for the past year:

Low   High   Unknown
1   2   3   4   5   X

3 - MIS ORGANIZATION, POLICIES & STRATEGIES

3.14   Why do people want to work at your MIS organization? (check all that apply)

    ____ Competitive salaries
    ____ Exciting challenges
    ____ Good team spirit, it's a fun place to work
    ____ Secure work place
    ____ Upward career mobility
    ____ Unknown

____ _____

3.15   Identify major reasons for abnormally low or high turnover.

_____

_____

_____

_____

_____

3.16   How effective are the following reward mechanisms? (rate all that apply)

	Useless			Very Effective	
Promotions	1	2	3	4	5
Raises	1	2	3	4	5
Special awards	1	2	3	4	5
Special events (e.g. lunch with V.P.)	1	2	3	4	5
Added responsibility	1	2	3	4	5
Training/seminars	1	2	3	4	5
Perks/Special privileges	1	2	3	4	5
_____	1	2	3	4	5
_____	1	2	3	4	5

3 - MIS ORGANIZATION, POLICIES & STRATEGIES

3.17   What types of activities are generally rewarded? (check all that apply)

____ Fire fighting   ____ Satisfying users
____ Efficiency/productivity   ____ Making your boss look good
____ Quality work   ____ New ideas (i.e., innovativeness)
____ Meeting project schedules

____ _____

3.18   Do you measure your productivity or quality on an ongoing basis?

____ Yes ____ No

3.19   If you measure yourself, how do you do it?

_____

_____

_____

_____

3.20   Indicate the effectiveness of the following modes of communication. (rate all that apply)

	Useless				Very Effective
Grapevine					
Electronic Mail	1	2	3	4	5
Bulletin boards	1	2	3	4	5
Staff meetings	1	2	3	4	5
Newsletters	1	2	3	4	5
Formal chain of command	1	2	3	4	5
Status reports	1	2	3	4	5
Memos	1	2	3	4	5
Information exchange lunches	1	2	3	4	5

_____   12345

4 - MIS CULTURE ASSESSMENT

A - MIS WORKING ENVIRONMENT

How do you view the MIS department? (indicate 1-strongly agree to 5-strongly disagree)

	Strongly Agree			Strongly Disagree		
4.1)	1	2	3	4	5	MIS's vision and mission are clear to me
4.2)	1	2	3	4	5	MIS leadership is steady with their direction
4.3)	1	2	3	4	5	MIS policies are clearly defined
4.4)	1	2	3	4	5	MIS policies/standards are uniformly adhered to
4.5)	1	2	3	4	5	MIS leadership has a long term focus
4.6)	1	2	3	4	5	Complaining is held to a minimum
4.7)	1	2	3	4	5	MIS is rarely in crisis mode
4.8)	1	2	3	4	5	Project managers have the autonomy to get the job done
4.9)	1	2	3	4	5	There is a lot of consistency in how people work within MIS
4.10)	1	2	3	4	5	Loss of a few critical people would not have a significant impact
4.11)	1	2	3	4	5	There is a relentless drive to improve productivity
4.12)	1	2	3	4	5	There is a relentless drive to improve quality
4.13)	1	2	3	4	5	MIS play's by the book to get things done
4.14)	1	2	3	4	5	This is a kind and gentle organization to work for
4.15)	1	2	3	4	5	MIS has an open door policy
4.16)	1	2	3	4	5	This is an exciting time to be part of MIS
4.17)	1	2	3	4	5	Once a project plan is set, project managers manage closely to it
4.18)	1	2	3	4	5	MIS is able to take advantage of new technologies
4.19)	1	2	3	4	5	The MIS department is under control
4.20)	1	2	3	4	5	The MIS leadership is good at providing feedback
4.21)	1	2	3	4	5	MIS is able to attract top recruits

4 - MIS CULTURE ASSESSMENT

	Strongly Agree			Strongly Disagree		
4.22)	1	2	3	4	5	MIS is willing to take a calculated risk
4.23)	1	2	3	4	5	MIS can smoothly change leadership
4.24)	1	2	3	4	5	MIS leadership operates in a hands-off manner
4.25)	1	2	3	4	5	People within MIS trust one another
4.26)	1	2	3	4	5	Ideas do not have to be "invented here" to be successful
4.27)	1	2	3	4	5	MIS staff members are very energetic
4.28)	1	2	3	4	5	MIS staff is very open minded to new ideas
4.29)	1	2	3	4	5	MIS is not very political
4.30)	1	2	3	4	5	MIS likes to be pioneers with regard to new technology
4.31)	1	2	3	4	5	MIS is able to stick to it to make something happen
4.32)	1	2	3	4	5	The company values and properly uses specialists
4.33)	1	2	3	4	5	Few within MIS have mentally "retired on the job"
4.34)	1	2	3	4	5	Visible activities (e.g., coding) are not the only things rewarded
4.35)	1	2	3	4	5	There is a genuine willingness to help others
4.36)	1	2	3	4	5	MIS is devoid on gossip about others
4.37)	1	2	3	4	5	MIS does not have a "sink or swim" mentality
4.38)	1	2	3	4	5	The MIS bureaucracy rarely gets in the way of getting the job done
4.39)	1	2	3	4	5	We rarely need to write "CYA" memos
4.40)	1	2	3	4	5	Fridays are as productive as other workdays
4.41)	1	2	3	4	5	MIS leadership takes the time to understand issues before action
4.42)	1	2	3	4	5	"Plum" assignments usually go to the best able
4.43)	1	2	3	4	5	MIS is a nurturing organization
4.44)	1	2	3	4	5	People are praised for trying something new, even if it fails

4 - MIS CULTURE ASSESSMENT

	Strongly Agree			Strongly Disagree	

4.45) 1 2 3 4 5   Effectiveness is rewarded, not just activity

4.46) 1 2 3 4 5   Quality is rewarded

4.47) 1 2 3 4 5   Teams are rewarded as a unit

---

4 - MIS CULTURE ASSESSMENT

B - PERSONAL SITUATION

How do you personally feel about your job? (indicate 1-strongly agree to 5-strongly disagree)

	Strongly Agree			Strongly Disagree		
4.48)	1	2	3	4	5	I am willing to completely change my job if it is right for the company
4.49)	1	2	3	4	5	I don't mind working overtime when its truly called for
4.50)	1	2	3	4	5	I'm fully qualified for my current position
4.51)	1	2	3	4	5	I expect my career goals will be accomplished in this company
4.52)	1	2	3	4	5	I follow and comply to standards
4.53)	1	2	3	4	5	I believe that other people in MIS deal with me fairly
4.54)	1	2	3	4	5	If I have a question, I will not hesitate to ask a co-worker
4.55)	1	2	3	4	5	I feel it is acceptable to make mistakes, as long as I learn from them
4.56)	1	2	3	4	5	I expect the results of this survey to be valuable and enacted upon
4.57)	1	2	3	4	5	My answers would be the same, with or without my name on this survey
4.58)	1	2	3	4	5	I enjoy learning about and using new technology
4.59)	1	2	3	4	5	I think of myself as a team player
4.60)	1	2	3	4	5	I love to be thrown into different assignments, its' challenging
4.61)	1	2	3	4	5	I think of myself as a leader
4.62)	1	2	3	4	5	I do my best work as part of a team
4.63)	1	2	3	4	5	I usually have control over my job and related activities
4.64)	1	2	3	4	5	I enjoy helping others do their assignments better
4.65)	1	2	3	4	5	This organization is fun to work
4.66)	1	2	3	4	5	I have started to learn about new subject without my boss recomending it
4.67)	1	2	3	4	5	I feel that the company will provide the appropriate level of training

---

4 - MIS CULTURE ASSESSMENT

C - SOFTWARE ENGINEERING OPINIONS

Indicate your beliefs and assumptions about the following issues and topics:

	Strongly Agree				Strongly Disagree	
4.68)	1	2	3	4	5	Long term productivity will increase if quality is improved
4.69)	1	2	3	4	5	If the development process ain't broke try to fix it anyway
4.70)	1	2	3	4	5	It's my job to help IS management fix the development process
4.71)	1	2	3	4	5	Everybody is innovative/creative in some way
4.72)	1	2	3	4	5	Users will pay extra for quality work
4.73)	1	2	3	4	5	MIS Management tends to practice what it preaches
4.74)	1	2	3	4	5	Quality is everybody's responsibility
4.75)	1	2	3	4	5	MIS is a science, not an art
4.76)	1	2	3	4	5	It is important to be as complete as possible when producing systems
4.77)	1	2	3	4	5	What I do truly makes a difference to the organization
4.78)	1	2	3	4	5	It's not OK to take short-cuts to meet critical time constraint
4.79)	1	2	3	4	5	The users should be an integral part of the MIS team
4.80)	1	2	3	4	5	I am proud of the work I do
4.81)	1	2	3	4	5	I am given the authority to match my level of responsibility
4.82)	1	2	3	4	5	What I do can be measured
4.83)	1	2	3	4	5	Measurement data will not be mis-used with MIS

4 - MIS CULTURE ASSESSMENT

D - SE SKILLS/ABILITY

4.84) Indicate YOUR overall skill level on the following technical skills:

	Novice				Expert
Project Management	1	2	3	4	5
Systems Analysis	1	2	3	4	5
Software Design	1	2	3	4	5
Programming	1	2	3	4	5
Testing	1	2	3	4	5

4.85) Indicate YOUR skill level on the following general business skills and techniques:

	Novice				Expert
Verbal communications	1	2	3	4	5
Written communications	1	2	3	4	5
Presentation	1	2	3	4	5
Facilitation	1	2	3	4	5
Meeting skills	1	2	3	4	5
Listening	1	2	3	4	5
Interviewing	1	2	3	4	5
Problem solving	1	2	3	4	5
Interpersonal skills	1	2	3	4	5
Leadership	1	2	3	4	5
Administration	1	2	3	4	5
PC	1	2	3	4	5
Mainframe	1	2	3	4	5

4 - MIS CULTURE ASSESSMENT

4.86) Indicate YOUR level of experience (internal or external to the company) with the following development techniques:

	Tried		Use		Expert
Data Flow Diagraming	1	2	3	4	5
Decomposition Diagramming	1	2	3	4	5
Matrix Analysis	1	2	3	4	5
Entity Relationship Modeling	1	2	3	4	5
Consensus Building (JAD)	1	2	3	4	5
Structure Charting	1	2	3	4	5
Structured Walkthroughs	1	2	3	4	5
Structured Programming	1	2	3	4	5
Structured Testing	1	2	3	4	5
Flow Charting	1	2	3	4	5
Data Normalization	1	2	3	4	5
Data Structure Diagramming	1	2	3	4	5
Prototyping	1	2	3	4	5
Real-time Modeling	1	2	3	4	5
Object-oriented Modeling	1	2	3	4	5
Critical Path Scheduling	1	2	3	4	5
PERT Charting	1	2	3	4	5
GANTT Charting	1	2	3	4	5
_____	1	2	3	4	5

5 - SKILLS & ABILITIES

5.1   To what extent do YOU understand the business areas?

Not at All   Very Well   Unknown
1   2   3   4   5   X

5.2   How well does your organization attempt to match the skills of the MIS staff with assignments?

Not at All   Very Well   Unknown
1   2   3   4   5   X

5.3   Indicate the effectiveness of training used by MIS.

	Useless				Valuable
Instructor-led classes	1	2	3	4	5
Video tape/CD classes	1	2	3	4	5
CBT classes	1	2	3	4	5
Outside training classes	1	2	3	4	5
Conferences & seminars	1	2	3	4	5
Internal coaches/mentors	1	2	3	4	5

5 - SKILLS & ABILITIES

5.4   Indicate YOUR level of experience (internal or external to the company) with the following development techniques:

	Tried		Use		Expert
Data Flow Diagraming	1	2	3	4	5
Decomposition Diagramming	1	2	3	4	5
Matrix Analysis	1	2	3	4	5
Entity Relationship Modeling	1	2	3	4	5
Consensus Building (JAD)	1	2	3	4	5
Structure Charting	1	2	3	4	5
Structured Walkthroughs	1	2	3	4	5
Structured Programming	1	2	3	4	5
Structured Testing	1	2	3	4	5
Flow Charting	1	2	3	4	5
Data Normalization	1	2	3	4	5
Data Structure Diagramming	1	2	3	4	5
Prototyping	1	2	3	4	5
Real-time Modeling	1	2	3	4	5
Object-oriented Modeling	1	2	3	4	5
Critical Path Scheduling	1	2	3	4	5
PERT Charting	1	2	3	4	5
GANTT Charting	1	2	3	4	5
_____	1	2	3	4	5
_____	1	2	3	4	5
_____	1	2	3	4	5
_____	1	2	3	4	5

5 - SKILLS & ABILITIES

5.5   Indicate YOUR level of experience (internal or external to the company) with the following types of automated development tools. Name those tools used on the line provided.

	Tried		Use		Expert
Matrix Engine	1	2	3	4	5
Analysis & Design tool (e.g., IEW, Excelerator)	1	2	3	4	5
Code Generator	1	2	3	4	5
4GL	1	2	3	4	5
Project Management Tool (e.g., Timeline, Project Workbench)	1	2	3	4	5
Project Estimator (e.g., Estimacs)	1	2	3	4	5
Spreadsheet (e.g., Lotus)	1	2	3	4	5
Word Processor	1	2	3	4	5
Data Dictionary	1	2	3	4	5
Configuration Management	1	2	3	4	5

5 - SKILLS & ABILITIES

	Tried		Use		Expert
Testing (data generation or test monitor)	1	2	3	4	5
Expert System Shell	1	2	3	4	5
Screen Painter	1	2	3	4	5
Report Writers	1	2	3	4	5
Other	1	2	3	4	5
Other	1	2	3	4	5

CAP GEMINI AMERICA

5 - SKILLS & ABILITIES

5.6   Indicate YOUR skill level on the following technical skills:

	Novice				Expert
Systems Analysis	1	2	3	4	5
Software Design	1	2	3	4	5
Programming	1	2	3	4	5
Testing	1	2	3	4	5

5.7   Indicate YOUR skill level on the following general business skills and techniques:

	Novice				Expert
Verbal communications	1	2	3	4	5
Written communications	1	2	3	4	5
Presentation	1	2	3	4	5
Facilitation	1	2	3	4	5
Meeting skills	1	2	3	4	5
Listening	1	2	3	4	5
Interviewing	1	2	3	4	5
Problem solving	1	2	3	4	5
Interpersonal skills	1	2	3	4	5
Leadership	1	2	3	4	5
Administration	1	2	3	4	5
PC	1	2	3	4	5
Mainframe	1	2	3	4	5

6A - DEVELOPMENT WORK PRACTICES

6a.1   To what extent has a rigorous (i.e., concise, consistent, complete, coherent) engineering-like approach been adopted within MIS?

Not At All				To Great Extent	Unknown
1	2	3	4	5	X

6a.2   To what extent is there enforcement of this approach?

Not At All				To Great Extent	Unknown
1	2	3	4	5	X

6a.3   If a Systems Development Methodology exists, how effectively is it being used?

Ineffective				Very Effective	Unknown
1	2	3	4	5	X

6a.4   Does the MIS organization have a Standards Manual?

____ Yes   ____ No   ____ Unknown

6a.5   Are the standards enforced?

Not at All				To Great Extent	Unknown
1	2	3	4	5	X

6a.6   How current are the standards in the manual?

Out of Date				Very Current	Unknown
1	2	3	4	5	X

6a.7   How effective is MIS at removing defects before releasing systems to production?

Inept				Very Effective	Unknown
1	2	3	4	5	X

6A - DEVELOPMENT WORK PRACTICES

6a.8   Will a project be stopped/halted if tests prove it should not be placed into production?

____ Yes ____ No ____ Sometimes ____ Unknown

6a.9   When does coding typically start?

____ Day one of a project
____ Whenever the users start getting worried
____ Whenever the MIS manager starts getting worried
____ Before the mid-point of a project
____ After the mid-point of a project
____ After detail design
____ Unknown

____ _____

6a.10   How often do you reuse the designs or actual coded modules?

Never				Always		Unknown
1	2	3	4	5		X

6a.11   To what extent is software documented?

Not At All			To Great Extent		Unknown
1	2	3	4	5	X

6a.12   If documentation is not well documented, why has this occurred? (check all that apply)

____ Not enough time
____ Keying in documentation takes a lot of time and I don't type very fast
____ My programs are self documenting
____ Any competent programmer could understand my code
____ My programs will only be used once
____ Documentation will become obsolete due to changes during testing and debugging
____ I don't like to document
____ No one reads documentation

____ _____

6a.13   How is software developed?

One Person Working Alone			High Reliance On Teams		Unknown
1	2	3	4	5	X

6A - DEVELOPMENT WORK PRACTICES

6a.14   How effectively does MIS perform the following development activities?

ANALYSIS

	Not Performed			Poorly		Very Well
Gather requirements	0	1	2	3	4	5
Analyze processes	0	1	2	3	4	5
Analyze data	0	1	2	3	4	5
Analyze future impact	0	1	2	3	4	5

DESIGN

Layout screens	0	1	2	3	4	5
Layout reports	0	1	2	3	4	5
Design logic	0	1	2	3	4	5
Identify controls	0	1	2	3	4	5
Specify interfaces	0	1	2	3	4	5
Normalize data	0	1	2	3	4	5
Create data structures	0	1	2	3	4	5
Design event flow	0	1	2	3	4	5
Design communications infrastructure	0	1	2	3	4	5
Package into code units	0	1	2	3	4	5

CONSTRUCTION

Detail module detail	0	1	2	3	4	5
Code programs	0	1	2	3	4	5
Compile/link programs	0	1	2	3	4	5
Document programs	0	1	2	3	4	5
Unit test programs	0	1	2	3	4	5

TESTING

Develop test plans	0	1	2	3	4	5
Requirements Mapping	0	1	2	3	4	5
String (event) Tests	0	1	2	3	4	5
Integration Test	0	1	2	3	4	5
Systems Test	0	1	2	3	4	5
User Acceptance Tests	0	1	2	3	4	5
Operations Tests	0	1	2	3	4	5
Base Software Package Validation Test		1	2	3	4	5
Stress test	0	1	2	3	4	5

INSTALLATION

Create user guide	0	1	2	3	4	5
Create training matls	0	1	2	3	4	5
Release to operations	0	1	2	3	4	5
Post impl support	0	1	2	3	4	5
Project post-mortem	0	1	2	3	4	5
		1	2	3	4	5

6a.15   How effectively does MIS perform the following package selection/implementation activities?

	Not Performed	Poorly			Well	Very
Investigate candidates	0	1	2	3	4	5
Analyze available candidates	0	1	2	3	4	5
Prepare RFPs	0	1	2	3	4	5
Select package	0	1	2	3	4	5
Negotiate contract	0	1	2	3	4	5
Customize package	0	1	2	3	4	5
Install package	0	1	2	3	4	5
Set parameters	0	1	2	3	4	5

6a.16   List in sequence of priority five areas of the software life cycle (e.g., project specification, testing) you would like to see improved.

1)_____

6A – DEVELOPMENT WORK PRACTICES

2)_____

3)_____

4)_____

5)_____

6a.17   List five areas where you believe your management and or technical approach to software development is strong.

1)_____

2)_____

3)_____

4)_____

5)_____

6B - PROJECT MANAGEMENT WORK PRACTICES

6b.1   How effectively does MIS perform the following project management activities?

	Not Performed		Poorly			Very Well
Obtain project funding	0	1	2	3	4	5
Manage to proj budget	0	1	2	3	4	5
Meet project schedule	0	1	2	3	4	5
Control change requests	0	1	2	3	4	5
Manage/coordinate project deliverables	0	1	2	3	4	5
Report proj status to the users	0	1	2	3	4	5
Report proj status to MIS mgt	0	1	2	3	4	5
Make project mid-course corrections	0	1	2	3	4	5
Meet user requirements	0	1	2	3	4	5
Satisfy user expectations	0	1	2	3	4	5

6b.2   Identify the degree to which the following planning components are typically defined or identified:

	Not Defined					Well Defined
Project scope	0	1	2	3	4	5
Project objectives	0	1	2	3	4	5
Formal project workplans	0	1	2	3	4	5
Deliverables	0	1	2	3	4	5
Milestones	0	1	2	3	4	5
Estimating assumptions	0	1	2	3	4	5
Project risks	0	1	2	3	4	5

6B - PROJECT MANAGEMENT WORK PRACTICES

6b.3   Indicate methods used to estimate software projects. (check all that apply)

____ Effort sizing tools (parametric models)
____ Comparison with similar past projects (analogy)
____ Multiple expert judgements (consensus, Delphi)
____ Bottom up detail task estimating (work breakdown structure)
____ Design to cost (allocating cost top down and fitting the work)
____ Independent, 3rd party estimates
____ Top down deliverables estimating
____ Wild approximate guesses (seat of the pants)
____ None

6b.4   Which of the following are normally estimated and planned before a project begins:

____ Effort (e.g., hours)   ____ CPU resources
____ Cost (e.g., project travel)   ____ Schedule (e.g., due dates and milestones)
____ None

6b.5   Indicate methods used to plan and track software projects.

____ Project management system   ____ Lotus spreadsheets
____ Milestone/Deliverable checklists   ____ None

6b.6   How long would it take to determine the exact status of a project? (check appropriate)

____ Minutes   ____ Weeks
____ Hours   ____ Unknown
____ Days

6b.7   Which of the following MIS activities require a formal cost/benefit analysis? (check all that apply)

____ Large development projects (over 6 man-months)
____ Small development projects (under 6 man-months)
____ Large enhancement projects (over 6 man-months)
____ Small enhancement projects (under 6 man-months)
____ Adaptive maintenance projects (i.e. adding a function)
____ None

6B - PROJECT MANAGEMENT WORK PRACTICES

6b.8   What is the typical size of a lowest level task or activity that is estimated and performed:

____ Less than 8 hours	____ 1 - 2 weeks
____ 9 - 20 hours	____ 2 weeks - 4 weeks
____ 21 - 40 hours	____ > 1 month
____ Unknown	

6b.9   At what level are project dependencies planned?

____ Task/Activities	____ Phase
____ Major deliverable	____ Sub-project
____ Milestone	____ Not planned for
____ Unknown	

6b.10   How far ahead are projects typically committed (in terms of cost and schedule)?

____ No commitment	____ Only for the next phase
____ Only for the next milestone	____ For multiple phases
____ Only for major deliverable	____ For the entire project
____ Unknown	

6b.11   How often are the following items captured (check the appropriate columns):

	Daily	Weekly	2 Wks	Mthly	Phase End	Mile-stone	Proj End	Never
Effort (hours)	____	____	____	____	____	____	____	____
Cost (dollars)	____	____	____	____	____	____	____	____
CPU resources	____	____	____	____	____	____	____	____
Schedule dates	____	____	____	____	____	____	____	____
_____	____	____	____	____	____	____	____	____

6b.12   How tightly controlled are most projects?

Very Loose				Very Tight		Unknown
1	2	3	4	5		X

6B – PROJECT MANAGEMENT WORK PRACTICES

6b.13   List in sequence of priority five areas of software project management (e.g., plannin
tracking, control) that you would like to see improved.

1)_____

2)_____

3)_____

4)_____

5)_____

6C - MAINTENANCE WORK PRACTICES

6c.1   How effectively does MIS perform the following maintenance activities?

	Not Performed	Poorly				Very Well
Identify problem causes	0	1	2	3	4	5
Analyze/understand existing code	0	1	2	3	4	5
Make changes	0	1	2	3	4	5
Test changes	0	1	2	3	4	5
Satisfy user expectations	0	1	2	3	4	5
Control the maintenance activity	0	1	2	3	4	5

6c.2   How do you know when it time to rewrite an application?

_____ By the number of user complaints/request
_____ By an analysis of support costs

_____ _____

6c.3   How well maintained is the documentation through the maintenance process?

Not Maintained			As good if not better than dev		Unknown
1	2	3	4	5	X

6c.4   How are defects and system problems recorded?

_____ Formally, for all of MIS   _____ Informally by area
_____ Formally, by project   _____ Not recorded
_____ Unknown

_____ _____

6C - MAINTENANCE WORK PRACTICES

6c.5   How are maintenance activities planned?

____ Using the development methodology   ____ Based on past projects
____ Using a maintenance methodology   ____ Unique for each job
____ Unknown

____ _____

6c.6   How are changes put into production?

Continuous Stream of Changes				Batched Releases		Unknown	
1	2	3	4	5		X	

6c.7   How do you view the maintenance activity? (check all that apply)

____ An exciting/challenging job   ____ A comfortable job
____ A dead end job   ____ A thankless job
____ A stepping stone to management   ____ An activity that effects the bottom line

____ _____

6c.8   Overall, how effective is MIS at maintaining applications?

Ineffective				Very Effective		Unknown	
1	2	3	4	5		X	

7 -- MIS/USER RELATIONSHIP

7.1   How does MIS refer to you?

    ____ Users   ____ Customers
    ____ Clients   ____ Partners
    ____ Them

____ _____

7.2   List any new products or services likely to have a significant future impact on software development and maintenance?

_____

_____

_____

_____

7.3   How often is the proper level of user involvement found on a development project?

Never   Always   Unknown
1   2   3   4   5   X

7.4   How much MORE you feel your are <u>willing</u> to do?

              What Ever
None   MIS Needs   Unknown
1   2   3   4   5   X

7.5   How much MORE do you feel you are <u>able</u> to do?

              What Ever
None   MIS Needs   Unknown
1   2   3   4   5   X

7.6   What is your current level of contact with MIS?

None   Daily   Unknown
1   2   3   4   5   X

7 -- MIS/USER RELATIONSHIP

7.7   How comfortable do you feel working with MIS?

Very Comfortable			Uncomfortable		Unknown
1	2	3	4	5	X

7.8   To what degree do you understand MIS concepts?

Not At All			Very Well		Unknown
1	2	3	4	5	X

7.9   Assess the overall MIS/user relationship.

Hostile			Supportive		Unknown
1	2	3	4	5	X

Informal			Formal		Unknown
1	2	3	4	5	X

Distant			Friendly		Unknown
1	2	3	4	5	X

Rigid			Loose		Unknown
1	2	3	4	5	X

7.10   List any recent events which have effected the User/MIS relationship. (positive and/or negative)

_____

_____

_____

7.11   How do you view software?

As a Necessary Evil			As a Strategic Weapon		Unknown
1	2	3	4	5	X

As a cost			As an asset		Unknown
1	2	3	4	5	X

7 -- MIS/USER RELATIONSHIP

7.12   How well has MIS met your requirements?

Not at
All   Completely   Unknown
1   2   3   4   5   X

7.13   How well has MIS satisfied your expectations?

Not at
All   Completely   Unknown
1   2   3   4   5   X

7.14   Indicate your overall level of satisfaction with MIS service you receive?

                    Very
Unhappy   Happy   Unknown
1   2   3   4   5   X

7.15   How often do you do your own programming?

Never   Always   Unknown
1   2   3   4   5   X

7.16   If you do your own programming, WHY do you?

____ Unavailability of MIS resources
____ They can do it better
____ They can do it faster

____ _____

7.17   When is MIS "at their best"?

_____

_____

7.18   When is MIS "at their worst"?

_____

_____

CULTURE IMPACT POINT WORKSHEET

_____ 1) Where on the industry technology innovation curve is the technology?

        20 pts - Bleeding edge (top 5%)
        10 pts - Leading edge   (next 25 %)
        0   pts - Common stuff   (next 50%)
        5   pts - Old stuff   (last 20%)

_____ 2) What portion(s) of the systems development lifecycle is/are effected? Add 3 points for each of the following that apply: (maximum of 12)

        Planning   Installation
        Analysis   Package selection implementation
        Design   Maintenance
        Construction   Operations
        Testing   Technical Support
        Quality Assurance

_____ 3) How does the technology look on the surface to the staff (i.e., initial perception)?

        10 pts - Boring, confusing, or complex
        0   pts - Like any other SE technology
        -10 pts - Glitzy or fun

_____ 4) How are people who are experienced in the new technology paid in the local MIS marketplace?

        15 pts -   Paid less and loosing ground
        5   pts -   Paid less
        0   pts -   Paid the same
        -5 pts -   Paid more
        -15 pts -   Paid more and gaining ground

_____ 5) What type of technology change is it?

        20 pts - Replacement of existing technology
        15 pts - New technology to the organization
        5   pts - Building on an existing technology

CULTURE IMPACT POINT WORKSHEET

RATED BY: _____ DATE: __/__/__

TECHNOLOGY: (Indicate technology category being rated)

____ Systems Development Methodology (SDM)
____ Planning toolkit
____ Data modeling tool
____ Matrix engine
____ Portfolio planner
____ Prototyping tools
____ Analyzing tool
____ Designing tool
____ Expert system shell
____ Application (code) generator
____ 4gl
____ Programming workbench
____ Testing toolkit
____ Conversion toolkit
____ Restructuring tools
____ JAD process
____ Self directing teams

____ Project financial analyzer
____ Project estimator
____ Project management tool
____ Change control
____ Measuring program & tools
____ Configuration management
____ Data dictionary
____ Information repository
____ IPSE Environment
____ General purpose graphics
____ Form/word processor
____ Spreadsheet
____ Code rating utilities
____ Re-engineering tools
____ Structured decision making
____ QA/QC group

BASE CIP POINTS: _____

MULTIPLIER: _____%

CIP RATING: _____

CULTURE IMPACT POINT WORKSHEET

____ 6) How does the new technology change the basic development or maintenance ideology?

40 pts - Complete replacement of existing ideology, re-education of staff, may require reassignments, and new hires with experience in new technology to act as "seeds."
25 pts - Complete new ideology, education of staff, may require reassignments, and new hires with experience in new technology to act as "seeds". No existing base of ideology to replace.
15 pts - Partial replacement of existing ideology, but still areas for "non-convertees" to migrate to.
0 pts - No change to ideology, business as usual, simply automating a function without changing how to do it.

____ 7) Add the appropriate points for the types of major cultural changes that need to occur.

25 pts - For changes in a belief (e.g., higher productivity results from better quality)
15 pts - For changes in a behavioral patterns (e.g., "but, we always do it this way")
10 pts - For changes in assumptions (e.g., users don't want to work with us)

____ 8) Add the appropriate points for any of the following changes in social interaction caused by the new technology.

5 pts - Increased or reduced level of interaction within the MIS staff
5 pts - For each new method of interaction introduced as a result of the new technology (e.g., E-Mail)
10 pts - Increased level on interaction with the user community

CULTURE IMPACT POINT WORKSHEET

_____ 9) Add the appropriate points for each of the following organizational situations caused by the new technology:

20	pts -	Reorganization of MIS staff
5	pts -	For each new position created (e.g., toolsmith, liaison)
5	pts -	For each organizationally separate MIS department that will be using the technology
5	pts -	For each geographically separate MIS department that will be using the technology (in addition to the above 5 points)

_____ 10) How understandable is the new technology to MIS management?

20	pts -	Extremely technical, most (if not all) management will never understand the technology
10	pts -	Significantly complex or mundane that management will not want to understand the technology
0	pts -	Easily understood technology

_____ 11) How long will it take to fully implement the new technology?

20	pts -	Less than 6 months
15	pts -	6 to 12 months
10	pts -	1 - 2 years
5	pts -	2 - 3 years
0	pts -	Over 3 years

_____ 12) How difficult will the new technology be to communicate and for the staff to understand?

40	pts -	Extremely technical, most (if not all) will never fully understand the technology
20	pts -	Significantly complex or mundane that staff will not want to understand the technology
0	pts -	Easily understood technology

CULTURE IMPACT POINT WORKSHEET

MULTIPLIERS

_____%   Percentage of the MIS staff who will directly use the technology (i.e., hands-on interaction)

+ _____% = .25 * _____%   Percentage of the MIS staff who will be indirectly affected by the technology (include above percent who will directly use technology if effected by it)

+ _____% = .20 * _____%   Percentage of MIS management who will be politically concerned with the success of the technology

+ _____% = .10 * _____%   Percentage of User Community served who will have visibility to the technology
====

_____%   (To be multiplied by Base CIP rating to give final number)

CULTURE IMPACT POINT WORKSHEET

_____ 13) How apparent are the organizational benefits (e.g., increased quality)?

   20 pts -   Very long term, very hard to quantify
   0   pts -   Not readily apparent, but no one will seriously question the benefits
   -10 pts -   Apparent on the first use of the technology

_____ 14) Subtract 15 points for each of the following personal benefits attributed to the new technology.

   - Increases job mobility
   - Makes work a little more fun
   - Improved personal satisfaction from "doing the job right"
   - Increased credibility with the user community
   - Enhances career development/enhancement

_____ 15) After an appropriate introduction period, what is the anticipated initial perception of the change for the target audience. Add 1 point for each negative perception percentage point. Add 1/2 point for each neutral perception percentage point.

   ____% Positive perspective

   ____% Neutral perspective

   ____% Negative perception
   ====
   100%

B

Sample SE Environment Requirements Report

SAMPLE SE ENVIRONMENT REQUIREMENTS REPORT

Attached is a sample Software Engineering Requirements report for the XYZ Company. It is presented here to show the depth, nature, and quality of the physical deliverable produced as a result of the IC/VISION approach. The base information in this report originated from actual client engagements.

Please note, each organization is different and has special needs, thus many of the requirements in this report will not apply to your situation. This sample is provided as a starting point to understanding the SE/CASE vision deliverable. It is not meant to be the standard for all to copy.

SOFTWARE ENGINEERING ENVIRONMENT VISION REQUIREMENT REPORT
XYZ COMPANY - JUNE 19XX

I.   INTRODUCTION/SCOPE

II. FUNCTIONAL REQUIREMENTS

     A. MIS DECOMPOSITION DIAGRAM
     B. FEATURE LIST

III. OPERATIONAL REQUIREMENTS

     A. RECOMMENDED DEVELOPMENT APPROACH(ES)
     B. RECOMMENDED TECHNIQUES
     C. METHODOLOGY REQUIREMENTS
     D. REQUIRED TOOL CATEGORIES
     E. VENDOR REQUIREMENTS

IV. TECHNICAL REQUIREMENTS

     A. TARGET/DEVELOPMENT PLATFORMS
     B. PERFORMANCE REQUIREMENTS

V.   ORGANIZATIONAL REQUIREMENTS

     A. ORGANIZATIONAL CHANGES
     B. POLICIES AND PROCEDURES
     C. SUPPORT COMPONENTS

VI. CULTURAL REQUIREMENTS

     A.   SPECIFIC CULTURE DIMENSIONS
     B.   SKILL REQUIREMENTS

I. INTRODUCTION/SCOPE

This report was commissioned by XYZ Company in June 19XX. It defines the complete set of vision requirements for XYZ Company's new development and maintenance environment. These requirements will be used by the CASE Implementation Task Force to help select methodologies, techniques, and tools. The requirement lists will also form the foundation for vendor Request(s) For Proposals (RFPs) and subsequent rating checklists.

This report is broken out by requirement categories. Section III through VI represent each of the different categories:

FUNCTIONAL REQUIREMENTS - These requirements provide the scope of activities to be included in the development and maintenance and additional features and special requirements pertaining to the activities.

OPERATIONAL REQUIREMENTS - These requirements specify how the development and maintenance activities will be carried out. They list the desired development approach(es), techniques, methodology(ies), and tool categories.

TECHNICAL REQUIREMENTS - These requirements list the hardware and performance requirements for both the development and target platforms.

ORGANIZATIONAL REQUIREMENTS - These requirements list any organizational changes that need to be made.

The scope of this report includes the development and maintenance activities of the Management Information Systems Operations Services (MIS) and the Phoenix Engineering departments. Maintenance activities only include maintenance to systems built with the new development approaches. Computer operations, technical support, and end-user development activities are also outside the scope of the new environments. Requirements have been "tempered" in accordance with the new corporate-wide Quality Assurance Program (QAP).

II.   FUNCTIONAL REQUIREMENTS

A.   MIS DECOMPOSITION DIAGRAM

The diagram on the next 7 pages is a functional breakdown
of the data processing activities performed by XYZ
Corporation. Please note: the Engineering Department has
traditionally performed their own software activities
relying on MIS only for special development efforts and the
integration of their software with core systems. These
activities are part of the scope of this study. They are
included in anticipation of a possible future
reorganization combining the two departments.

The diagram begins with the corporate organization chart
and decomposes work activities by function, often blurring
activity and responsibility. The main purpose of this
diagram is to list and organize the functional requirements
for inclusion into the development and maintenance
environments.

B.   FEATURE LIST

The following requirements expand the above activities and
have been prioritized in three categories: MUST HAVE,
IMPORTANT, NICE TO HAVE.

MUST-HAVE REQUIREMENTS

- The ability to track projects at the activity level. In
addition, this data needs to tie into the existing labor
tracking system. The interface may initially be manual for
one to two years, but should be automated by End-Of-Year
(EOY) 92.

- A cost per seat not to exceed $30,000, including
additional hardware and software. Hardware and software
maintenance costs are not included in this limit.

- The activities must be measurable from both a quality and
productivity perspective.

- At least 30% of the development staff needs to be using
at least one of the new approaches by EOY 90, 50% by EOY
91, and the rest by EOY 92.

- ....

- .....

IMPORTANT REQUIREMENTS

- The internal repository (or encyclopedia) standard needs
to share application information (both data and process
objects) with our Phoenix department. Phoenix is currently
using the DEC environment for development and uses the ATIS
standard.

- The environment should allow users direct involvement in
the development process. As team members, they will be
using the prototyping, project management, and testing
tools. Thus, these tools need to be easy to use and well
documented.

- Quality Assurance and Quality Control activities need to
be tightly integrated into the development environment
(even though they are the responsibility of corporate
planning and control).

- Need to provide support for a package software selection
process (currently 35% of new systems).

- ....

- .....

- ..

NICE-TO-HAVE REQUIREMENTS

- Inclusion of contact sensitive helps on all tools.

- Need to provide support for Spanish and French language
screens and data input.

- All interfaces (User, Developer, Application to
Application) need to conform to SAA standards.

- Need the ability to integrate system deliverables from
contractors using non-standard methods and tools.

- Need to limit the total number of different vendors
involved.

- All documentation output should look professional.

- ....

- .....

- ..

III.   OPERATIONAL REQUIREMENTS

A.   RECOMMENDED DEVELOPMENT APPROACH(ES)

XYZ Corporation currently uses a more traditional, written specification approach for all projects. This approach will stay in effect for the next few years for small enhancement and "bug fix" modifications. The standards manual will be updated using the recently purchased Small Project and Maintenance life cycle Methodology as a guide.

For on-line, process-oriented systems requiring consensus among multiple department or groups, an evolutionary prototyping approach will be used. This approach will adhere to the Rapid Applications Development (RAD) philosophy.

For the remainder of the enhancement and development IS projects, a structure analysis and design approach will be used.

All projects will follow PMC (Project Management Concept), the standard project management approach developed by the XYZ Engineering Department. Individual approaches will be modified to conform to this internal standard.

B.   RECOMMENDED TECHNIQUES

Evolutionary Prototyping

     Joint Application Design
     Screen Painting
     Report Writing
     Data Modeling (Chen)
     Data Flow Diagramming (Gane & Sarson)
     4GL coding
     User System Testing
     Timeboxing

Structure Analysis And Design

     Data Flow Diagramming (Gane & Sarson)
     Data Modeling (Chen)
     Structure Charting
     ....
     ....
     ..

C. METHODOLOGY REQUIREMENTS

The following methodology requirements have not been
prioritized into categories. This will occur during the
selection process.

- If at all possible, both development approaches (SA&D and
RAD) should be under the umbrella of one vendor. This
should provide common terminology and procedural interfaces
between the approaches.

- The methodology (ies) selected should be descriptive in
nature. The material should lay out each task in a
"cookbook" approach for the organization's relatively
inexperienced staff.

- Sample deliverables are a must.

- Estimating guidelines, including Minimum/Average/Maximum
effort estimates, would be useful.

- User participation activities need to be specified and
estimated within the methodology.

- It would be very useful if the manuals were packaged for
easy transportation in briefcases. Pull-out reference guides
would be an additional benefit.

- The methodology should be easily segregated by role (e.g.
DBA, User Management). XYZ MIS is very departmentalized,
with programming, analysis, and database design being
separate entities. The ability to extract a specific role
would help a lot.

- We must have the authority to use the methodology in
England for special projects with the International
Division. There should be no legal restrictions.

- Although a formal strategic planning process will not be
introduced to XYZ for the next 2 to 3 years, our selected
development methodology should include a planning component
or be tightly integrated to another planning methodology.

- The methodology vendor must be committed to the continued
development of the product and should be financially sound.

D. REQUIRED TOOL CATEGORIES

Strategic Planning

    Matrix Engine (mainly for analysis activities)

Development

    Process Analysis and Design
    Data Modeling
    Schema Generator
    COBOL Code Generator
    Screen & Report Painters
    Test Coverage Analyzer

Maintenance
    Code Rating Tool
    Logic/Impact Analyzer
    Source/File Comparison

Project Management
    Metrics/Estimating Tool
    PC-Based Repository (when available in the next year)
    Portfolio Manager
    Desktop Publisher

    E. VENDOR REQUIREMENTS

    The following vendor requirements will help protect our investment in methodology and tool purchases:

    - The vendor must have a D&B rating of at least AA and have been in business for a minimum of two years.

    - The majority of the organization's revenue should come from software engineering related products and activities. (this protects us from a large company from quickly abandoning ship if times turn tough for the vendors.

    - The vendor must have a well conceived plan for future advancements that matches with our general direction.

    - The vendor should be able to provide training and consulting for their product.

    - For tools, the vendor should have a phone hotline service during all business hours. Coverage is needed for MIS in the Eastern Time Zone and for Phoenix Engineering in the Mountain Time Zone.

    - There should be no legal restrictions on the normal use of the methodologies and tools.

TECHNICAL REQUIREMENTS

A.   TARGET/DEVELOPMENT PLATFORMS

- The development environment needs to directly support multiple target platforms. These platforms include: IBM PC, VAX Workstation, System 36 and 38s, and IBM 4381. COBOL will be used on all platforms. Generation of RPG on the 36 and 38 would be an added benefit.

- The prototyping mechanism needs to span all platforms with screen/report painting and screen control flow.

- The development platform should make full use of existing MIS IBM PCs. The VAX is available for departmental networking if needed.

- All tools must run on a machine which employs PC/DOS. Other environmental overlays may exist, but must be transparent to the user and be integrated with the product.

- The analysis set of tools must be able to support two or more individuals sharing a common repository.

- The environment needs to support target application based on IDMS, DB2, VSAM, and CICS technology.

- The environment needs to support distributed data bases.

- ......

- ....

- ..

B.   PERFORMANCE REQUIREMENTS

- The ability to generate at least 95% of the COBOL or PL/1 code directly from diagrams.

- No degradation of mainframe response times.

- ......

- ....

- ..

A. ORGANIZATIONAL CHANGES

- Combine the analysts and programming groups into one using matrix management techniques to staff projects.

- Establish a formal Development Center at Corporate to support the MIS and Phoenix Engineering departments.

- Formalize the Quality Assurance function. Initiate it through the Development Center, but spin it off as an independent group by EOY 91.

- Move the Information Center under the newly formed development center.

- ......

- ....

- ..

B. POLICIES/PROCEDURES

- Incorporate a Change Management procedure. It needs to be tightly integrated into the methodology(ies).

- Formalize the current Project Funding and Approval procedure.

- Update the existing Quality Control policies. Need to focus on the methodology deliverables and suggested review points.

- Create project estimating policies and procedures. This function will be centralized, with only a relatively small number of individuals trained in the estimating of concepts and tools.

- ......

- ....

- ..

C. SUPPORT COMPONENTS

- Tie the corporate personal development program to the software engineering education and training requirements. Assign an MIS manager responsibility to monitor the plan.

- Create a monthly quality award program. Tie software engineering/CASE initiative to the QAP program.

- Integrate new initiatives into the annual bonus reward system. Make team level objectives a major component.

- ......

- ....

- ..

A. CULTURE DIMENSIONS

- Make sure that the majority of the staff wants to change before the culture transition begins in earnest.

- Once started, give the staff a full year to "see the light" before we start releasing resisting staff members.

- Implement the following new dimensions to our existing culture:

INNOVATIVENESS
Look at challenges from new/different perspectives
Reuse successful approaches/ideas,
    not necessarily created from scratch
Take calculated risk

QUALITY AWARENESS
Focus on user community service
Focus on the process not the deliverables
Measure quality

TEAMWORK
Look for individual strengths to exploit
Recognize synergy
Form a common purpose
Provide opportunities to exploit, explore, & develop talents
Use the word "we" more often
Consider self-directing teams

OPEN COMMUNICATIONS
Provide safe forums to surface ideas
Do not allow MIS to become more political
Use your ears often, listen to others
Make it OK to be wrong
    Almost every bad idea has an element to be built on
    Learn from mistakes

SHARED LEADERSHIP
Expect/allow for multiple pacesetters
    Cannot be forced or formalized
    If no one pops up we will stagnate
Recognize leadership is different from administration
Allow yourself to be lead by others

B. SKILL REQUIREMENTS

- Improve the following MIS departmental skills:

SE/CASE Skills
Data Flow Diagraming
Matrix Analysis
Entity Relationship Modeling
Consensus Building (JAD)
Structured Walkthroughs
Structured Testing
Prototyping

```
GANTT Charting
PC

General Business Skills
   Written communications
   Facilitation
   Meeting skills
   Listening
   Interviewing
   Interpersonal skills
   Leadership
```

- Tie the attainment of specific skills to increases in pay. Institute a pay for skills policy.

- Reinvigorate the training curriculum.

- ......

- ....

- ..

```
RESPECT/TRUST
   Grant amnesty to others
   Develop confidence/trust in each other
   Deal with others with honesty and integrity
   Recognize and respect differences

MOTIVATION
   Focus on value-added activities
         Helping
         Being helped
   Don't overdo it, pace the momentum
   Be selfish, learn from others
```

- ......

- ....

- ..

Index

ABOUT THE AUTHORS

TOM FLECHER is manager of Culture Transition Services for CAP GEMINI AMERICA and has been heavily involved with emerging IS concepts and techniques for more than 15 years. Throughout his career, Mr. Flecher has acquired valuable hands-on experience by applying these newly emerging concepts on multimillion dollar projects. Mr. Flecher received his MB with an MIS concentration from Indiana University.

JIM HUNT is President of James W. Hunt and Associates, an Atlanta-based consulting firm. He is an expert in CASE implementation, system implementation and downsizing.